To Barbara,
    with love and
        on you st
            Sue and Mark
                xxxx   x.

CHAPEL AND SWASTIKA

To Reverend Barbara Greenwood,
with very best wishes
on your ordination,

Dr David Chapman
5th July 2009

CHAPEL AND SWASTIKA: ERRATA (p. 223)

NOTES AND REFERENCES

Introduction

[1] Cited in Raoul Lemprière, *Portrait of the Channel Islands*, 2nd edn (London: Hale, 1975), p. 15.

[2] The small size of the islands (given here in square miles) must constantly be borne in mind: Jersey (45); Guernsey (24); Alderney (3); Sark (1.25).

[3] Still a useful introduction is Alan Wood and Mary Seaton Wood, *Islands in Danger* (London: Evans, 1955).

[4] Charles Cruickshank, *The German Occupation of the Channel Islands* (Channel Islands: Guernsey Press, 1975).

[5] R. D. Moore, *Methodism in the Channel Islands* (London: Epworth, 1952) contains a short chapter on Methodism during the German Occupation. Diane Moore, *Deo Gratias: A History of the French Catholic Church in Jersey: 1790-2007* (St Helier, Les Amitiés Frano-Britannique de Jersey, 2007) contains a chapter on the German Occupation. Otherwise there are no studies of the churches in the Channel Islands during the German Occupation.

[6] For example: L.G. Dantinne, *The Catholic Church in Belgium under the German Occupation* (London: Lincolns-Prager, 1944); Nicholas Atkin, *Church and Schools in Vichy France 1940-1944* (London: Garland, 1991); W.D. Halls, *Politics, Society and Christianity in Vichy France* (Oxford: Berg, 1995); Jacques Duquesne, *Les Catholiques français sous l'Occupation* (Paris: Bernard Grasset, 1996); Bernard Comte, *L'honneur et la conscience: catholiques français en résistance 1940-1944* (Paris: Editions de l'atelier, 1998); Emile C. Fabre, *God's Underground* (St Louis: Bethany, 1970); Horsta Malinowski-Krum, *Frankreich am Kreuz: Protestanten Frankreichs unter deutscher Okkupation, 1940-1944* (Berlin: Wichem-Verlag, 1993).

[7] Hazel R. Knowles-Smith, *The Changing Face of the Channel Islands Occupation: Record, Memory and Myth* (Basingstoke: Palgrave MacMillan, 2007).

[8] Madeleine Bunting, *The Model Occupation: The Channel Islands under German Rule, 1940-1945* (London: Harper Collins, 1995), p. 332. For a definitive study of the treatment of Jews in the Channel Islands see Frederick Cohen, *The Jews in the Channel Islands during the German Occupation 1940-1945* 2nd edition (Jersey: Jersey Heritage Trust, 2000).

[9] Channel Islands Study Group, *Nos Iles: A Symposium on the Channel Islands* (Teddington, 1944), p. 23.

[10] Jersey introduced stringent Sunday trading laws in 1904 and Guernsey in 1911 as self-regulation by traders was no longer working in the islands.

Chapel and Swastika:

*Methodism in the Channel Islands
during the German Occupation
1940-1945*

David M. Chapman

ELSP

Published in 2009 by
ELSP
16A St John Road
St Helier
Jersey   JE2 3LD

Printed and bound in the UK
on behalf of
JFDi Print Services Ltd.

Origination by
Seaflower Books, Jersey
www.ex-librisbooks.co.uk

ISBN 978-1-906641-08-5

**All enquiries and correspondence concerning
this book should be directed to the author:**

David M Chapman

davidm.chapman@btinternet.com

CONTENTS

ACKNOWLEDGEMENTS

The Chair of the Channel Islands District of the Methodist Church and Superintendent of the Jersey Circuit, Rev. David Coote, for permission to access files in the Methodist Collection in the Jersey Archives.

Staff at the Island Archives, Guernsey, and the Jersey Archives for their assistance in accessing materials.

Dr Peter Forsaith at the Methodist Studies Centre, Oxford Brookes University for his assistance in accessing the *Methodist Recorder* archives and other Methodist materials.

Miss Susan Laker, Deputy Librarian at the Priaulx Library, Guernsey, for assistance and access to material relating to the German Occupation in her possession.

Rev. Herbert White, Wellington, Somerset, for permission to use materials in the Herbert White Collection, German Occupation Museum, Guernsey.

Mr Richard Heaume for his assistance at the German Occupation Museum, Guernsey.

Rev. David Le Seelleur; Mr Reg Jeune CBE; Rev. David Hart, Superintendent of the Bailiwick of Guernsey Circuit.

*   *   *   *

Photographs on pages 27, 29, 79, 112 are copyright the Jersey Heritage Trust and are reproduced with permission.

Photographs on pages 29, 33, 108, 187 are copyright the Island Archives, Guernsey, and are reproduced with permission.

ABBREVIATIONS

CIOS	Channel Islands Occupation Society
GA	Guernsey Archives
GEP	*Guernsey Evening Press*
JA	Jersey Archives
JEP	*(Jersey) Evening Post*
LM	Leaders' Meeting
LPM	Local Preachers' Meeting
MR	*Methodist Recorder*
QM	Quarterly Meeting
TM	Trustees' Meeting

Introduction

The British Channel Islands of Jersey, Guernsey, Alderney and Sark, together with a number of smaller dependencies, lie approximately seventy miles due south of Weymouth within sight (on clear days) of the Cherbourg peninsula in Normandy. Historically, the islands once formed part of the Duchy of Normandy which accounts for their Norman French constitution, customs and patois. Victor Hugo famously described the islands as *morceaux de France tombés à la mer et ramassés par l'Angleterre* (little pieces of France fallen into the sea and gathered up by England).[1] But, although the Bailiwicks of Jersey and Guernsey owe allegiance to the British sovereign as successor to the Dukes of Normandy, they are independent jurisdictions each with their own legislature, the States of Jersey and the States of Deliberation in Guernsey.

French influence on the islands remained strong until improved sea links with Britain resulted in the rapid growth of the English language and culture in the latter part of the nineteenth century. During the First World War, islanders were exposed to external influences on an unprecedented scale as hundreds of local men served with the British Army in France – the first time many had ventured beyond their native community. In the 1930s the islands were known chiefly for their distinctive breeds of cattle and the export of Jersey potatoes and Guernsey tomatoes. Besides horticulture and agriculture, tourism was a significant source of income as large numbers of British holidaymakers took advantage of the mild climate, attractive scenery and sandy beaches.

The Second World War might have had little direct impact on the sedentary way of life in the Channel Islands had events on the Western Front followed the same pattern of trench warfare as in the 1914-18 conflict. However, in May and June 1940 German troops swept through Holland, Belgium and northern France before occupying the Channel Islands, hastily abandoned by the British Government as militarily untenable. The islands remained under German control until the very end of the war in Europe in May 1945.

Basking in the defeat of France, the first German soldiers to set foot in the Channel Islands saw this as a stepping-stone to the invasion of Britain.

For propaganda reasons, the islands, being British soil, assumed an importance disproportionate to their tiny size, signalling to the neutral nations (especially the United States) that Britain stood on the threshold of defeat.[2] From airports in Guernsey and Jersey Luftwaffe aircraft flew raids against targets in the West Country as part of an air campaign in the summer of 1940 intended to bring Britain to her knees. However, the Luftwaffe's failure to achieve air superiority over the Royal Air Force prompted the postponement of invasion plans, leaving the Channel Islands in German hands as a militarily insignificant, but politically prestigious, spoil of war.

What had begun as an unexpected opportunity afforded by the collapse of France thus settled into a long-term military occupation in which Germany needlessly sank immense resources into turning the Channel Islands into an impregnable fortress capable of withstanding frontal assault from air and sea. Plans for the invasion of Britain having been abandoned, the islands became a remote outpost of the Third Reich, permanently garrisoned by a complete infantry division in one of the most heavily fortified sections of the Atlantic Wall. The driving force was Hitler's personal obsession with defending the islands which raised their military profile to the highest strategic level. Such was the islands' prestige value, not only had the civilian administration to contend with local German officialdom, but at times Berlin interfered for political reasons that had little to do with the immediate situation, as when those born in Britain were deported to Germany in September 1942 and February 1943 in reprisal for Britain's internment of German civilians in Iran.

Loyal to the British Crown, but at the same time insular, clannish and strongly attached to their land, islanders found themselves living cheek by jowl with an enemy whose numbers swelled alarmingly. Faced with a foreign invader, many instinctively retreated into their traditional Norman French way of life as growers, smallholders or fishermen until circumstances returned to normal. Given the unique circumstances, there was little alternative. Unlike the other occupied territories, where German forces were never in complete physical control, the Channel Islands were so densely crowded with military personnel that active resistance was virtually impossible. Besides, most island men of military age were serving in the British armed forces.

Partly for these reasons, but also because Nazi policy was based on respect for the Anglo-Saxon race, the German Occupation of the Channel Islands was relatively benign in comparison with many other parts of Europe. Nevertheless, islanders were conscious that their well-being depended upon

continuing acquiescence to the military authorities. Failure to obey German orders would have resulted in severe retribution. Murderous air raids on both Jersey and Guernsey on the eve of the Occupation left islanders in no doubt as to the treatment they could expect should they offer any resistance. The presence of large numbers of forced labourers, mostly Russian and Polish, was a further reminder of the Third Reich's brutality. Islanders who gave trouble could expect severe punishment.

The history of the German Occupation of the Channel Islands is well documented.[3] Indeed, almost every aspect of the Occupation has been thoroughly investigated with the curious exception of religious activity. Even the official history of the Occupation makes no reference to religion, an omission that is all the more surprising given its importance in island life and the unique position of the churches as the only public institution relatively free from interference by the German authorities.[4] Occupation studies generally ignore the churches, as if islanders' religious activities were a private affair with no bearing on civic life.[5] Yet, as sociologists of religion remind us, religious activities have social and political dimensions as well as a spiritual function. Whilst there are several useful studies of European churches under German Occupation during the Second World War, none of them refer to the Channel Islands.[6]

Even when religious activities receive a rare mention in Occupation studies the treatment is cursory to say the least. In a recent academic study of the Occupation Hazel Knowles-Smith dedicates a single paragraph to the role of the churches – revealingly in a chapter entitled 'Pastimes and Entertainments'.[7] Madeleine Bunting at least recognises that the churches had an influential public profile in the islands. In her controversial study of the Channel Islands under German rule, Bunting strongly criticises the churches for failing to speak out against the occupying forces. According to Bunting, the churches meekly followed the example of civilian leaders by avoiding confrontation. Noting the large number of Methodist churches in Guernsey, she finds 'no evidence that they took any stand on the treatment of slave labourers or Jews'.[8] For Bunting, their silence on public issues constitutes a damming indictment of the churches during the Occupation.

Yet the position of the churches during the Occupation is more complex than Bunting allows. Whilst it is true to say that clergy generally were no more outspoken than civilian leaders, this was because in the early days of the Occupation they were warned that anti-German statements from the pulpit would not be tolerated. Given the ample manpower resources at the disposal of the occupying power, it would be naïve to imagine that island

clergy could have criticised German policy without immediately being arrested and their churches closed. A principled stand would have been a noble but futile gesture that could have made no difference to the plight of those concerned but would have deprived islanders of religious activities that had spiritual, social and political value. Doubtless, there would also have been reprisals against the civilian population. Criticising the churches for their silence on public issues during the Occupation without taking account of the circumstances in the islands is both unfair and misleading. In fact, as we shall discover, when unrealistic expectations of martyrdom are set aside there is evidence to suggest that the churches provided a ready outlet for passive resistance to the enemy.

Before and during the Occupation, the main Christian traditions in the Channel Islands in terms of membership were the Church of England and Methodism.[9] Roman Catholics formed the third largest group, and there were several smaller congregations, among them Baptists, Reformed, Pentecostalists and the Salvation Army. Whilst the Church of England was established by law, Methodism was influential in island life and culture. Moreover, Methodism had more churches (chapels as they were usually known) in the islands than any other denomination. Stringent Sunday trading laws that prohibited the opening of shops and public houses (and even the sale of petrol) were due largely to Methodist influence.[10]

The present study examines for the first time how Methodism was able to function during the Occupation, making reference to other churches where appropriate for purposes of comparison. The first chapter sketches the history of Methodism in the Channel Islands by way of background to the project. The events of the summer of 1940 are then examined from the point of view of their impact on religious activities (Chapter 2). Detailed consideration is given to Methodist worship (Chapter 3) and church life (Chapter 4), and the consequences of living in close proximity to the enemy (Chapter 5). The effect of deteriorating social conditions on church life is also investigated (Chapter 6). Whilst ecclesiastical finances seldom receive close attention from historians, the funding of Methodism during the Occupation (Chapter 7) sheds light on the role of the churches as an outlet for passive resistance. Strict Methodist discipline (Chapter 8) and the continuing investment of human resources in children's work (Chapter 9) illustrate islanders' commitment to the future. The full story of Methodism during the Occupation includes the mission to evacuees in Britain, as well as the Methodist contribution to religious life in the internment camps housing islanders deported to Germany (Chapter 10). Finally, consideration

is given to how Methodists prepared for, and responded to, the Liberation (Chapter 11) and its aftermath (Chapter 12).

Sixty years after the Liberation, a study of Methodism during the German Occupation of the Channel Islands is timely since a considerable amount of material is now available to anyone wanting to research religious activity during this period. Island archives in Jersey and in Guernsey contain a wealth of documentation, including captured German files and the records of the civil authorities. The Methodist collections in particular contain a large number of contemporary records deposited by churches within the past decade. The Methodist obsession for recording every aspect of church life means that researchers have access to reliable contemporary sources that allow events to be followed as they unfolded. In some cases even routine announcements made from Methodist pulpits week by week have been preserved.

Accordingly, the present volume is based primarily on contemporary records, including diaries, though selective use has been made of personal reminiscences by those who experienced the Occupation. A deal of caution is required in assessing the reliability of these witnesses since inevitably memories become blurred by the passage of time. For this reason, personal reminiscences have been used sparingly and then only to add detail and colour to written sources. Perhaps in time more of the verbal history of Methodism during the Occupation will find its way into print.

Admittedly, an account of Methodism during the German Occupation of the Channel Islands constitutes just one aspect of what remains an under-researched period in European church history in the twentieth century. Unfortunately, however, the other denominations cannot be considered here if the project is to remain within manageable bounds. Nevertheless, despite its necessarily limited focus, the present volume goes some way towards filling a lamentable gap in Occupation studies and the history of Methodism in the Channel Islands.

Chapter 1

The Rise of Methodism

Channel Islanders have practised their religion since prehistoric times. Neolithic dolmens and similar stone formations have been excavated and a number of grave goods unearthed that show the inhabitants of the islands believed in an afterlife and equipped their dead with provisions for the final journey. Following the discovery of various cultic relics and the study of solar alignments, it has recently been suggested that these prehistoric sites were used principally for worship and that the burial of the dead was incidental to this purpose.[1]

During the Roman period (*c*.100BC to 400AD) the Channel Islands were a strategic trading post on the cross-channel route between northern Gaul and southern England. In 1982 divers discovered the remains of a Gallo-Roman trading vessel under layers of silt in the entrance to St Peter Port harbour. However, despite the excavation of numerous artefacts in the commercial area of the town, no evidence has yet been found to shed light on religious practices in the islands in Roman times. Whether travellers between Gaul and England might have brought Christianity to the islands remains an intriguing possibility.

The earliest Christian missionaries known to have set foot in the Channel Islands were sent by the Celtic Church in the sixth century but virtually no reliable information has survived from this period.[2] Traditional accounts suggest that Guernsey was evangelised around 550 by Sampson, bishop of Dol in Brittany, whilst Jersey was evangelised by Helier, whose feast day (16 July) is still celebrated in the island. Parish names in both islands commemorate the activities of these and other Celtic saints. Another of them, Magloire, nephew of Sampson, converted Sark and founded a monastery. He also established a community of hermit monks on a small island midway between Guernsey and Sark which subsequently became known as Herm.

Adopting their usual strategy, the Celtic missionaries in the Channel Islands abolished pagan festivals and organised the building of parish

churches, many of them on sites formerly associated with pagan worship. Ecclesiastically, the islands were incorporated into the diocese of Coutances, later part of the Duchy of Normandy, though their remoteness meant the old religion was difficult to eradicate. Despite efforts at suppression, pagan customs and superstition proved resilient amongst islanders long used to appeasing the gods of earth and sea in order to ensure their continuing survival. For centuries pagan customs co-existed alongside Christianity until improvements in education in the latter part of the nineteenth century undermined the credibility of folklore.

When King Philip II of France wrested the Duchy of Normandy from King John of England in 1204 the Channel Islands remained in the possession of the English Crown. However, because of strong cultural ties with Normandy, ecclesiastically the islands continued to be part of the diocese of Coutances in the province of Rouen. In 1496 Pope Alexander VI transferred them to the diocese of Salisbury but this arrangement never took effect. In 1499 Pope Alexander cancelled his original instruction and instead transferred the islands to the diocese of Winchester. Henry VII duly informed the bishop of Winchester; but it seems the bishop of Coutances continued to exercise ecclesiastical authority in the islands for several more decades until Elizabeth I issued an Order in Council in 1569 confirming the position of the islands within the diocese of Winchester. By this time, the English Church was in the painful throes of reform.

The impetus for reform in the Channel Islands sprang directly from the continent and not via England. The earliest preachers of reformed doctrines in the islands were Huguenot, French Protestants of Calvinist persuasion who sought refuge from persecution in France.[3] Vacancies among the parish clergy were filled by these French ministers, who then introduced Protestant forms of worship from France and Geneva. When Mary restored Roman Catholicism as the state religion in 1553 most French ministers in the islands fled to Geneva where they came under the influence of a particularly austere form of Presbyterianism. Although the accession of Elizabeth in 1558 secured the Protestant character of the English Church, there followed a century-long feud in the Channel Islands between loyalists upholding the ecclesiastical authority of the bishop of Winchester and French Calvinists, who succeeded in establishing a key component of Presbyterian order in the shape of a powerful consistory court.[4]

Rather than impose the *Book of Common Prayer* on unruly Channel Islanders, Elizabeth was persuaded to give the returning French clergy a free hand to determine forms of worship and ecclesiastical governance on

the grounds that a strong dose of Calvinism would guarantee the islands remained a bulwark against Catholic France. Unfortunately for Elizabeth, the Calvinists proved no more willing to acknowledge the royal supremacy than they had been to accept papal authority. James I eventually reasserted the crown's authority in Jersey by enlisting a new Governor, John Peyton, who insisted upon the king's right to appoint clergy. In 1618 a Dean loyal to the king was installed and in 1623 Prayer Book worship was imposed in all parish churches. In Guernsey, where Calvinism was more deeply entrenched, attempts to install clergy loyal to the king proved unsuccessful.

Following the restoration of the Stuart monarchy in 1660, an Order in Council extended the Act of Uniformity to the Channel Islands, thereby reasserting the authority of the bishop of Winchester over clergy and parish churches. In Guernsey resistance to the Prayer Book was quelled only by threats of armed intervention. Presbyterianism having been vanquished, the 1662 *Book of Common Prayer*, translated into French by Jerseyman Jean Durel, became the exclusive vehicle for worship in the parish churches of the Channel Islands.

For at least the next hundred years the Church of England struggled to maintain an effective presence in the Channel Islands, many islanders being suspicious of a form of religion imposed by external authority. Moreover, the poverty and isolation of island parishes made them unattractive to prospective incumbents with the result that clergy vacancies were numerous and difficult to fill. A shortage of Anglican priests able to speak French further limited the effectiveness of the parish churches amongst the lower social classes, who generally spoke no English. Sometimes former Roman Catholic priests from France were appointed to island parishes since their orders were acceptable to the Church of England, and they could be understood by islanders. But the dubious quality of renegade French priests led to a number of scandals that further weakened the influence of the Church. Finally, a new and alarming challenge to the Church of England appeared on the horizon towards the end of the eighteenth century in the guise of Methodism, which threatened to exploit islanders' non-conforming tendencies.

In his magisterial study of the rise of Methodism, the historian David Hempton identifies a number of factors that influenced the movement's development in the British Isles.[5] According to Hempton, Methodism prospered in communities where squire and parson's combined influence on the social order was weakest. In rural counties such as Sussex, where

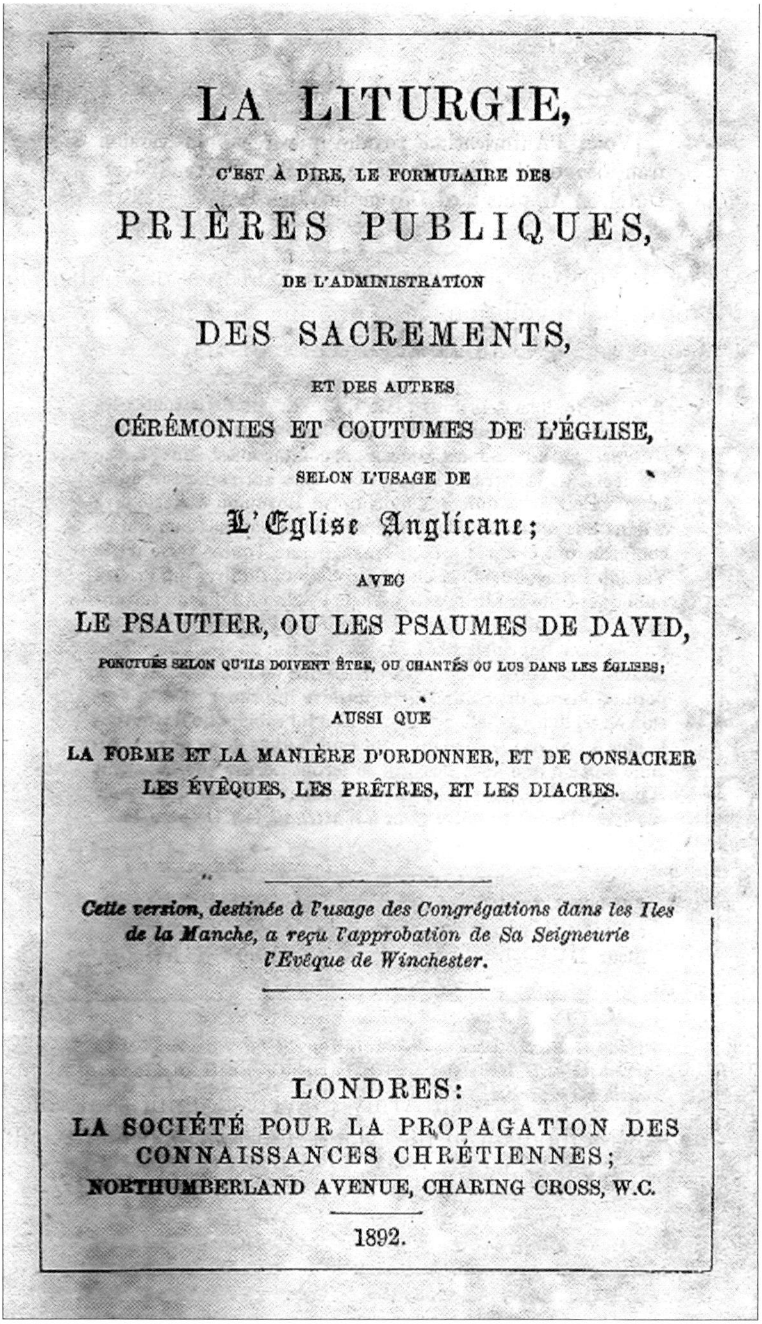

LA LITURGIE,

C'EST À DIRE, LE FORMULAIRE DES

PRIÈRES PUBLIQUES,

DE L'ADMINISTRATION

DES SACREMENTS,

ET DES AUTRES

CÉRÉMONIES ET COUTUMES DE L'ÉGLISE,

SELON L'USAGE DE

L'Eglise Anglicane;

AVEC

LE PSAUTIER, OU LES PSAUMES DE DAVID,

PONCTUÉS SELON QU'ILS DOIVENT ÊTRE, OU CHANTÉS OU LUS DANS LES ÉGLISES;

AUSSI QUE

LA FORME ET LA MANIÈRE D'ORDONNER, ET DE CONSACRER
LES ÉVÊQUES, LES PRÊTRES, ET LES DIACRES.

*Cette version, destinée à l'usage des Congrégations dans les Îles
de la Manche, a reçu l'approbation de Sa Seigneurie
l'Evêque de Winchester.*

LONDRES:

LA SOCIÉTÉ POUR LA PROPAGATION DES
CONNAISSANCES CHRÉTIENNES;
NORTHUMBERLAND AVENUE, CHARING CROSS, W.C.

1892.

Figure 1.1: The 1662 Book of Common Prayer *was translated into
French by Jerseyman Jean Durel for use in the Channel Islands*

squire and parson effectively controlled an essentially agricultural economy, it was difficult for Methodism to gain a foothold. Here the livelihood of agricultural workers depended upon their conforming to the will of the landowner, who invariably regarded Methodism as a threat to social stability and profits. Conversely, Methodism tended to flourish in places where the social order was more fluid and the economy diverse so that workers were not dependent upon a single employer. Thus the heartlands of Methodism came to be located in the rapidly expanding urban areas of Northern England where the industrial revolution was gathering strength.

Beyond the burgeoning industrial areas, Methodist preaching also found fertile soil in socially isolated and close-knit communities where the principal occupation involved facing constant danger. Such communities, which set particular store by superstition and the religious interpretation of natural phenomena, were more easily persuaded to seek signs of divine providence in their lives. Moreover, a strong sense of corporate identity often meant that the recruitment of significant figures yielded further conversions. Mining and fishing communities were especially receptive to Methodist preachers, as were soldiers serving in the British Army. Being itinerant, fishermen and soldiers were valuable converts because they proved effective carriers of Methodism to fresh locations. Finally, Methodism prospered on the Celtic fringes of England where the influence of the established church was historically weak. Thus remote Cornwall with its mining and fishing communities became Methodism's southern redoubt. In Scotland, where a few wealthy landowners controlled vast areas, Methodism made little headway, though the isolated fishing communities on the East coast proved more receptive, as did the Shetland Islands.

Applying Hempton's theory about the spread of Methodism explains why the movement flourished in the Channel Islands despite initial opposition. Following the conventional pattern, Methodism first took hold within Jersey's deep-sea fishing community. Then, at a crucial juncture, soldiers serving in the British Army played a significant role in the consolidation of Methodism in the island. Once established, Methodism exploited the relative weakness of the Anglican Church by appealing to a large section of the population that had never been effectively evangelised. At the same time, Methodism was fiercely opposed by a tacit alliance between irreligious islanders and a conservative establishment that felt equally threatened by the prospect of a Methodist awakening.

At first, the remoteness of the Channel Islands from England, the difficulty of sea communication and the language barrier all meant that

Methodism was slow to reach the islands in the eighteenth century. Long before there was a Methodist society in Jersey, Methodism was already established in North America, introduced by British and Irish settlers following the transatlantic trade route. When Methodism finally arrived in the Channel Islands it was via the fishing fleet that plied between Jersey and the fishing grounds off Newfoundland on the eastern coast of Canada. In 1779 or 1780 a number of Jerseymen in Newfoundland with the fishing fleet attended revival meetings in St John's led by Laurence Coughlan, an Anglican priest and Methodist preacher serving as a missionary with the SPCK.[6] Two fishermen in particular, Pierre Le Sueur (1747-1819) and Jean Tentin, were strongly influenced by Coughlan and returned to Jersey with an awakened spiritual conscience.[7]

Tentin later left Jersey, but not before he and Le Sueur had gathered a small circle of believers at great personal cost. Le Sueur was ostracised and his business ruined on account of his activities. Even his wife was initially hostile until, after experiencing spiritual conversion, she joined the two men in praying for religious revival. Given the hostile conditions, the flame of Methodist renewal might soon have been extinguished had it not been for a providential sequence of events. A Congregationalist sea captain from Poole, John Brown, preached to the fledgling Methodist group on his regular visits to the island, as did a blind Baptist preacher named Bestland. Between them they kept the group together though, since neither spoke French, Le Sueur was obliged to translate.

Then in November 1783 Le Sueur met a small group of Methodist soldiers, recently arrived in Jersey, who sought the company of like-minded Christians. As a result of the Calvinist preaching of Brown and Bestland, Le Sueur was initially suspicious of their allegiance to John Wesley. But reassured by their explanation of the Methodist doctrine of grace, he agreed that Wesley be asked to send a bilingual preacher to the island. A letter was promptly dispatched to Jasper Winscomb, a Methodist preacher in Winchester where the soldiers had recently been stationed, asking him to exert his influence with Wesley.

When John Wesley received Winscomb's appeal he happened to have with him Robert Carr Brackenbury (1752-1818), a Cambridge graduate whose wife had recently died. Brackenbury was a cultured man of independent means, willing and able to devote his energies to the Methodist cause. In December 1783 Wesley sent Brackenbury to Jersey accompanied by Alexander Kilham to begin Methodist work in the island. Soon Wesley was writing to him:

I rejoice to hear you have had a safe passage, and that you have preached both in Guernsey and Jersey. We must not expect many conveniences at first: hitherto it is a day of small things. I should imagine the sooner you begin to preach in French the better: surely you need not be careful about accuracy. Trust God, and speak as well as you can.[8]

The establishment of a Methodist society in Jersey under the ministry of Brackenbury led to Methodism being introduced to Guernsey. In the autumn of 1785 two Jersey sisters, both Methodist converts, visited the home of their brother, Pierre Arrivé, in St Peter Port. Deeply distrustful of Methodism, Arrivé subsequently modified his views and invited Brackenbury to come across to Guernsey. The urbane preacher was so warmly received that soon afterwards he wrote to Thomas Coke urging him to find a French-speaking preacher for Guernsey. Coke immediately decided to visit Brackenbury in Jersey to assess the situation. In the absence of anyone more suitably qualified, they decided to send a young Jersey Methodist, Jean de Quetteville, who arrived in Guernsey in February 1786 following a short mission conducted by Coke. The Conference that summer accepted de Quetteville as an itinerant preacher. Later the same year, he was joined by Adam Clarke.

Nominally, Thomas Coke was bishop and General Superintendent of the Methodist Episcopal Church in the United States but his ambitions for Methodism were global. For Coke, the Channel Islands had a strategic importance far beyond their tiny size. In particular, he saw the possibility of a mission to Catholic France using Methodist preachers raised in the islands. Accordingly, in 1786 Coke launched Methodism's first financial appeal in support of 'overseas missions' in various strategic locations in the world, including the Channel Islands. At first, the prospects for a French mission seemed promising. As early as 1791, William Mahy became the first Methodist preacher raised in the Channel Islands to be sent as a missionary to France. However, the mission never prospered and eventually came to an end in the final years of the nineteenth century.

Whether John Wesley shared Coke's vision for a mission to France is not certain, though he made a short visit to the Channel Islands in August 1787 in order to encourage Methodist work.[9] In Alderney, where his ship was unexpectedly obliged to take shelter in a gale, he preached on the beach to a small congregation. In Guernsey he received hospitality from Henri de Jersey, a prosperous fruit and cider farmer who frequently entertained

Brackenbury and de Quetteville. Here Wesley preached 'in a large room to as deeply serious a congregation as ever I saw' (a not infrequent refrain in his journal). Likewise, in St Helier he addressed 'an exceeding serious congregation'. In Jersey he also ventured to preach in the country parishes: 'Mr Brackenbury interpreted sentence by sentence, and God owned his word, though delivered in so awkward a manner, but especially in prayer. I prayed in English, and Mr B. in French.'

Despite the respect shown to Wesley as a venerable churchman, opposition to Methodism in the Channel Islands was fierce, though probably no worse than elsewhere in the British Isles, even if those on the receiving end were convinced otherwise. A Jersey preacher later recalled:

> I doubt whether there exists a place in all the British dominions, where the opposition has been so long and obstinate as in this island. For many years hardly was there one quiet meeting throughout the country; laughing, throwing peas, stones, dirt, rotten eggs, breaking of windows and tiles, insulting the women, and hooting through the streets, were the common attendants on our assemblies.[10]

Opposition was encouraged by Anglican clergy, for whom Methodism constituted unwelcome competition, though irreligious islanders generally required little incitement to attack Methodist gatherings. As elsewhere, magistrates were disposed to blame Methodist preachers for the disorder that often followed their preaching.

Beyond the fear of physical assault, the most serious problem facing Methodism in the Channel Islands in the eighteenth century was the requirement for militiamen to drill on Sundays. From a Methodist perspective, this was inappropriate on the Lord's Day, interfered with religious observance and encouraged carousing. From the perspective of the authorities, however, refusing to drill on Sundays appeared unpatriotic at a time of heightened fears of French invasion. Methodists in the Channel Islands were regularly fined for refusing to muster on Sundays until in 1799 Thomas Coke successfully appealed to the Privy Council for them to be exempt from routine military duties on Sundays.

Despite opposition and a comparatively late start, Methodism in the Channel Islands quickly became an established feature of British Methodism recognised by the Conference. The islands first appear on the official list of ministerial stations for 1786: Robert Carr Brackenbury and Adam Clarke being the itinerant preachers in Jersey; and Jean de Quetteville in Guernsey.

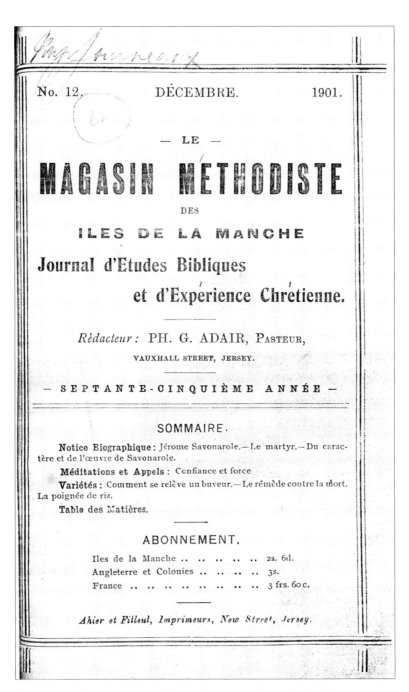

Figure 1.2: Le Magasin Méthodiste des Iles de la Manche *was published monthly between 1817 and 1901*

By the following year, 200 members were reported in Jersey and 100 in Guernsey and Alderney. In 1797 the Channel Islands became a separate administrative district of British Methodism comprising five ministers and a total membership of 681.[11]

The rapid growth of Methodism in the Channel Islands during the nineteenth century can be attributed principally to the availability of itinerant Wesleyan preachers who spoke French and were willing, albeit sometimes under duress, to serve a tour of duty in the 'Norman Isles'. Publication of a monthly journal, *Le Magasin Méthodiste des Iles de la Manche*, underscored Methodism's commitment to its mission in the islands. Modelled on John Wesley's *Arminian Magazine*, *Le Magasin Méthodiste* contained sermons and edifying contemporary stories of divine works and providence as well as news of overseas missions.[12]

William Toase ministered for nine years in the Channel Islands, later admitting: 'There I suffered more than ever I did in all the Circuits together, where I served.'[13] Even so, he regarded his call to the islands as providential. In 1805 he was appointed to the Doncaster Circuit where he felt compelled to learn French, though he had no inkling where it would lead. Two years later he was sent to the Channel Islands where he met and married his wife. He left Guernsey after a two-year tour of duty but eventually returned in 1815 as General Superintendent, his task to impose order on the chaotic state of Methodism. Resentful at being asked to serve a second tour of duty in the islands, in the end he relented 'solely in obedience to the wishes of the Conference'.[14]

Imposing discipline on Methodism in the Channel Islands was a tall order, made more difficult by the truculence of islanders. At his first quarterly meeting as General Superintendent, objections were raised about the cost of supporting English ministers and their families in the islands. Toase was criticised for preaching from written notes, though he insisted these were merely section headings.[15] Discipline among the local preachers was virtually non-existent: Toase convened a preachers' meeting only to discover they had never before met together. Worse still, they were 'as ignorant of our discipline as if they had never heard a Methodist preacher'.[16]

Problems of discipline apart, Methodism continued to expand in the Channel Islands in the nineteenth century as the increasing number of chapels confirms. The first Methodist building in Jersey was a ruined Roman Catholic chapel, which Le Sueur bought and restored in 1784.[17] In the course of the next five years the Methodist society raised £400 to purchase a more

suitable property but the States of Jersey would not register a contract of sale to a body that it steadfastly refused to recognise. So in 1790 a house in King Street, St Helier, was purchased in the name of one of the Methodist members and adapted for worship. The first purpose-built chapel was erected at St Ouen in 1809 and thereafter 23 chapels were built in the next 50 years. In Guernsey, the first purpose-built Methodist chapel was situated in Rue Le Marchant near the Royal Court in St Peter Port. Adam Clarke preached the dedicatory sermon on 20 April 1789.[18] The Bailiff, William Le Marchant, was supportive of the project to the extent that he contributed £50 towards building costs and even rented a pew for himself and his family, though it is not known whether he attended services.[19] Two more chapels opened in 1814, and a further 18 were added in the next 50 years.[20]

Figure 1.3: Chapelle des Pas, Jersey, the first Methodist church in the Channel Islands

Correspondingly, Wesleyan Methodist membership in the Channel Islands grew from 795 in 1800 to a peak of 4,079 in 1870, though a decade later it had fallen back to 3,507.[21] In 1901 the Wesleyan Methodist District Synod reported 3,326 members, 118 fewer than the previous year but still a healthy number. At Methodist Union in 1932, Wesleyan membership in the

District totalled 3,150, a slight decline (5.3 percent) since the turn of the century but as yet no cause for concern.[22] When those belonging to the smaller Methodist denominations were added, the combined total stood at 4,076. Thus, on the eve of the Second World War, Methodism in the Channel Islands was still in a strong position, though the combined membership statistics obscured an underlying decline across the uniting traditions.

A lack of itinerant preachers proficient in the French language seriously hindered the non-Wesleyan Methodist denominations in establishing themselves in the Channel Islands. First to arrive were the Bible Christians, who in 1823 sent three itinerant preachers (two of them young women) on a mission to the islands. A succession of preachers followed but the work never extended beyond St Helier and St Peter Port. By 1868 there were still only 197 Bible Christians in Jersey and 40 in Guernsey. When the Bible Christians eventually united with two other Methodist traditions in 1907 to form the United Methodist Church they had 582 members in Jersey and 268 in Guernsey.[23] But the loss of a distinctive denominational identity led to decline, and by 1932 there were only 261 United Methodists in Jersey.

Next to arrive in the islands were the Primitive Methodists. Sailors from Guernsey attending Primitive Methodist revival meetings in South Shields in 1832 asked for a preacher to be sent to their island. The first Primitive Methodist preacher in the Channel Islands, George Cosens, a West Indian, arrived around the time of an outbreak of cholera, which served to heighten religious interest amongst the population. In 1839 a chapel was opened in Aquila Road, St Helier, but this turned out to be the only Primitive Methodist cause in Jersey. Again, a lack of preachers able to speak French prevented the movement from making headway in the country parishes. At the time of Methodist Union in 1932 there were 207 Primitive Methodists in Jersey. In Guernsey Primitive Methodism struggled for years and by 1932 had only one chapel with 71 members. It closed soon afterwards. A cause was established in Alderney in the middle of the nineteenth century but did not last long.

The Methodist New Connexion was the first splinter group in Wesleyan Methodism following the death of John Wesley in 1791 but the last to reach the Channel Islands. In 1836 a dispute between the minister and elements of the congregation at Ebenezer in St Peter Port concerning the authority of the Wesleyan Conference led to the resignation of several class leaders and more than one hundred members. The breakaway faction acquired premises and threw in their lot with the Methodist New Connexion. William Booth,

one of the connexion's most effective evangelists, made three preaching tours in Guernsey between 1854 and 1860 before leaving his co-religionists to found the Christian Mission, forerunner of the Salvation Army. In 1862 the Methodist New Connexion opened St Paul's church, flagship premises occupying a prime site in St Peter Port. The building could accommodate 950 people, though its size owed more to denominational pride than to any practical requirements.

Until the latter part of the nineteenth century, Methodist worship in the Channel Islands was conducted mainly in French, though a few churches were English-speaking, and some held services in both languages. For practical reasons, separate Wesleyan circuits for French and English work were established in both main islands. Since the itinerant preachers in the French circuits usually spoke no English, they could not be stationed elsewhere. By the beginning of the twentieth century, English was rapidly replacing French as the preferred language in business and education which put pressure on the churches to modernise. As always, young people provided the catalyst for change since they tended to prefer church services in English. On the eve of the Occupation, French was seldom used in Methodist worship in Jersey and in steep decline in Guernsey (see Chapter 3).

Alderney and Sark

The first Methodist missionary to set foot in Alderney was Adam Clarke in 1787, a few months before the visit of John Wesley. Several islanders opened their homes for Methodist preaching, though cooling ardour made it difficult to sustain meetings of converts between Clarke's infrequent visits. When a Methodist society was eventually formed it attracted the usual assortment of individuals and religious experience, invariably reported in stock terms: at one early meeting a Roman Catholic man was said to have been strongly convicted of his sins by Methodist preaching before experiencing forgiveness during the following week's sermon.[24] When the requirement for militia drill on Sundays was relaxed, the Governor of Alderney formed Methodists into a single company, nicknamed Gideon's Army, which was allowed to drill during the week.[25]

In 1790 the first Methodist chapel in Alderney was dedicated by Jean de Quetteville.[26] This proved too small for the congregation and was replaced by a larger chapel in 1813. A gallery was added in 1839, increasing capacity to 380. If this creates the impression of rapid growth in Methodism, the

RECUEIL

DE

CANTIQUES

A L'USAGE DES

ÉGLISES MÉTHODISTES

DES ILES DE LA MANCHE

———

NOUVELLE ÉDITION AVEC SUPPLÉMENT

———

LONDRES
WESLEYAN CONFERENCE OFFICE
2, CASTLE-STREET, CITY-ROAD
ET CHEZ LES PASTEURS MÉTHODISTES DES ILES
DE LA MANCHE

—

1893

Figure 1.4: The Wesleyan Methodist Conference published a collection of French hymns for use in the Channel Islands

4 Que mon âme et vive et te loue,
Par ton Esprit, toujours plus humblement ;
 Sauveur à qui je me dévoue,
 Fais-moi vivre éternellement.

CANTIQUE 58.

Air 6. (6. 6. 8. 6.)

1 JÉSUS, Seigneur de tous,
  Si propice et si doux,
Si riche en faveur des croyants,
 Entends tes suppliants.

2 Par tes attraits vainqueurs,
  Attire à toi nos cœurs ;
Que les trésors de ton amour
  Soient ouverts en ce jour.

3 Ta perçante clarté
  Voit notre pauvreté ;
Subviens à nos besoins pressants
  Par tes dons abondants.

4 Nous invoquons ton nom ;
  Dieu si riche et si bon,
Notre cœur soupire après toi ;
  Réponds à notre foi.

CANTIQUE 59.

Air 8. (8. 8. 8. 8.)

1 INSPIRE-MOI, divin Sauveur,
  Ton zèle et ta fidélité ;
Fais régner la foi dans mon cœur.
Avec ta sainte humilité.

Figure 1.5: A hymn from the Wesleyan Methodist French hymnbook

reality was somewhat different. As elsewhere in the British Isles, Methodists in the Channel Islands built to anticipate future needs often based on unrealistic expectations.

In 1850 William Toase visited Alderney to observe the situation of Methodism following the sudden increase in population from just over 1,000 to more than 3,000 as a result of an Admiralty scheme to build an immense breakwater to protect Royal Navy vessels patrolling the English Channel. The sudden influx of labourers, many of them hard-drinking men, had a serious impact on social conditions. Toase described the religious state of the island as 'deplorable'.[27] He undertook an energetic programme of preaching and pastoral visitation, targeting the many 'backsliders from Methodism' whose chief pastime was the consumption of gin and brandy. Realistically, the availability of 1,700 seats in island churches was far in excess of actual needs, though Toase (with the optimism characteristic of nineteenth-century clergy) believed more would be necessary as the population was still rising.[28] At its peak in 1860 Wesleyan Methodist membership stood at a modest 161 but completion of the breakwater scheme led to a slump in the population of Alderney and its economic fortunes with a corresponding decline in Methodism.

Thereafter, Methodism in Alderney struggled, though from time to time numbers increased as a result of the permanent garrison being temporarily reinforced in response to heightened political tensions with France. The Wesleyan congregation was never able to pay for its resident minister, who therefore had to be financed by the Wesleyan Methodist Home Missions department. In 1933 Methodist membership in Alderney stood at just 36.

The first Methodist missionary to visit Sark was Jean de Quetteville in 1792. One of his first hearers was Jean Vaudin, who promptly offered accommodation and the use of his home for services. Before long there were regular visits from Methodist preachers in Guernsey who stayed with Vaudin or another of the converts. Vaudin became the first class leader on Sark and provided land for the building of the first Methodist chapel, which opened in 1797. There were two tiny rooms above the entrance to house preachers visiting from Guernsey.[29]

In 1833 a Methodist preacher from Jersey began the first Sunday school on Sark. Two years later a gallery was installed in the chapel, increasing its capacity to 200. Since the indigenous population stood at just 550 people, the extension was presumably intended to cater for the presence of 250 Cornish miners working the silver mines on Little Sark. However, there was

no profit to be made in the enterprise and the miners soon returned home, leaving Methodism with a chapel far too large for its needs.

For the next hundred years Methodism on Sark continued uneventfully on its way with little change in the small Methodist community. In 1925 a new chapel, seating a more modest total of 120, was built on a freehold site financed by Methodism in Guernsey. Even this was probably too large for the actual size of congregation. In 1939 the membership stood at just 20.

Chapter 2

Islands at War

When Britain and France declared war against Germany on 3 September 1939 few places in Europe could have felt more remote from hostilities than the Channel Islands. Apart from the introduction of conscription for men of military age, life continued much as before, the introduction of rationing and lighting restrictions being the only visible signs of wartime, though air raid wardens frequently complained that people were not taking the blackout as seriously as they should.

If so, Channel Islanders were hardly alone in shrugging off the threat of enemy attack. The 'phoney war' that continued into the spring of 1940 encouraged a sense of complacency throughout Britain and France, an attitude compounded by widespread confidence that the Maginot Line was impregnable. Constructed by the French in the 1930s, this impressive chain of fortifications stretched the entire length of their border with Germany. Beyond that, the British Expeditionary Force stood ready to defend the Franco-Belgian border and Channel ports. But, with neither side seemingly willing to seize the initiative, the Western Front settled into stalemate. Advertisements in British newspapers, including the *Methodist Recorder*, encouraged holidaymakers to take advantage of the lack of travel restrictions to enjoy a summer holiday in the Channel Islands.

The European war had little immediate effect on Methodism in the Channel Islands. In September 1939 there were four circuits in Jersey, the largest being the Jersey (Grove Place) Circuit with eighteen churches and four ministers. The flagship church, in Grove Place, St Helier, comfortably sat 1,400 people, though the entire circuit at that time mustered fewer than 900 members. The Jersey (Wesley) Circuit comprised two ministers and six churches, the largest of which (Wesley chapel, membership 103) could accommodate 940 people. Prior to Methodist Union in 1932 both circuits were Wesleyan Methodist, Grove Place being the French-speaking circuit and Wesley the English circuit. Aquila Road church in St Helier was the

island's only Primitive Methodist chapel, a status reflected in the fact that even in 1939 it continued to exist as a separate circuit with its own minister. Lastly, the Jersey (Great Union Road) Circuit was served by one minister, who looked after three churches that had originally been Bible Christian. The main church in Royal Crescent, St Helier, could seat 900 people – nearly three times the circuit membership on the eve of war.

Figure 2.1: Grove Place Methodist Church,
St Helier, from a 19th century drawing

In the Bailiwick of Guernsey there were three circuits. The Guernsey (English) Circuit comprised four ministers and ten churches plus a rented mission hall in Cornet Street, St Peter Port. Two of the smaller churches began life as Bible Christian chapels, the rest were former Wesleyan Methodist causes. Ebenezer church, the largest building in the circuit, had seats for 900 people. The Guernsey and Sark (French) Circuit boasted four ministers and 16 churches, all of them formerly Wesleyan Methodist. The largest of these, in Victoria Road, could accommodate a congregation of 700, though in 1939 there were only 84 members. A retired minister looked after the chapel on Sark, living in a rented cottage. Remote Alderney formed

a separate circuit consisting of one minister and a single church. So as to avoid complete isolation, the Alderney minister was required on two Sundays in each year to exchange pulpits with colleagues in Guernsey.

Germany's invasion of Poland on 1 September 1939 coincided with the start of the Methodist year when, under the itinerant system peculiar to Methodism, ministers commenced duties in the circuit to which they had been appointed by the preceding Conference. Since, at that time, ministers typically served only three or four years in a particular circuit, the annual turnover of staff in larger circuits was anywhere between a quarter and a third. In 1939 four ministers arrived in the Channel Islands to take up new appointments.

Two Jersey circuits welcomed a new superintendent minister (appointed by the Conference to be in overall charge of a circuit). Donald Stuart (1886-1948) was born into a Wesleyan Methodist ministerial family. After training for the ministry at Richmond College, he served in a number of circuits before becoming superintendent of the Jersey (Wesley) Circuit.[1] An avowed Pacifist, Stuart became embroiled in a bitter conflict with lay officials which posed the most serious internal threat to Methodism during the Occupation and led to his suffering a nervous breakdown from which he never fully recovered.

Clement Mylne (1885-1970) was the last ministerial candidate to be accepted by the Bible Christians before their merger with two other Methodist denominations in 1907.[2] After ministerial training at Shebbear College, the following year he was sent to the Chao Tong Fu Circuit in West China where he began studying the Chinese language in order to work among the Nosu tribe. In 1927 ill-health forced him to return permanently to England where he served in a number of circuits in the London area before becoming superintendent of the Jersey (Great Union Road) Circuit. Mylne was imprisoned by the German authorities in 1943 for illegally possessing a radio.

In the Bailiwick of Guernsey there were two ministerial changes. Edgar Calvert arrived in Alderney to assume pastoral charge of what would once again become a garrison church serving the battalion sent to reinforce this lonely outpost of the British Empire. Philip Romeril was stationed in the Guernsey (English) circuit. Altogether, there were eight ministers in each of the main islands, plus one on Alderney and a retired minister on Sark. There were also two retired ministers in Jersey and three in Guernsey (See Appendix).

Three other Methodist ministers may conveniently be introduced at this

*Left, Figure 2.2: Rev. Donald Stuart, photographed in 1941 for identity card
(Jersey Archive D/S/A/4/A11380 Courtesy of the Jersey Heritage Trust)
Right, Figure 2.3: Rev. Sidney Beaugié (Herbert White Collection)*

point. William Ward was appointed superintendent of the Jersey (Grove Place) Circuit in 1938. Then aged 66, he was the oldest serving Methodist minister in Jersey. His previous ministry in Primitive Methodism included three tours of duty in West Africa.[3] On finally returning to England, he became national Home Missions Secretary for Primitive Methodism. Following Methodist Union in 1932, he was appointed Chairman of the Wolverhampton and Shrewsbury District. His experience and gifts proved invaluable to Jersey Methodism during the Occupation.

The superintendent of the Guernsey and Sark (French) Circuit was Sidney Beaugié (1879-1966), a native of Jersey whose family were stalwarts of the French circuit. After obtaining a double first in Mathematics at Oxford, he was accepted for the Wesleyan ministry. Through his ability to preach in French, he had already served a tour of duty in Guernsey (1923-28). In 1933 he returned to the French circuit as superintendent. Beaugié proved to be a resourceful leader when it came to steering Methodism through the

uncharted waters of the Occupation.[4]

Residing in the Guernsey (English) Circuit was a minister without appointment, John Leale (1892-1969), who led the civilian administration of the island from October 1940 to the end of the Occupation. Leale was born into a prosperous Guernsey family.[5] On graduating from Cambridge, he entered the Wesleyan ministry in 1913. His first ministerial appointment was in the Manchester and Salford Mission but, because of ill-health, he returned to Guernsey in 1922 without pastoral responsibilities. In 1930 he was elected a people's Deputy in the States of Deliberation and four years later was appointed a Jurat.[6] When the executive was streamlined in order to cope with the expected arrival of German forces, Leale was appointed a member of the Controlling Committee then its President. In the Liberation honours announced in December 1945 he received a knighthood for his services to the island during the Occupation.

The four Jersey circuits together with the three in the Bailiwick of Guernsey comprised the Channel Islands District of the Methodist Church, one of 47 districts in British Methodism which constituted an administrative tier between the Conference and its 1,200 circuits. The Conference, held annually, is the highest authority in British Methodism, and the majority of its members are elected representatives of the districts. Being comparatively small, in the 1930s the Channel Islands District was represented at the annual Conference by one minister and a layperson.

The Methodist Conference alone has the authority to approve major institutional reforms affecting circuits – an arrangement that safeguards Methodist interests against local power struggles but in the extraordinary circumstances of July 1940 made it difficult for Methodism in the Channel Islands to adapt to the circumstances of enemy occupation. Cut off from communicating with the Conference, Methodists in the Channel Islands would have to decide for themselves what institutional changes would be necessary so that Methodism could continue to function. But, in the face of competing convictions, how could the unity and discipline of Methodism be preserved without the authority of the Conference? The role of the Chairman of the District would be crucial.

Among the ministers stationed in each district one was designated by Conference as Chairman of the District. Besides fulfilling normal ministerial duties, he presided over the District Synod, comprising ministers and lay representatives from the circuits, and was responsible to the Conference for ministerial discipline. In 1939 the Chairman of the Channel Islands District

was 58 year-old Frederick Flint, superintendent of the Guernsey (English) Circuit. Flint served as an army chaplain during the First World War, and his varied experience in ministry included a period in the London Mission (East End) Circuit.[7] Under the system of distributed authority that is characteristic of Methodism, the powers of the District Chairman were strictly limited. Whilst Methodists might look to Flint for leadership in a time of crisis, they would not hesitate to point out the limits of his authority should they disapprove of his actions. In practice, this meant that churches and lay officials had a veto over proposals of which they disapproved.

Nevertheless, during the Occupation, Flint skilfully exercised a personal ministry of oversight that was commonly accepted among Methodists as a lawful substitute for the authority of the Conference. On several occasions Flint's decisive leadership came to the rescue of Methodism. In particular, his intervention in the affairs of the Jersey (Wesley) Circuit in 1941 almost certainly avoided disaster.

The Secretary of the District Synod (and constitutionally the Chairman's deputy) was Walter Fell, superintendent of the Jersey (Aquila Road) Circuit

Left, Figure 2.4: Rev. Frederick Flint, photographed in 1941 for identity card (Courtesy of Island Archives, Guernsey)
Right, Figure 2.5: Rev. Walter Fell, photographed in 1941 for identity card (*Jersey Archive D/S/A/4/A3945* Courtesy of the Jersey Heritage Trust)

29

since 1935. Fell began his ministry in Primitive Methodism and had already served a tour of duty in the Channel Islands.[8] When Flint was deported to Germany in 1942, Fell automatically became Acting Chairman of the District. Though they could hardly have foreseen such circumstances, those who drafted the Methodist constitution prevented a power struggle arising as a result of Flint's deportation. The transfer of authority from Flint to Fell preserved the authority of the Conference, thereby avoiding a power vacuum in which churches acted unilaterally. Had that happened it would have been difficult for the Conference to reassert its authority over congregations after the Liberation.

In normal times the District Synod met twice a year to consider business required by the Conference and to discuss matters of common interest. The Channel Islands District seldom troubled the rest of British Methodism with its affairs, though in 1938 the Synod formally asked Conference to enquire of His Majesty's Minister of Health why certain ministers stationed in the islands found themselves at a disadvantage under Government health provision on their return to Britain.[9] The Synod met as usual in May 1940 but the prohibition on inter-island travel during the Occupation prevented further meetings until 1946.[10]

Whether the District Synod might have had a significant role to play in Methodism during the Occupation had it been allowed to meet is difficult to say, though on the whole this seems unlikely. Since the ability of the Synod to intervene in the internal affairs of circuits was limited, there is no reason to suppose that it could have made a decisive difference to the administration of Methodism, though it might have been able to put its weight behind initiatives for rationalisation. As things stood, with the Synod out of action, the distributed authority structures that tied the hands of the District Chairman made it equally impossible for superintendents to impose reforms without the consent of churches. In a situation that demanded decisive action, Methodism was stuck with an essentially consultative decision-making process more suited to peacetime conditions. That Methodism in the Channel Islands did not grind to a halt during the Occupation was due in no small measure to the heroic efforts of ministers, local preachers and lay officials in maintaining structures that remained burdensome even after modest reforms were agreed in July 1940.

The need for Methodism in the Channel Islands to face up to strategic decisions was not entirely due to the Occupation. On paper, even before the war there was a strong case for rationalising the number of circuits, churches and ministers, not least because Methodist Union in 1932 brought together

competing denominations under the umbrella of a single polity. For instance, there was little justification for maintaining four separate circuits in an island the size of Jersey. However, a combination of loyalties and longstanding local rivalries meant that the vast majority of Methodists were determined to preserve the status quo whatever the cost.

The number and size of church buildings also made little sense. Following national trends, Methodists in the Channel Islands had overstretched themselves in building places of worship on a grand scale, partly as a matter of denominational prestige and partly in anticipation of future needs based on unrealistic assumptions about the projected growth of Methodism. Guernsey Methodism could accommodate a total of 8,842 people at Sunday worship (20 percent of the population), whereas the combined Methodist membership in 1940 was 2,176 (5.1 percent of the population).[11] In Jersey, Methodist pews could seat 10,948 (21 percent of the population) in contrast to a total membership of around 1,800 (3.5 percent of the population). Even when generous allowance is made for adherents and Sunday school children the fact remains that, even before the Occupation, Methodism had more places of worship than were needed.

The cost of maintaining expensive buildings was a constant drain on resources but, without the will to reorganise, rationalisation was generally piecemeal and imposed by circumstances. St Paul's church in St Peter Port was sold in 1938 because of insurmountable structural problems. Otherwise, trustees were implacably opposed to any development that would lead to the closure of their chapel – a situation common in British Methodism in the 1930s.

Since rationalisation was off the agenda, the most pressing issue facing Methodism in the Channel Islands in the opening months of the war was how to maintain public worship given the shortage of local preachers resulting from conscription and other forms of wartime service. Since local preachers led the majority of Sunday services, a reduction in their number placed a greater burden on individuals. To make matters worse, petrol rationing disrupted public and private transport.

Yet congregations often did not appreciate the situation. In January 1940 William Ward, superintendent of the Jersey (Grove Place) Circuit, placed a notice in the quarterly preaching plan reminding churches of current difficulties and seeking their assistance. The message was repeated in even stronger terms in the preaching plan for July-September 1940, printed before the Occupation:

Our local preachers – loyal and willing always, are giving of their utmost to make the continuation of *all* the Sunday Services possible. Through national calls and service the lessened number of preachers available is making heavier demands on those still with us. We ask, therefore, that the Churches will assist the brethren, as may be required, by helping them to and from their appointments.[12]

Blackout regulations posed a further problem in winter months since churches had difficulty in ensuring that no lights were shown. The only solution was to alter the time of evening services during the winter; but this was deeply unpopular and confusing for people long used to Sunday being regulated by fixed hours of worship. It should also be remembered that most Methodist churches at this time held their principal service on Sunday evening. Alarmed at falling attendances, Ward reminded congregations: 'Special attention is called to the alterations in times of services.' Before long, however, remembering the time of the service would be the least of the problems facing Methodists in the Channel Islands.

The phoney war on the Western Front came to an abrupt end on 10 May 1940 when German forces launched a massive attack, advancing unchecked through Holland and Belgium towards Paris and the Channel ports. Armoured columns poured through the supposedly impenetrable Ardennes Forest on the northern edge of the Franco-German border, bypassing the Maginot line and driving a wedge between British and French forces. At the end of the month, the British army was hastily evacuated from Dunkirk. The fall of Paris on 14 June signalled the imminent defeat of France. Among the hordes of refugees fleeing the city was Herbert Bishop, minister of the English-speaking Methodist church in the Rue Roquépine, who headed south towards Limoges.[13] Suddenly, Channel Islanders were forced to decide between being overrun by German forces or else evacuating to England.

Around this time, Douglas Ord (1898-1978), minister in the Guernsey (English) Circuit began to keep a diary that would eventually run to more than a thousand typed pages kept hidden under the floorboards of the choir stalls at his Brock Road church in St Peter Port.[14] Paul Sanders, an academic historian of the Occupation, describes Ord's unpublished diary as 'arguably the most significant document to have emerged from the Channel Islands' Occupation'.[15]

Ord was an extraordinary example of a Methodist minister with scholarly interests. He served as a soldier with the British army in France during the

Figure 2.6: Rev. Douglas Ord, photographed in 1941 for identity card (Courtesy of Island Archives, Guernsey)

First World War. After being taken prisoner by the enemy, he then spent much of his time extending his knowledge of German and learning Russian from fellow prisoners before eventually escaping from captivity.[16] After the war he entered the Wesleyan ministry and served in a number of circuits before arriving in Guernsey in 1938.

Following the fall of Paris, Ord discussed the situation with his wife. He could not possibly leave his post until the sick and elderly had been evacuated; and since the chances of this happening were slim, his duty was to stay in Guernsey come what may. His wife would not leave without him.[17] The decision made, Ord took it upon himself to walk about the town in his clerical collar to help maintain calm: 'Continually people stopped me for advice with a naïve conviction that wisdom must, of necessity, repose in any cleric.'[18] Afterwards, he noted wryly: 'It is curious how, in times of crisis, people turn to a minister of religion when they ignore him at other times.'[19]

The clamour for evacuation increased even among those previously opposed to leaving the island. Ord observed that: 'The "patriot" responsible for the posters "Don't be Yellow!" has had a sudden fit of jaundice and has gone to England seeking a cure.'[20] Yet, despite conditions resembling panic, a little over half the civilian population finally decided to remain in Guernsey, encouraged by the most senior island officials, who considered total evacuation to be both impracticable and undesirable for the island's well-being. Inevitably, there was a sudden rush of weddings in June.[21]

On 24 June the staff of both Guernsey circuits met together to consider how to respond to the crisis. The superintendent of the Guernsey (English) Circuit and Chairman of the District, Frederick Flint, was absent in London attending a scheduled meeting of the stationing committee prior to the annual Conference. Another minister, Douglas Moore, was believed to be on his way back from a preaching visit to Manchester. Whilst some of those present urged evacuation, John Leale, attending at his own request, insisted

that any minister leaving his post would be deserting and threatened to seek a restraining order from the Attorney General against anyone who decided to leave. Despite the dubious nature of this threat, Leale's rhetoric had the desired effect. Stiffened by his resolve, the meeting telegraphed Flint in London: 'Evacuation has been checked. 17,000 gone. 25,000 remain. Inform Stationing Committee present staffs therefore intend staying unless evacuation is continued.'

Two days later, on 26 June, ministers and circuit stewards assembled for a further meeting, again in the absence of Flint but this time with Douglas Moore, recently returned from Manchester. Moore was convinced that the entire civilian population of Guernsey should be evacuated. Whilst in London on his way back to Guernsey he had visited the Home Office to urge more Government help in evacuating civilians from the Channel Islands. This time Leale was not present to press the case for remaining. Swayed by Moore, the meeting sent a telegram to the Secretary of the Methodist Conference: 'Local action has checked evacuation. Combined staffs meeting believe imperative pressure should be brought upon Government to resume and complete evacuation in interest of community.' It was agreed that Moore would travel to London next day to press the Government for a complete evacuation. On arrival, he immediately went to the Home Office where he was assured that evacuation would be speeded up.[22]

In Jersey, there was similar consternation as enemy forces sped through France. On 28 June at 8am ministers and circuit stewards from the four circuits gathered anxiously at the home of the Synod Secretary, Walter Fell, for a meeting with the Chairman of the District on his way home to Guernsey from the stationing committee. Flint informed them of his discussions in London. He had advised the stationing committee that if half the population evacuated it would be necessary to reduce ministerial staff. Furthermore, if enemy occupation became inevitable, some ministers would want to return to England, even though the Bailiff of Guernsey had assured him that island officials were staying at their post whatever happened.

Displaying exemplary leadership, Flint now declared that he was 'prepared to stay and look after the interests of the Methodist Church in the Islands, even if all the others went'.[23] Cecil Harrison, Jersey's Solicitor General and circuit steward in the Jersey (Aquila Road) Circuit, believed it 'the duty of all ministers to stay, and that, if they went, it would be a serious blow to the Methodist Church in Jersey'. One by one, ministers affirmed their intention to stay in the island. Since the Jersey (Grove Place) Circuit

stewards wanted time to consult with churches, the meeting agreed to reconvene the following week to make the final decision, but by this time the island had been occupied.

Having shored up things in Jersey, Flint arrived home in Guernsey later that same morning and immediately arranged a meeting of ministers and circuit stewards for the afternoon at Ebenezer. Once again he shared what had transpired at the stationing committee. The situation in Guernsey was more serious than in Jersey, especially in the English circuit which had been badly affected by evacuation. The stationing committee accepted that the present number of staff could not be sustained, irrespective of whether the island was occupied. Therefore, for financial and pastoral reasons, the youngest minister in each circuit, David Ball in the English circuit and Frederick Lines in the French circuit, were 'solemnly released' from their appointment in order to join their families in England. Whilst he did not resent their departure, Ord could not help but reflect that there were now only five ministers left in the island to undertake the work of eight.[24]

As soon as the meeting broke up, Ball and Lines left hurriedly for their respective homes in order to pack before catching the mail boat scheduled for that evening. They had barely forty minutes to gather what possessions they could before heading for the harbour. Ball, carrying only a few clothes and his ordination bible, was just a few yards from the gangplank when German planes suddenly appeared in the sky, swooping low over St Peter Port. He spent a terrifying hour sheltering in a nearby warehouse as aircraft attacked the harbour, destroying vehicles bringing boxes of tomatoes for export.[25] Twenty-nine people were killed and many more injured. A simultaneous raid on St Helier caused nine deaths. A few hours later, having suffered only minor damage, the mail boat left St Peter Port headed for Southampton with Ball and Lines among the passengers, shaken but uninjured. The following morning, the two ministers arrived in London on the boat train to be greeted at Waterloo Station by Douglas Moore, anxious for news of events.

Meanwhile, an eerie stillness settled over the Channel Islands following the devastating air raids. Shocked by what had happened, the population feared the worst. They did not have long to wait for the inevitable. On Sunday 30 June Douglas Ord led the evening service at his Brock Road church where the attendance was better than expected. Shortly after 7.30pm, just as he was pronouncing the benediction, the air raid siren sounded, this time heralding the arrival of the enemy. Ord stood watching at the vestry door as German transport planes flew low overhead on their final approach

Figure: 2.7: Notice in Jersey Evening Post *for Methodist services on Sunday 30 June 1940 (JEP)*

to the airport: 'What manner of men did they contain, and what [were] their intentions towards the first British people to pass under their occupation?'[26]

Later that evening, German officers met with the Bailiff and other island officials at the Royal Hotel in St Peter Port. Telephone communication with the mainland was severed. Early the next morning, 1 July, a surrender ultimatum was dropped on Jersey. Without waiting for the ultimatum to expire, an advance party occupied Jersey during the course of the afternoon.

The immediate task for island clergy in the first week of the Occupation was to bury the dead from the devastating German air raids. In the emotionally charged atmosphere following the raids, ministers had somehow to acknowledge in their eulogies the shock and grief of the population whilst not antagonising the occupying forces. Inevitably, Methodists were among the dead in both islands, and several Methodist ministers conducted funerals.

In communities as small as the Channel Islands most people knew at least one of the victims, and everyone felt outraged at such a callous act. Islanders were aware of their demilitarisation and assumed that the British Government had informed the Germans. But in fact the Government had not done so, fearing that any announcement would be regarded as an invitation to occupy the islands. Unaware, therefore, that the islands were demilitarised, the Germans launched air raids as an armed reconnaissance in order to test defences. At the

Methodist Church
AQUILA ROAD
(THE CHURCH OF GOOD FELLOWSHIP)

TO-MORROW (SUNDAY)

Rev. WALTER C. H. FELL

11.0 a.m.—" Strength and Beauty."
6.30 p.m.—" Voices in the Silence."
Evening Anthem.

Organist: Leonard Herivel, F.R.C.O.

Join with us in Worship !
It will help you ! !

METHODIST CH.
Grove Place

TO-MORROW (SUNDAY)
11.0 a.m.—MR. A. C. QUERÉE.
6.30 p.m.—MRS. M. A. 'VARD.

Grove Place Sunday School will open to-mo

Church Services as usual

WESLEY CHAPEL.

TO-MORROW (SUNDAY)

DIVINE WORSHIP.

PREACHERS:

11.0 a.m —REV. DONALD STUART.
Subject: " Things we cannot do without: (5) The Love of God."
6.30 p.m.—REV. RONALD E. SOUTH.

TUESDAY, July 2nd, at 7.30 p.m.
SERVICE OF INTERCESSION.
Led by Rev. Donald Stuart.

METHODIST CH.
GREAT UNION ROAD
TO-MORROW (SUNDAY)
11.0 a.m.—MR. J. WAKEFIELD.
6.30 p.m.—REV. C. N. MYLNE.
You are cordially invited.

METHODIST CH.
ROYAL CRESCENT

TO-MORROW (SUNDAY)
11.0 a.m.—REV. C. N. MYLNE.
6.30 p.m.—MR. E. C. A. LE CORNU.
A hearty invitation to all.

Seaton Pl. Methodist Mission

TO-MORROW (SUNDAY)

10.30 a.m.—Young People's Service.
6.30 p.m.—MR. J. DU FEU.

urgent request of the civil authorities in the islands, the British Government belatedly announced the demilitarisation on the BBC news shortly after the air raids, at the same time implying that the German Government had already been informed.

Swallowing the British Government's propaganda, the following week's *Methodist Recorder* declared that, as the demilitarisation of the Channel Islands had been announced 24 hours earlier, the German air raid was a heinous war crime. After criticising the chaotic evacuation of the islands (with justification), the *Recorder* exclaimed belligerently: 'It is to be hoped that the Government will sound the retreat no more.'[27] However, there would be many more retreats in the course of the war before Channel Islanders would taste freedom again.

Although the number of casualties was small in comparison to what was happening elsewhere in Europe, the psychological impact of the German air raids on Channel Islanders should not be underestimated. By this single show of strength the Germans demonstrated their ruthlessness. If this was how German forces treated unarmed civilians in the absence of provocation, what might they do in the event of active resistance? Confirming islanders' fears, the surrender ultimatum to Jersey threatened that every hostile action would be followed by bombardment. The futility of resistance was thus driven home to powerful effect – a point that must be remembered when ill-informed commentators criticise the passivity of islanders during the Occupation.

Despite the period of mourning, the immediate future of the churches had to be considered now that enemy occupation was a reality. On 2 July 1940 ministers and lay officials from the two Guernsey circuits met as an 'emergency committee' to make arrangements for their joint working. Ord arrived at the meeting having conducted the funeral of one of the air raid victims. Misleadingly, a local newspaper reported the outcome of the meeting under the headline 'Methodists Unite – One Circuit for Whole Island'.[28] In fact, the two circuits continued to operate as separate entities throughout the Occupation. To cover the vacancies caused by the departure of three ministers, the meeting approved a substantial reorganisation of pastoral charges across circuit boundaries which in peacetime would have taken years to negotiate.[29] To ease the workload of the remaining ministers, two churches in each circuit (Salem and Morley in the English circuit, Victoria Road and Forest in the French circuit) would close temporarily, their congregations amalgamating with others for the duration of the Occupation. In the privacy of his diary Ord voiced his hope that these arrangements

would turn out to be permanent.[30]

In Jersey the immediate impact of the Occupation so far as Methodism was concerned was not as great as in Guernsey. Since the evacuation was on a smaller scale and none of the ministers had left the island, there was no pressing need for reorganisation. Instead it was agreed that informal meetings between ministers and lay officials of the four circuits would continue from time to time in the form of an island council, though this would have no executive powers.

In the first week of the Occupation no one could yet tell what the future held in store. With unaccustomed speed, Methodists in both islands had managed to introduce modest emergency measures in response to the unprecedented situation caused by the evacuation of civilians and the arrival of German forces. Now all anyone could do was wait anxiously to see what the attitude of the military authorities would be towards the churches.

Alderney and Sark

When Edgar Calvert arrived in Alderney in 1939 he found himself in pastoral charge of a moribund church that had long struggled to develop its mission. According to Douglas Moore, 'It would be hard to find a more difficult and discouraging scene of Methodist activity.'[31] However, the arrival of an infantry battalion in Alderney in the autumn seems to have increased the size of the Methodist congregation. At least, Brock Road church in Guernsey lent a dozen hymnbooks to the Alderney Circuit 'to help them in the difficult situation arising from the presence of troops'.[32] Other churches may have done the same.

Any revival in the fortunes of Methodism in Alderney was short-lived. The garrison was abruptly withdrawn on 21 June 1940, and two days later virtually the entire civilian population was evacuated, leaving the incoming German forces with a free hand in the island. The majority of houses were commandeered for accommodation or storage purposes. A significant number were ransacked and destroyed. In time the island was heavily fortified using slave labour. Several prison camps were established, including a concentration camp for political prisoners from various European nations who wore the distinctive blue-and-white striped 'pyjama' uniforms of such places. Although there was no systematic killing of prisoners, the regime was brutal. A French woman, conscripted to work as a cook on Alderney, described her posting thus: '*Aurigny; île du silence, du cauchemar et de l'épouvante*' (Alderney, island of silence, of nightmare and of terror).[33]

According to a reliable source, German forces used the deserted churches in Alderney as food stores.[34] The Roman Catholic church was used as a depot. St Anne's Anglican parish church housed tinned goods, flour and wine, the Salvation Army hall flour, whilst the Methodist church provided storage for potatoes. The bells from St Anne's church were removed and taken to Cherbourg where they were discovered after the war and returned to the island. A soldier gave the church bible to a Lutheran padre for safekeeping. His widow eventually returned it to the island in 1998.

According to another source, German forces used the Methodist church in Alderney for their own religious services.[35] The same source suggests that the Methodist manse in Alderney was damaged when HMS *Rodney* shelled the island late in 1944. Whether part of the Methodist church was used for storage purposes, it seems probable that the Germans used it for religious purposes. In May 1945 a newspaper report claimed that, whereas the Anglican and Roman Catholic churches on Alderney had been desecrated, the Methodist chapel was used solely for 'divine worship'.[36]

Life on Sark in the autumn of 1939 carried on much as usual. With a retired minister, Rev. William Bunting, resident on Sark to conduct Sunday services and provide pastoral care, the small Methodist community was well served in comparison with similar-sized congregations elsewhere in the British Isles. The minutes of the leaders' meeting (written in French until 1938) reflect a leisurely way of life. In October 1938 the main item of business was to decide whether there would be an anthem at Christmas and if a watch-night service should be held as usual on New Year's Eve.[37] In February 1940 the meeting received two applications for church membership. One was from a Guernsey Methodist who had recently moved to Sark. The other was from a woman who 'through her husband asked to be enrolled as a member'. Both applicants were unanimously accepted, increasing the membership to a total of 20.[38]

The sudden and unexpected death of Bunting on 21 May 1940 plunged Sark Methodism into crisis. Sidney Beaugié, superintendent of the Guernsey and Sark (French) Circuit, had now to find local preachers willing to undertake the two-hour sea crossing in order to conduct Sunday services. To his great relief, Alf Tardif, a local preacher in the Guernsey (English) Circuit and leader of the Cornet Street mission in St Peter Port, accepted an invitation to become lay pastor on Sark with effect from 1 September. Until then, ministers and local preachers would travel from Guernsey by boat to lead Sunday worship.

It was not until 4 July that a small party of German officers crossed over from Guernsey to take possession of Sark. Following the lead set by the Dame of Sark, the redoubtable Sybil Hathaway, the vast majority of islanders had elected to remain in the island rather than abandon their homes. They were reassured to learn that most island activities could continue as before, albeit under close supervision. Julia Tremayne noted in her diary that islanders would be permitted to attend services at the Anglican parish church and at the Methodist chapel.[39]

However, the occupying forces promptly imposed a ban on travel between the islands, thereby preventing Methodist preachers from fulfilling their duties on Sark. With no one to occupy the pulpit, the Methodist chapel was obliged to close its doors until such time as the lay pastor could take up his appointment, assuming that the German authorities would permit him to do so. Later in July Julia Tremayne noted that Methodists on Sark were attending worship in the parish church because of travel restrictions on their own preachers.[40]

In the event, the closure of the Sark chapel was short-lived. The German authorities agreed to permit the Methodist lay pastor to reside on Sark, and in September 1940 Tardif commenced his duties. For the next five years, with only occasional relief from visiting ministers, Tardif conducted services twice each Sunday in the Sark chapel.

Life on Sark during the Occupation was uneventful so far as Methodism was concerned. Tardif, a devout and conscientious man, had been a student at Cliff College, Methodism's training centre for lay evangelists. Since his wife had evacuated in June 1940, he threw all his energies into his ministry on Sark, where he proved a popular pastor to the Methodist congregation. In December 1943 his modest stipend was increased by 5s per week, and in June 1945 the circuit awarded him an *ex gratia* payment of £50 in recognition of his services to Sark Methodism during the previous five years.[41]

To supplement his meagre income during the Occupation, Tardif worked in Hubert Lanyon's bakery. Lanyon was the designated recipient of the regular news summary compiled clandestinely from BBC broadcasts by the Guernsey Underground News Service (GUNS). Trusted Sarkees would be allowed to read the illicit news summary on their regular visits to the bakery. When Lanyon fell under suspicion following the theft of a bag of flour from German stores, Tardif, along with another bakery employee and fellow Methodist, William Giffard, and the Sark carrier, C.F. Wakley, took it in turns to fetch the bulletin from the harbour.[42]

When those responsible for producing the newssheet were eventually

betrayed, Lanyon was severely beaten by members of the German field police but he doggedly refused to reveal the names of his accomplices. He was imprisoned in Guernsey for six months before being allowed to return home. The ringleaders in Guernsey were imprisoned on the continent where one died in prison.[43] Tardif was badly shaken by the experience and after the war rarely spoke of his time on Sark. Following the Liberation, he resigned his post as lay pastor on Sark and two years later emigrated to New Zealand with his wife where he continued in Christian ministry.[44] Hubert Lanyon succeeded him as Methodist lay pastor on Sark.

Chapter 3

Worship and Preaching

The first orders issued by the German Commandant of the Channel Islands in July 1940 confirmed that 'Assemblies in Churches and Chapels for the purpose of Divine worship are permitted. Prayers for the British Royal Family and for the welfare of the British Empire may be said.' However, there were limits to what was permissible: 'Such assemblies shall not be made the vehicle for any propaganda or utterances against the honour or interests of or offensive to the German Government or Forces.'[1] Clergy would have to work out for themselves how to pray for the welfare of the British Empire without causing offence to the Third Reich.

By monitoring church services, as happened elsewhere in occupied Europe, the military police soon discovered that clergy were finding ways to circumvent the ban on anti-German rhetoric from the pulpit. The response was to lean on the civil authorities, a tactic often employed during the Occupation to play off islanders against each other. In July 1940 the Bailiff of Guernsey reminded denominational leaders that freedom of worship did not extend to using prayers and sermons to launch verbal attacks on the Third Reich. Frederick Flint, Chairman of the District, duly wrote to Methodist ministers:

> I am asked by the Bailiff to inform you that he is concerned lest there should be a serious curtailment of the freedom at present permitted for religious worship. He is informed that in speech and in prayer, some persons have made reference to '*the forces of evil*', and it is obvious such words may bear an objectionable significance for the Army of Occupation. If we desire to retain our present privileges, there must be unceasing care concerning the words used in sermons and prayers.[2]

Henceforth, ministers were in no doubt as to what would happen if they criticised the Third Reich from the pulpit. In Guernsey one clergyman was

so anxious to avoid incriminating himself that on the following Sunday instead of preaching a sermon he read a psalm. Douglas Ord was scathing: 'No self-respecting minister can evade his responsibilities that way.'[3] Whilst Ord expected German spies would operate within congregations, he believed that clergy must continue to exercise their ministry as best they could, finding more subtle means to convey an anti-German message.

Apart from monitoring sermons, the military authorities generally did not interfere with public worship. In September 1940 the Jersey (Aquila Road) Circuit noted that 'During the two months of German occupation which have so far elapsed it has been a matter for thankfulness that the services of churches have not been interfered with by the German Commandant. We trust that such freedom of worship will be allowed to continue.'[4] What islanders did not know was that their 'freedom of worship' was part of a benign strategy intended to encourage Britain to accept generous peace terms in exchange for giving Germany a free hand in Europe.

Yet there were already unmistakable signs of religious intolerance on the part of the German authorities. Days after announcing that church services could continue as normal, the Commandant wrote to Major Ferguson of the Salvation Army in Guernsey refusing permission to hold open-air meetings.[5] In January 1941, following orders from higher authority, the organisation was proscribed and its members forced to disband. Resigned to accepting the inevitable, many joined Methodist churches, though Marie Ozanne, a young Salvation Army officer, protested against the ban by reading the scriptures in uniform on the steps of the citadel in St Sampson's until warned to stop.[6]

In Jersey the authorities believed the Salvation Army was planning to defy the ban. On the last Saturday in January 1941 the usual weekly notice appeared in that day's *Evening Post* advertising services next day at the St Helier citadel.[7] In fact, the announcement was almost certainly the result of an oversight on the part of the newspaper rather than a deliberate provocation by the Salvation Army. Nevertheless, Teutonic pride at stake, the German Commandant immediately wrote to the Salvation Army in politely menacing terms: 'Will you kindly put an immediate stop to activity of this kind. I shall not prosecute on this occasion.'[8] The organisation was unable to resume activities until June 1945.[9]

After banning the Salvation Army in January 1941, the German authorities took no further interest in the religious activities of islanders until the following November when the island Commandant in Jersey wrote to the Bailiff asking for 'a list of the churches, religious communities, religious associations, sects and orders in Jersey' together with a copy of their 'rules'.[10]

The Attorney General, Duret Aubin, prepared a list of religious groups in the island, but claimed he could not provide information about their 'rules' without a more precise definition of the term.[11]

Unwilling to be drawn into legal argument with the wily Attorney General, the Commandant pursued a different line of enquiry: how were religious groups financed? What were their objectives and their politics?[12] After consulting the respective church leaders, Duret Aubin supplied the required information. The Church of England parishes were financed by 'grants, endowments, fees and voluntary contributions'. Their objectives were 'The conduct of Public Worship; the ministry of the Word and Sacraments; Pastoral Work.' Roman Catholic churches were financed by voluntary contributions with modest income from renting properties. Their objective was 'the spiritual welfare of persons of the Roman Catholic Faith'. Methodism, according to William Ward, superintendent of the Jersey (Grove Place) Circuit, was financed solely by voluntary contributions. Its objectives were: 'The propagation of the Gospel; the maintenance of Divine Worship; the culture of the Christian Life.' Likewise, the smaller Nonconformist churches supplied their statement of purpose. In each case the Attorney General noted 'No connexion whatsoever with politics'.[13]

The German authorities appear to have been satisfied by this information. At least, there were no more requests for information and no further action is recorded as having been taken against any of the religious groups on the list supplied by the Attorney General. Just how serious was the threat to religious activities cannot now be determined, though the occupying forces would not have hesitated to ban any group had it served their interest.

The organisation of Methodist worship during the Occupation generally followed the pre-war pattern, as a survey of contemporary preaching plans reveals. Published quarterly by the superintendent, the Methodist preaching plan provides information about services in a particular circuit. Besides indicating the times of services and the name of the minister or local preacher appointed to lead worship, the preaching plan contains various symbols denoting denominational festivals and occasions such as the celebration of the Lord's Supper. Sufficient preaching plans have survived from the Occupation to provide a detailed picture of Methodist worship.

In the 1930s Methodist worship in the Channel Islands, as elsewhere, generally took the form of a preaching service led by an ordained minister or, in most cases, by a local (lay) preacher. Nearly every church held morning and evening services on Sunday. However, even before the shortage caused

Eglise Methodiste

Circuit de Langue Française de

Guernesey et Sercq.

Tableau Trimestriel

JANVIER, FEVRIER, MARS 1945

Pasteurs :

SIDNEY E. BEAUGIÉ, M.A., The Manse, Baugy, Vale.
Tel. 4264.
(*Surintendant*)

HENRY J. FOSS.

A. E. TARDIF, Rosebud Cottage, Sercq.

Economes du Circuit :

EDWIN MAHY, Furzedale, Le Valle.
EDWIN FALLA, Bon Air, Le Valle.

Trésoriers :

Fonds Auxiliaire.—M. A. W. Collenette.
Missions à l'Etranger.—M. B. Brehaut, Rue des Landes, Forêt.
Mission Intérieure.—M. J. C. Langlois, H.M.'s Procureur's Office, Manor Place.
Fonds des Pauvres.—M. N. T. Mahy, Crowndale, Vale.
Comité de Sercq.—M. Pierre Le Maitre, Bordeaux.
Union des Ecoles du Dimanche.—M. W. C. Ozanne, c/o Advocate Martel, Court Row.

Secrétaires :

De l'Assemblée Trimestrielle.—M. F. J. Le Page, Helston, St. Martin.
Assemblée des Prédicateurs Locaux.—
M. A. E. Heaume, Les Boulains, Câtel.
Conducteurs de Classes.—M. B. P. Brehaut, Rue des Landes, Forêt.
Missions à l'Etranger.—M. Carré, Royston, Castel.
Mission Intérieure.—M. W. F. Bougourd, Newton, Port Soif, Le Valle.
Chapelles.—M. A. A. Mahy, Southwood, St. Samson.
Union des Ecoles du Dimanche.—M. le Pasteur Foss.
M. L. Mahy, Southwood, St. Samson.
Tempérance.—M. Geo. Le Feuvre
Young Methodism Department.—

✠ **EGLISE METHODISTE** ✠

Circuit "Grove Place,"
Jersey.

TABLEAU TRIMESTRIEL

Octobre, Novembre, Decembre.

1941.

Pasteurs :

W. J. WARD, 22, Vauxhall Street (Tel. 263).
A. T. SKYRME, 6, St. Mark's Crescent (Tel. 2464).
D. L. COLLINGS, O.H..M.S.
J. W. J. SCOTT, "Craig Choyle," Old Beaumont Hill (St. A. 290)
A. M. FREEMAN, Prospect House, St. Martin (Gorey 268).
Pastor P. H. HANKS, 11, Roseville Street.

Economes du Circuit :

M. J. LUCAS, Junr., Ambleside, Tower Road (Tel. 366).
M. H. G. LUCE, Southdown, Samarès (Tel 1131).

Tresoriers :

Fonds Auxiliare ... ... M. P. J. NOEL, Holmlea, Midvale Road.
Missions à l'Etranger ... ... M. J. LUCAS, Ambleside, Tower Road.
Missions à l'Intérieur ... ... M. W. R. HERIVEL, Stopford Road.
Women's Auxiliary ... ... Mme. LUCAS, Ambleside, Tower Road.

Secretaires :

Assemblée Trimestrielle ... M. P. G. LE MOIGNAN, Cardiff House, St. Peter.
Missions à l'Etranger ... M. le Pasteur A. T. SKYRME, St. Mark's Cres.
M. L. PICOT, Sunnedene, Mount Bingham.
M. le Pasteur A. M. FREEMAN, St. Martin.
Women's Auxiliary ... Mlle. C. ALEXANDRE, 135, St. Saviour's Road.
Missions à l'Interieur ... M. le Pasteur W. J. WARD, 22 Vauxhall Street
M. E. J. AHIER, 27, Duhamel Place.
Conducteurs de Classe ... ... M. A. C. QUEREE, Lake Vale, St. Ouen.
Chapelles ... ... M. P. G. LE MOIGNON, Cardiff House, St. Peter.
Education ... ... M. le Pasteur A. T. SKYRME, 6 St. Mark's Crescent.
M. P. E. NOEL, 71 Rouge Bouillon.
Temperance ... ... M. le Pasteur J. W. J. SCOTT, "Craig Choyle."
M. A. DE B. BRETON, First Tower.
Assemblée des Prédicateurs Laïques ... M. A. DE B. BRETON, 1, Yaralla Villas.
Guilds ... ... M. PH. DU FEU, Tunbridge House, George Town.

Filleul et Queen, Imprimeurs, New Street, Jersey.

Left, Figure 3.1: Guernsey and Sark (French) Circuit preaching plan, January – March 1945 (Author's Collection)
Right, Figure 3.2: Jersey (Grove Place) Circuit preaching plan, October – December 1941 (Author's Collection)

by enlistment and evacuation, there were insufficient preachers to provide a comfortable margin in drawing up the quarterly preaching plan. The evacuation of three preachers in the Jersey (Grove Place) Circuit in June 1940 made the task of compiling the preaching plan even more difficult than usual.[14]

To help alleviate the shortage of preachers, in September 1940 Flint gave permission for a group of young people in the Guernsey (English) Circuit to form a 'mission band' that would conduct Sunday services.[15] The band grew in size until there were sometimes 15 or 20 involved in leading worship – more than in the congregation at smaller chapels. At least two members of the mission band began training as local preachers as a result of taking part in services. The mission band conducted services throughout the Occupation before disbanding in the summer of 1945.[16] In the Jersey (Grove Place) Circuit a mission band also operated in the latter part of the Occupation.[17]

Besides a shortage of preachers, the scarcity of transport posed an immediate problem for Methodism in the summer of 1940 since the military authorities cancelled bus services and imposed a ban on private motoring. Bicycles became the standard mode of transport during the Occupation, but over a period of time even these wore out, and spare parts were virtually unobtainable. All kinds of ingenious alternatives to tyres were tried out, including rope, but with limited success. When bicycles eventually fell apart or were commandeered, preachers were obliged to walk considerable distances in order to lead worship.

In October 1940 the superintendent of the Jersey (Grove Place) Circuit, William Ward, launched a novel scheme to help ease transport difficulties: 'To enable preachers to fulfil their preaching appointments, despite lack of ordinary means of transport, an arrangement has been made to hire a horse and cab fortnightly for this purpose, and the Quarterly Meeting requests each Church to take a retiring collection toward the expenses incurred.'[18] Once established, the scheme was judged a great success, continuing in subsequent years until even this form of transport became impossible to provide.[19]

More difficult to resolve was the disruption to worship caused by blackout and curfew regulations that required alterations in the times of evening services in the autumn and winter. Concerned at the likely effects of a second winter of disruption, in October 1940 Ward published an 'Important Notice' in the preaching plan: 'It is hoped that the alteration in the times of Sunday Services will be regarded as a call to sacrifice both convenience and inclination and [that church members will] heartily support

		JANVIER.			
		COVENANT 5 *SUNDAY*	12	19	26
* GROVE PLACE ... *Jeudi*	11 3½ 3½	Freeman Ward s Ward	Hanks Struthers EX Hanks	Le Cornu Scott Ward	Ward Skyrme Ward
* AUGRES ... ... *Mardi*	10¾ 3 3	E. J. Ahier Colback	Renouf J. B. Le Quesne Skyrme	Huelin De La Perrelle	Sarre Ward Skyrme
* LA ROCQUE ... ... *Mardi*	11 3½ 3½	Bree Bull. Skyrme	En. Le Feuvre Freeman	Skyrme Skyrme Skyrme	Bree Webley
GEORGETOWN ... *Jeudi*	11 3½ 3½	G. L. Hanks Hanks	Skyrme s Chapman Ward	J. T. Du Feu Hanks Hanks	E. J. Ahier Howells Hanks
BETHEL ... ... *Mercredi*	11 3½ 3	Ward s Howells	Freeman En. Le Feuvre Ward	E. J. Ahier Goodsman	E. P. Ahier Hanks Ward
* SION ... ... *Jeudi*	11 3 3½	Sterling Skyrme	Sarre Hanks Skyrme	Ford Ward	Gallichan Swinnerton Skyrme
* TABOR ... ... *Jeudi*	11 3½ 3½	E. P. Ahier Boxall Scott	Jeune Wakefield	Swinnerton W. Queree Scott	Ed. Le Feuvre Scott
* GALAAD ... ... *Jeudi*	11 3½ 4½	Ford De La Perrelle Skyrme	Noel E. J. Ahier	Scott Watson Skyrme	Breton Nutley
* FRERES ... ... *Mardi*	10½ 3 3	Le Cornu W. Queree	Scott Siouville Freeman	P. Le Ruez Freeman	Huelin *G.B.* Freeman
* CARMEL ... ... *Mardi*	10½ 3 3	Savage Savage Freeman	Ward Renouf	Mourant Noel Freeman	Siouville A. C. Queree
* EDEN ... ... *Mercredi*	10½ 3 3	P. Le Ruez Freeman Freeman	Huelin De la Perrelle	Siouville Jeune Freeman	Mourant Renouf
* ST. MARTIN ... *Jeudi*	10½ 3 3½	Hanks Huelin	Swinnerton Ward Freeman	Savage Savage	Skyrme Freeman Freeman
* EBENHEZER ... *Jeudi*	10¾ 3½ 3	Skyrme J. T. Du Feu Freeman	H. B. South Cobley	Ward Colback Freeman	De La Perrelle S. J. Picot
* BETHLEHEM ... *Mardi*	10¾ 3 3½	Scott Robson Scott	Green A. C. Queree	Hanks Elson Scott	J. B. Le Quesne Jeune
BETHESDA ... ... *Mardi*	10¾ 3 3½	A. C. Queree Ed. Le Feuvre	W. Queree Mourant Scott	Boxall Boxall	A. C. Queree N. Le R. Scott
* PHILADELPHIE *Mercredi*	10¾ 3½ 3½	Noel Scott Scott	P. Le Ruez Robson	H. B. South Sterling Scott	Freeman En. Le Feuvre
* ST. OUEN ... ... *Mercredi*	11 3 3½	G. Huelin Maillard	F. Du Feu Scott Scott	Freeman Robson	Hanks Perchard Scott
SIX RUES ... ... *Jeudi*	10¾ 3 3½	Mourant Le Cornu	E. P. Ahier Ed. Le Feuvre Scott	Maillard P. Le Ruez	Scott Webb Scott
L'ETACQ, *Jeudi*					

Figure 3.3: Extract from Jersey (Grove Place) Circuit preaching plan, January 1941 (Author's Collection)

the priceless privilege of public worship. If the times planned are deemed unsuitable, the Churches should consult the preachers planned for them, before any alteration is made.' [20]

The problems posed by blackout and curfew regulations were never satisfactorily resolved during the Occupation. Compiling the preaching plan during winter months was made complicated by the fact that everyone had to be indoors before curfew. Churches gradually brought forward evening services as autumn days grew shorter, reversing the process in spring. Inevitably, congregations found it difficult to remember the times of services, leading to frustration on all sides, especially when stewards neglected to inform preachers, who then failed to arrive at the appointed hour. Only when restrictions were lifted at the end of hostilities did the problem resolve itself.

Preaching

Despite logistical difficulties, Methodist congregations continued to gather for worship week by week throughout the Occupation. As the name suggests, the principal feature of the preaching service was the sermon, and Methodists expected to hear a substantial address that was faithful to the Gospel and relevant to their situation. How, then, did preachers respond to the spiritual needs of islanders during the Occupation?

Certainly, preachers were encouraged to acknowledge the current situation. At the height of the Dunkirk crisis in May 1940, Rev. Henry Foss addressed preachers in the Guernsey and Sark (French) Circuit on 'the special needs of congregations in the present circumstances'.[21] Douglas Moore emphasised the importance of choosing an appropriate theme for sermons. Addressing preachers in August, Beaugié made the same point: 'Since we last met [...] we have passed through strange times and it is more important than ever that we should preach the right message. We have a great opportunity; God help us to use it rightly.'[22]

Local preachers in the Guernsey (English) Circuit met shortly after the Dunkirk evacuation, though the minutes convey no impression of any special challenge facing preachers.[23] In December 1940 their conversation focussed on the need for greater unity in the world, especially amongst Nonconformists – a subject that can hardly have been uppermost in the mind of most islanders.[24] Even in spring 1941 they discussed nothing more specific to the current situation than 'the Church and her mission in the world of the future'.[25] Eventually, in September 1941 preachers reflected on their experience of leading worship during the Occupation. If the minutes are to

be believed, congregations were content with their efforts: 'the brethren related that in their services the greater blessing was experienced in preaching. The Word of God and the hymns seemed to have greater meaning and freshness, fitting the need of these difficult times.'[26]

Whether congregations entirely shared this point of view is difficult to say. Circuits recorded their thanks to preachers from time to time but it would have been churlish to do otherwise in the circumstances.[27] Only one dissentient voice is preserved in contemporary records. In August 1944 the acting superintendent, Philip Romeril, shared with preachers a letter from the organist at Brock Road 'expressing criticism and suggestions in regard to preaching and the conduct of public worship'.[28] The preachers were inclined to lay the blame for any failings on those of their number who did not attend preachers' meetings. Romeril was asked to write a letter urging preachers to attend future meetings 'in order to help our fellowship and our preaching'. In fact, the organist's complaints may not have been directly related to the Occupation since the standard of preaching is a perennial issue in Methodist congregations.

Establishing precisely how preachers responded to spiritual needs during the Occupation is made difficult by the fact that the content of sermons can only be gleaned from isolated references. There are no verbatim accounts extant, and any notes that preachers may have made have long since perished. J. Allés Simon, a respected local preacher in the Guernsey and Sark (French) Circuit, kept a meticulous record of his preaching appointments between 1899 and 1946, providing us with a rare glimpse into Methodist worship during the Occupation.[29] On 5 May

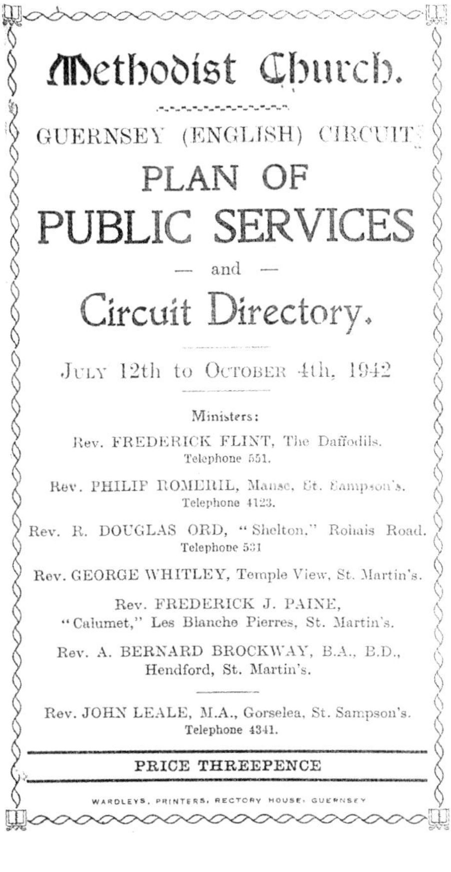

Figure 3.4: Guernsey (English) Circuit preaching plan, July – October 1942 (Author's Collection)

Methodist Church.

GUERNSEY (ENGLISH) CIRCUIT

PLAN OF
PUBLIC SERVICES
— and —
Circuit Directory.

JULY 12th to OCTOBER 4th, 1942

Ministers:

Rev. FREDERICK FLINT, The Daffodils.
Telephone 551.

Rev. PHILIP ROMERIL, Manse, St. Sampson's.
Telephone 4123.

Rev. R. DOUGLAS ORD, " Shelton." Rohais Road.
Telephone 531

Rev. GEORGE WHITLEY, Temple View, St. Martin's.

Rev. FREDERICK J. PAINE,
"Calumet," Les Blanche Pierres, St. Martin's.

Rev. A. BERNARD BROCKWAY, B.A., B.D.,
Hendford, St. Martin's.

Rev. JOHN LEALE, M.A., Gorselea, St. Sampson's.
Telephone 4341.

PRICE THREEPENCE

WARDLEYS, PRINTERS, RECTORY HOUSE, GUERNSEY

1940, with the British army reeling from defeat in Norway and North Africa, he urged the congregation at Castel to be soldiers of Jesus Christ (2 Timothy 2.3), a biblical text he subsequently used many times. Preaching at Les Adams on 2 May 1943 (when the end of hostilities seemed distant), he assured the congregation: 'We know that in everything God works for good with those who love him, who are called according to his purpose' (Romans 8.28). On 3 December 1944, at an extremely low point in the Occupation, he urged the same congregation to 'Pray constantly' (1 Thessalonians 5.17).

His careful selection of biblical texts suggests that Simon was a powerful preacher. On 19 July 1942 he preached at Galaad on 'My times are in thy hand' (Psalm 31.15). Whilst it is impossible now to reconstruct the content of the sermon, the rest of the verse provides a clue as to its general drift: 'deliver me from the hand of my enemies and persecutors!' Since all preachers reuse their sermons, the same text crops up from time to time in his preaching diary. In fact, he had preached on this text in the same church in 1928.

Judging by the number of times the biblical reference occurs in his preaching diary, another of Simon's favourite sermons was based on the story of Elijah and the widow of Zarephath. His chosen text was the response of Elijah to the starving widow: 'For thus says the Lord, the God of Israel, "The jar of meal shall not be spent, and the cruse of oil shall not fail, until the day that the Lord sends rain upon the earth"' (1 Kings 17.14). It is easy to imagine him applying this text to the contemporary situation in order to assure the congregation of God's providence.

In Jersey preachers made similar efforts to respond to the situation. At the Free Church ministers' meeting in August 1940 the Presbyterian, F.B. Struthers, presented a paper on 'Preaching during the Occupation'. According to Struthers, the task of the preacher was: to teach; to bring comfort 'since many people were in need of consolation'; and to win people for Christ. He urged colleagues to preach on the central themes of Christian faith 'as a dying man to dying men'.[30]

Doubtless, clergy of all denominations tried in some way to address the spiritual needs of their flock, though the innocuous sermon titles occasionally found in newspaper or pulpit notices provide little clue as to their content. In January 1945 Walter Fell preached to the congregation at Aquila Road on 'Self-Possession' and 'Facing the Future', themes which may well have been slanted towards the contemporary situation, though it is more difficult to imagine a similar angle in a subsequent sermon entitled 'The Old-fashioned Gospel in this New-fangled World'.[31] In January 1944 Peter Hanks, lay pastor

in the Jersey (Grove Place) Circuit, preached at Georgetown on 'The Christ who goes on'. The following month his subject was 'What is man?'[32] Whilst titles such as these suggest weighty theological topics, their application to contemporary spiritual needs can only be surmised.

The diary of Nan Le Ruez in the Jersey (Grove Place) Circuit contains several appreciative references to sermons. On 2 January 1944 she was greatly encouraged to hear a sermon based on Joshua 1.9: 'Be strong and of a good courage; be not afraid, neither be thou dismayed; for the Lord thy God is with thee whithersoever thou goest.' The following week the preacher's uplifting text was Philippians 4.5-6: 'The Lord is at hand. Have no anxiety about anything, but in everything by prayer and supplication with thanksgiving let your requests be known to God.'[33] In November 1943 she was grateful for Ward's sermon on Psalm 37.1: 'Fret not yourself because of the wicked.' These and similar references in contemporary diaries suggest that preachers often selected biblical texts that could be developed in ways appropriate to the current situation.[34]

Given the importance of hymn singing in Methodism, the preacher's choice of hymns was equally important to congregations for the message they conveyed. Unfortunately, there is scant evidence to indicate the kind of hymns that were popular during the Occupation. According to Leslie Roussel, a local preacher in the Guernsey and Sark (French) Circuit, top of any poll of popular hymns chosen by preachers during the Occupation would have been Cecil Frances Alexander's hymn:

> Jesus calls us! o'er the tumult
> Of our life's wild restless sea,
> Day by day His sweet voice soundeth,
> Saying: Christian follow Me.[35]

Another popular hymn portraying the Christian life in terms of the fight against evil was that by Henry Kirke White:

> Oft in danger, oft in woe,
> Onward, Christians, onward go;
> Fight the fight, maintain the strife,
> Strengthened with the Bread of Life.[36]

Probably for the same reason, a personal favourite of Roussel's was Charles Wesley's 'Soldiers of Christ arise and put your armour on'. The

separation of families as a result of the evacuation and deportation made Isabel Stevenson's hymn a perennial favourite:

> Holy Father, in Thy mercy,
> Hear our anxious prayer;
> Keep our loved ones, now far distant,
> 'Neath Thy care.[37]

When the tide of war eventually turned in favour of the Allies, causing the Germans to become jittery, the threat posed by informers made preaching even more of a risky business, especially if preachers made reference to war news that could only have been obtained by means of clandestine radios. The consequences of arrest for a wireless offence could be serious, and targeting clergymen sent a powerful message to the civilian population (see Chapter 6).

Two tragic episodes illustrate the danger facing clergy. Clifford Cohu, retired army chaplain and acting rector of St Saviour's church in Jersey, kept a wireless hidden in the organ loft. Fearless and indiscreet, he cheerfully passed on the latest war news to everyone he met as he cycled into town. Eventually, he was arrested and imprisoned, first in France then in Germany. On his release he was immediately re-arrested by the SS and transferred to a 'work education camp' where he died within a few days as a result of a brutal beating. The prisoners who removed his body found a tiny bible clasped to his breast.[38] In Guernsey in 1942 after numerous warnings Marie Ozanne was arrested and imprisoned without trial for preaching in uniform in the open air despite the prohibition on Salvation Army activities. Though released within a few weeks, her health was badly affected by the experience, which probably included being beaten in order to keep her quiet. She died in hospital in February 1943.[39] The message to other island clergy was clear.

Douglas Ord had no intention of being imprisoned by the Germans for a second time in his life, though he certainly wanted to address the spiritual needs of his congregation. According to Ambrose Robin, a senior civil servant and member of Brock Road church, Ord was a gifted preacher and communicator.[40] Aware of the risks involved, Ord chose to illustrate his sermons with encouraging, if oblique, references to the latest war news. In May 1943 he referred to a dam in north Wales which burst of its own account 'unlike some dams' (a reference to the Dambusters' raid a few days earlier).[41] A favourite device was to retell historical incidents that had contemporary parallels. In September 1942 he preached at Brock Road on Sennacherib's

failed attempt to gain control of Egypt (Isaiah 37), illustrating the theme with reference to Napoleon's retreat from Egypt in 1799 which prevented him from staying at the famous Shepherd Hotel in Cairo. (In fact, the hotel was not built until 1814.) A few days earlier, the BBC had broadcast news of the German retreat from Egypt. According to reports, Rommel had been hoping to make his headquarters in the Shepherd Hotel.[42]

Ord was heartened by the favourable response to his veiled mention of topical war news, though he remained careful not to take risks.[43] Even so, there were times when his emotions got the better of him. Shortly before Christmas 1943 he felt moved to include a reference to Winston Churchill in the prayers of intercession. Had there been an informer in the congregation, the German authorities would have had something specific to act on.[44]

Aside from the constant fear of informers, the physical strain on preachers was considerable because of the number of services and the harsh conditions. Leslie Roussel averaged ten to twelve preaching appointments each quarter throughout the Occupation, cycling in his estimation a total of 1,600 miles in order to lead Sunday services.[45] Even in normal circumstances this would have been demanding. During the Occupation, cycling or walking even short distances without adequate food quickly drained preachers' reserves of energy. In October 1944 Beaugié walked from his manse in the Vale parish in the north of Guernsey to Rocquaine chapel in the southwest of the island (a round trip of 12 miles) in order to conduct a wedding.[46]

For elderly preachers there was little prospect of retirement unless infirm. In 1943, at the age of 71, William Ward in Jersey celebrated the Golden Jubilee of his ministry, and he was by no means the oldest preacher.[47] William Corbet was the doyen of preachers in the Guernsey and Sark (French) Circuit. In April 1885, aged seventeen, he preached his first sermon (in French) in a cottage at Cobo. For many years he regularly took twelve preaching appointments a quarter and only gave up preaching in 1942 because of failing eyesight and transport difficulties. On 15 April 1945 he celebrated his diamond jubilee of preaching by leading the evening service at La Moye.[48] Though confined to an invalid carriage, Rev. Bernard Brockway in Guernsey regularly preached during the Occupation.[49] That services were seldom cancelled during the Occupation because of a shortage of preachers testifies to the commitment of ministers and local preachers under the most arduous conditions.

The Lord's Supper, Denominational Festivals, Church Attendance

Until liturgical reforms in the 1970s it was customary in Methodism for the sacrament of the Lord's Supper to be 'administered' after the conclusion of the normal preaching service. Consistent with the normal pattern, most Methodist chapels in the Channel Islands celebrated the Lord's Supper once a quarter. In larger churches twice a quarter was common, though Grove Place church in St Helier continued to hold a monthly communion service during the Occupation, as did Brock Road, Ebenezer and St Sampson's in the Guernsey (English) Circuit. Most congregations would have used the order contained in the *Book of Offices* (1936). In February 1940 the Sark chapel finally invested in a dozen 'communion books'.[50]

Deteriorating social conditions during the Occupation are reflected in the difficulties faced by churches in celebrating the Lord's Supper. For Anglicans and Roman Catholics, locating wafers and communion wine was increasingly difficult, though ordinary wine could be used if necessary. Roman Catholic priests occasionally obtained permission to travel to France in order to purchase fresh supplies.[51] Church candles were also a rarity. As was customary, Methodist churches used ordinary bread at the Lord's Supper, though in such miniscule amounts that congregations sometimes complained. When stocks of non-alcoholic communion wine ran out, Methodists resorted to using tap water coloured by vegetable dye. In February 1945 flour stocks were exhausted, leaving islanders without bread for three weeks until the arrival of a Red Cross ship. At Les Capelles in the Guernsey and Sark (French) Circuit, 'It was decided to hold communion services without bread or wine while the present emergency existed.'[52]

Denominational festivals continued to function more or less as normal during the Occupation, albeit without the usual quota of visiting preachers from the mainland for special Sundays in support of Overseas Missions, Home Missions, Temperance and Social Welfare, and the National Children's Home and Orphanage. The unashamed purpose of these festivals was to raise funds, and Methodists in the Channel Islands were noted for their endeavours (see Chapter 7). Besides fundraising, festivals also fulfilled an educational role. When churches in the Jersey (Grove Place) Circuit observed Temperance and Social Welfare Sunday in November 1941 Rev. John Scott set an examination paper on the subject of temperance, the winners receiving cash prizes.[53] To a casual observer, maintaining the cycle of denominational festivals might have seemed pointless when the islands were cut off from

the Methodist connexion. However, doing so demonstrated a firm belief that life would eventually return to normal. Thus festivals acquired patriotic overtones, and none more so than harvest festival.

In the mostly rural communities of the Channel Islands harvest festival constituted the high point in the Methodist calendar when vestigial folk religion ensured the presence of those otherwise seldom involved in Christian worship. Paradoxically, despite an acute shortage of food which presented a challenge in creating traditional displays of produce, harvest festival became even more important during the Occupation as many more islanders than normal responded to the opportunity to give thanks for divine providence.

Churches went to elaborate lengths to celebrate harvest. Ken Lewis, a young civil servant and diarist, was impressed with the 1941 harvest festival at Les Camps in the Guernsey and Sark (French) Circuit: 'although it was wartime we had a lovely lot of stuff.'[54] At harvest festival in 1943, Brock Road was 'wonderfully decorated' with generous gifts of flowers, fruit and vegetables, which afterwards were distributed to the needy. Ord thought the display all the more remarkable for a town church.[55] Even in the final autumn of the Occupation, the decorating committee at St Andrew's in the same circuit confidently gathered to receive the usual harvest gifts.[56] At another Methodist chapel in September 1944 Ord was amazed to note the harvest gifts – matches, a petrol lighter, flints, salt, eggs, saltwater, strawberries, goat's milk, butter, saccharine and logs.[57]

Two other Methodist festivals need only brief mention. Congregations continued to hold the annual Covenant service during the Occupation, usually on the first Sunday of the New Year. However, a casualty of the curfew was the watch-night service, generally held at a late hour on New Year's Eve as a spiritual alternative to secular celebrations. Aquila Road church in Jersey arranged a watch-night service in lieu of the normal evening worship on the last Sunday of 1940.[58] This was repeated in subsequent years until in 1943 and again in 1944 a temporary relaxation in the curfew enabled the watch-night service to revert to a more traditional time.[59] Georgetown in the Jersey (Grove Place) Circuit held a watch-night service during the afternoon of New Year's Eve.[60]

Occupation hagiography suggests that church attendance during the Occupation was buoyant as islanders sought comfort in religious activities. A short article on church life during the Occupation published in July 1945 for the benefit of Channel Island evacuees in Britain states blandly that 'The

services of the Church of England, the Free Churches and the Roman Catholic Churches were well attended.'[61] Frank Stroobant in his published memoirs recalled 'a marked increase in church and chapel congregations' during the Occupation.[62] In fact, however, attendance at worship during the Occupation was generally not as high as these accounts might suggest.

So far as Methodism is concerned, denominational festivals and other special services usually attracted a reasonable congregation but at other times church attendance could be poor, especially during cold weather (see Chapter 6) but also in summer. In August 1942 Ambrose Robin noted just 24 adults and 4 children in the morning congregation at Brock Road and 'not many more' at the evening service in the main Anglican parish church of St Peter Port.[63] Roy Rabey later recalled 'reduced congregations' because of the evacuation in June 1940.[64]

A feature of church attendance during the Occupation was the higher proportion of women in congregations, a trend already evident in many English churches at least since the First World War. In November 1941 Ambrose Robin noted that 'Men are conspicuous by their absence at religious services in the town.'[65] In February 1943 he counted only nine men in a congregation of 44.[66] In February 1944 he observed three men in a congregation of 30.[67] The following month there were just five men in a congregation of 58.[68] At times he felt like 'an intruder at a mothers' meeting'.[69] These figures incidentally confirm the low numbers attending worship. In Anglican parish churches a shortage of men and boys led to some choirs being composed entirely of women and girls.[70] According to the churchwarden, the sparse morning congregation at St Sampson's parish church in Guernsey on 30 June 1940 included only one other man besides himself.[71]

The shortage of men in worship may be attributed in part to their disempowerment as a result of the Occupation. Even without that added factor, patriarchal attitudes within the male population discouraged men from attending activities in which there would be a majority of women. Nevertheless, the fact that ministers, local preachers and lay officials in Methodism were almost always male suggests that women were not especially empowered during the Occupation, except possibly in running their own midweek meetings (see Chapter 4).

Despite fluctuating attendance, sustaining public worship across the denominations was a major (and largely voluntary) undertaking that involved many thousands of people every week throughout the Occupation. Methodists in particular invested considerable energy in their annual cycle

of denominational festivals for religious, social and political reasons. By attending services and other church activities, islanders identified themselves with an authority beyond the control of the occupying forces. Given the relative freedom granted to the churches, religious activities were one of the few safe outlets for expressing passive resistance to the Occupation.

Services in French

The 1930s saw a steep decline in the use of French in Methodist worship in Jersey. By 1940 none of the ministers in the island could preach in French, and most local preachers preached comfortably in English even if they also spoke French. Nan Le Ruez, who began preaching during the Occupation, always preached in English whereas her grandfather preached exclusively in French.[72]

A survey of the Jersey (Grove Place) Circuit preaching plan for the period 1940 to 1945 reveals that French was rarely used. The symbol 'F' denotes '*Service en Français*'. Between January and March 1940 only 21 of the 468 services (4.5 percent) were in French. Figures for the same quarter in following years show that French was used in less than one percent of services.[73] Most churches averaged one or two French services per quarter; four was exceptional. By 1939 there were just two French services a quarter at St Martin's but only during the winter months.[74] These ceased altogether in 1940. In four other churches (Philadelphie, Georgetown, Bethel and Galaad) no French services were held during the Occupation.

Local church records provide a further glimpse into the decline of French. Already, before the war, the majority of churches had ceased using French to record their affairs. Even where French was still used, some English was creeping in, as the records of St Ouen's church illustrate. In 1939 the trustees received a donation for '*l'ouvrage pour le boiler room et la cheminée. Il est aussi décidé de construire un car park sur une piece de terre.*'[75] At St Martin's the leaders' meeting stopped using French to record their minutes in 1924. In 1941 the trustees similarly decided that in future their minutes would be written in English 'as the French language was so little used now in the circuit'.[76] At Carmel, the secretary to the trustees dutifully recorded the minutes in French almost to the end of the Occupation. When it came to meetings, however, he translated the minutes into English for the benefit of others. In January 1945 the trustees agreed that he might as well write the minutes in English.[77] By the end of the Occupation, few churches were still recording their meetings in French.[78] The circuit stewards also concluded

that the future lay with the English language. In June 1945 the quarterly meeting 'unanimously agreed that, in future, the circuit plan will be printed wholly in English'.[79]

In the Guernsey and Sark (French) Circuit the French language continued in regular use during the Occupation, though English was by now predominant. Sidney Beaugié and Henry Foss preached in fluent French and each was serving his second tour of duty in the islands. On the preaching plan, the asterisk (*) denotes 'Service Anglais'. Between January and March 1940 194 Sunday services (46.6 percent) were conducted in French. Table 3.1 contains a breakdown of these figures:

Table 3.1: Services in the Guernsey and Sark (French) Circuit, January – March 1940

Church	Services in French	Services in English
Victoria Road	-	26
Wesley	-	26
Les Camps	-	26
Forest	-	26
Sion	18	8
Torteval	23	3
Les Adams	23	3
Rocquaine	24	2
Carmel	12	14
St Andrew's	7	19
Castel	9	17
Galaad	16	10
Les Capelles	11	15
Vale	11	15
La Moye	14	12
Sark	26	-
TOTAL	**194**	**222**

A clear pattern emerges from these figures. In the town churches (Victoria Road and Wesley) and in the southern parishes (St Martin's and Forest) Sunday services were conducted exclusively in English. Conversely, French was almost always used in churches in the Western parishes (Torteval, Les Adams and Rocquaine) and in Sark. In churches in the central and northern

parishes (Castel, Les Capelles, Vale, Galaad, St Andrew's) both languages were used, though English was more common. Two churches held an equal number of services in French and in English: Carmel held a service in each language every Sunday; at La Moye the morning service was in English whereas the evening service was in French (except for the Sunday school anniversary when both were in French).

Figures for the same quarter in subsequent years reveal a modest decline in the number of services in French.[80] In churches where both languages were used the balance shifted decisively in favour of English. Following the Liberation, the number of French services declined steeply. From 1945 the preaching plan appeared in English; the asterisk now denotes 'French Service'. Table 3.2 contains a breakdown of Sunday services in the last quarter of 1945. Every church registers a significant decrease in the number of French services since 1940. The figure for the Sark chapel is conjecture since there is no asterisk to indicate its worship was conducted in French, though it seems unlikely to have switched to English overnight.

Table 3.2: Services in the Guernsey and Sark (French) Circuit, 14 October 1945 – 6 January 1946

Church	Services in French	Services in English
Victoria Road	-	-
Wesley	-	13
Les Camps	-	26
Forest	-	14
Sion	7	19
Torteval	13	13
Les Adams	17	9
Rocquaine	18	8
Carmel	6	20
St Andrew's	4	22
Castel	3	23
Galaad	9	17
Les Capelles	6	20
Vale	3	23
La Moye	4	22
Sark	26 (?)	-
TOTAL	**116**	**249**

Methodists in Guernsey mostly stopped recording their affairs in French before the Second World War, though occasionally French was still heard in meetings. In February 1944 Beaugié conducted the oral examination of a local preacher on trial entirely in French.[81] The fact that the minutes (written in English) draw attention to the use of French suggests that by this time it was becoming unusual. Indeed, preachers seemed less than familiar with the proper form. In 1941 it was noted that local preachers were confusing congregations by leading them in different versions of the Lord's Prayer. Beaugié arranged for 50 copies of the Lord's Prayer in French to be printed and distributed around the churches for the use of preachers.[82]

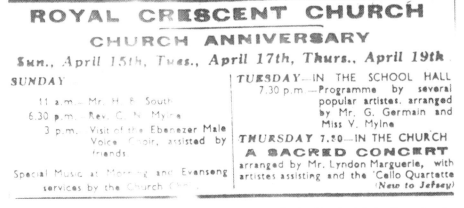

Figure 3.5: Church anniversary was an important festival in the Methodist calendar

The transition to English, though gradual, was inexorable. The congregation at Les Capelles (229 members) was the largest in the circuit. Between January and March 1940 there were 11 Sunday services in French and 15 in English. During the same quarter in 1941 there were 10 in French and 16 in English. In the first quarter of 1942 and again in 1943 there were only eight services in French compared with 18 in English. In the spring of 1943 the congregation were consulted about reducing still further the number of French services, though the consultation revealed a substantial majority in favour of maintaining the existing pattern.[83] In the first quarter of 1944 there were nine services in French and 17 in English. In the first quarter of 1945 there were 10 services in French but in the last quarter of 1945 this fell back sharply to just six.

The dramatic decline in the use of French in Methodist worship in Guernsey from the middle of 1945 can be attributed to a conscious desire to accommodate the needs of returning evacuees, who spoke only English.

Figures 3.6, 3.7, 3.8: Decorative panels at Galaad Chapel in the Jersey (Grove Place)
Circuit (Jersey Methodist Circuit)

Even before evacuees returned, Methodist leaders in the Channel Islands realised that the future lay with the English language. Roy Rabey's father had long been used to preaching in French. However, in 1943 he resolved to preach in English because that would be the language of the returning evacuees.[84] Even in the Western country parishes of Guernsey change was in the air in the summer of 1945. When Sion chapel reopened its Sunday school in July 1945 a notice in the newspaper invited children to 'bring hymnbooks and English bibles'.[85]

The return of evacuees may have hastened the demise of French as a vehicle for Methodist worship in the Channel Islands, but the ascendancy of English was already ensured by an irresistible combination of social factors affecting the population as a whole. Whereas in parts of Wales Nonconformist worship became a vehicle for the preservation of the Welsh language, Methodist identity in the Channel Islands was not bound up with the French language. Church records contain no indication of a concerted effort by Methodists to preserve the use of French in worship even if older church members regretted its passing.

Chapter 4

Church Life

B esides allowing church services, the first orders issued by the German Commandant of the Channel Islands in July 1940 permitted cinemas, public houses, concerts and other forms of entertainment to continue as before, provided that: 'Such Assemblies shall not be made the medium for any propaganda or utterances against the honour or interests of, or offensive to, the German Government or Forces.'[1] However, these 'privileges' were dependent upon the good behaviour of the population and could be withdrawn at any time for reasons of 'military necessity'.

In September 1940 military necessity led to a ban on public dances, causing resentment amongst the civilian population for whom such events were a valued pastime.[2] In this instance, the orders emanated from the German authorities in Paris and applied to the whole of occupied France, including (for administrative purposes) the British Channel Islands, irrespective of local factors. In May 1941 the Military Governor in Paris lifted the prohibition, and public dances were once again permitted, albeit only in registered premises.[3] This episode illustrates how the leisure activities of islanders were subject to interference by the occupying power for reasons that made little sense in the Channel Islands.

As it happens, the ban on public dances did not have much impact on Methodism since at that time the Methodist Conference prohibited all forms of dancing on church premises. An inherited puritanical streak caused Methodists to frown upon dancing as an activity almost as unsuitable for church members as frequenting public houses.

Although attitudes in Methodism were beginning to change by the 1940s, suspicion of worldly pleasures accounts for the importance of midweek church activities, especially fellowships, in the leisure time of Methodists during the Occupation. Recognising the danger posed by boredom, Methodist churches actively promoted edifying spiritual alternatives to secular activities that would put their members in temptation's way. In

particular, sustaining a strong musical tradition meant that choir practice and sacred concerts featured prominently in the social calendar of Methodists. Should the military authorities prohibit these activities, the effect on Methodism would be serious. In particular, ministers feared that members of their congregation would find less wholesome forms of entertainment that undermined their allegiance to Christianity.

A few weeks after public dances were forbidden, church activities suddenly came under threat for reasons that had nothing to do with the situation in the Channel Islands. Following instructions issued by the military authorities in Paris, on 14 October 1940 the German Commandant of the Channel Islands published an order prohibiting all public meetings except those licensed by the authorities. To confuse matters, no one seemed to know whether church activities, including musical concerts, constituted public meetings within the terms of the order. To be on the safe side, most church groups unilaterally suspended their meetings pending further information.

In an attempt to clarify the situation, on 8 November the Commandant published a further 'Order relating to Associations, meetings, distinctive emblems and beflagging', which confirmed that: all unlicensed societies and associations were banned; all public meetings remained prohibited; and no new associations or societies were permitted. Furthermore, the population was forbidden to wear 'distinctive apparel and uniform emblems'. Strictly interpreted, this last regulation would have widespread implications since a ban on 'distinctive apparel and uniform emblems' covered a multitude of attire. Douglas Ord was disconcerted to be asked by a member of his Brock Road congregation whether he intended to discard his clerical collar and whether she would have to forego wearing her Wesley Guild lapel badge.[4] Here was a classic example of the German authorities issuing unenforceable orders that made them appear ridiculous.

Confirmation of the ban on unlicensed activities prompted a flurry of applications from clubs, societies and churches requesting permission to continue as before. The Dean of Guernsey wrote to the Bailiff on behalf of the town church asking that its weekly programme of variety entertainment at Ozanne Hall Mission be allowed to carry on: 'As you probably know these entertainments are drawing large audiences, and are proving a great source of enjoyment to the poorer class of people in the town.'[5] A note scribbled in the margin by the Bailiff authorises an urgent request to the German authorities for a permit so that the following week's concert could go ahead.

Between 11 and 13 November 1940 the Bailiff of Guernsey wrote three separate letters to the German authorities enclosing applications from various organisations for a licence under the terms of the order 'regarding meetings, emblems and flags'. Amongst various religious groups seeking exemption from the order were: the Guernsey (English) Circuit; the Guernsey and Sark (French) Circuit; the Elim Pentecostal churches; the Salvation Army; the Christian Science reading room; the Spurgeon Memorial Baptist Church; St Andrew's Presbyterian Church; and the Dean of Guernsey on behalf of the island's Anglican churches.[6] In Jersey the Bailiff similarly wrote to the German authorities requesting permission for various church groups to carry on with their activities.[7]

Whereas churches invariably received permission to continue their midweek activities, certain religious, quasi-religious and military organisations were proscribed or strictly controlled. In January 1941 the Bailiff of Guernsey was informed that the Salvation Army, the Freemasons, the Oddfellows Society and the Ex-Servicemen's Club were all proscribed.[8] Members of the St John's Ambulance Brigade were not permitted to wear uniform, though social activities could continue providing advance notice was given.[9] In Jersey, where the same orders were enforced, there was confusion over whether the prohibition applied to the YMCA. The German Commandant referred the matter to higher authority, but any subsequent correspondence on the subject has not survived.[10]

At first, the ban on new societies was rigorously enforced. In May 1941 an application to set up a sporting club in Guernsey was rejected on the grounds that no exceptions could be permitted 'as the great number of existing associations gives ample opportunity for the practice of sports'.[11] The following month the Southern Social Club wrote to John Leale asking for permission to re-open for cards, darts and billiards. The club was strictly teetotal 'and no political debates ever take place'. Leale supported the application, but the German authorities eventually turned it down.[12] Later, the ban on new associations was partially relaxed. In May 1944 approval was given for a public meeting in Jersey to discuss forming a ladies' netball league, though any proposed new association would require a permit and its rules would have to be approved by the authorities.[13]

For ideological reasons, the prohibition on Freemasonry extended to abolishing the lodges. The civil authorities in both islands received instructions to liquidate assets held by the Freemasons, much to the disgust of the Bailiff of Guernsey, Victor Carey, who protested vigorously to the German Commandant: 'British Freemasons are non-political and political

discussion is strictly forbidden. That circumstance and that the activities of all the Lodges in Guernsey have been suspended throughout the Occupation, should, I think, dispel any idea that anti-German influence is or will be exerted or attempted by the continuance in being of these Lodges.'

If the Freemasons had to be suppressed, he argued, it should be done by German order rather than by legislation in the States of Guernsey. 'It would be asking a lot of those members of the legislature who are Freemasons, to violate their undertakings, by voting their associations out of existence.' Finally, he cited the Hague Convention: Freemasonry was essentially a charitable institution and as such protected under the terms of the convention.[14] But the Germans were unwilling to compromise on so serious an ideological principle. In Jersey and in Guernsey the States eventually approved legislation giving them legal ownership of the assets in question.[15]

Victor Carey's appeal on behalf of Freemasonry is the only known instance of his intervening with the German authorities in support of a particular group. No such protest was made against the registration of anti-Jewish laws in the States of Guernsey, even though they directly affected the lives of people and not just the ownership of property. Had the Bailiff leapt to the defence of other groups, his intervention on behalf of Freemasonry might not now appear so self-serving. As it is, Carey's outraged concern for the sensitivities of Freemasons does nothing to enhance his reputation among those who criticise his dealings with the occupying forces.

Be that as it may, the liquidation of assets held by Freemasons and others demonstrates the extraordinary lengths to which the German authorities were prepared to go in order to eliminate perceived threats to their interests. Against this backdrop, it is evident that the churches enjoyed a privileged position. Once licensed, their midweek activities were able to continue with minimum interference. What is more, public events organised by the churches, such as concerts and plays, were also permitted, subject only to the programme being approved by the censor's office. Thus the churches provided one of the few public spaces in which islanders were able to assemble relatively freely in order to express their religious, cultural and social identity.

Midweek Fellowships

The principal midweek activity for Methodists in the Channel Islands was the Wesley Guild, an evening meeting for both sexes held on church premises for social, educational and devotional purposes. Although most Guild members were active Methodists, others who did not usually attend worship

were welcome to join, thus affording an opportunity for evangelism. Reflecting the habits of a more formal era, the Wesley Guild had an elaborate constitution involving several officers, an executive committee, and various sub-committees responsible for organising a cycle of devotional, literary and musical evenings, all dutifully recorded for posterity by the secretary. Guild meetings continued in Jersey and Guernsey during the Occupation, though in a few cases meticulous sets of minutes dry up for the duration, as if secretaries feared the consequences of committing their thoughts to paper.[16]

Figures for the Jersey (Wesley) Circuit reported in March 1945 and set out below in Table 4.1 illustrate how the Wesley Guild expanded in the final year of the Occupation in response to the growing need for a midweek church activity suitable for young people.[17] Guild meetings at Samarès recommenced in the autumn of 1943 after an interval of several years. In December 114 members were reported.[18] Judging by the programme, the intention was to provide a safe diversion from the drabness of daily life. The schedule for 1943/44 reflects the interests of pre-war years – beetle drive, Spelling Bee, 'I was there', round the camp fire, record requests, games evening, Gentlemen entertain the Ladies. Probably the most controversial meeting was a literary evening when the motion to be debated was 'That the Parish of St Clements is backward at going forward.'[19]

Table 4.1: Wesley Guilds in the Jersey (Wesley) Circuit in March 1945

Church	Guild Membership	Average Attendance	Increase since 1944
Wesley	56	29	21
First Tower	20	15	2
St Aubin	57	32	19
Samarès	128	50	-3

Whilst the Wesley Guild programme at Samarès may not have been intellectually stimulating, the fact that one hundred copies were printed and distributed indicates considerable interest in midweek church activities within and beyond the regular congregation. This may have resulted in a weakening of the Guild's links with the church. In January 1944 one of the church officers urged stronger ties so as to encourage Guild members 'to find the way to the source of all happiness – a closer walk with God'.[20] As a means towards this end, it was suggested that members of the Wesley Guild take responsibility for leading a Sunday service.

A similar renewal of interest in the Wesley Guild in the Jersey (Grove Place) Circuit confirms that midweek church activities were increasingly important among Methodists as the Occupation progressed. In the autumn of 1940 a number of Guilds were obliged to cease meeting because of problems created by the blackout. Several resumed meeting in the autumn of 1943 in response to repeated requests from young people for some kind of midweek church activity.

For instance, Wesley Guild meetings at Bethlehem chapel ceased altogether between 1940 and 1942. However, in September 1943 a group of young people decided to restart the Guild. At the first meeting Rev. John Scott gave an address but, according to Nan Le Ruez, spoiled the evening by going on too long.[21] Despite this minor setback, a programme was drawn up which included an evening on characters from the Old Testament, meetings for Home Missions and Overseas Missions, and finishing with a sacred concert given by young people. The programme for 1944/45 included evenings on elocution, favourite hymns and another sacred concert. Potentially, there were opportunities to address more weighty issues, such as 'What the Occupation has taught me' and 'Knotty Problems of the Occupation', though the choice of title suggests a light-hearted approach.[22]

Unusually, St Martin's church did not consider Guild meetings to be worthwhile during the Occupation. In September 1945 Guild members met for the first time since June 1940. The minutes of the last meeting were read, and it was noted that a decision to install a clock in the vestry in memory of a deceased member had not been carried out in the previous five years because of 'wartime conditions'.[23] However, such a long hiatus was exceptional. As the Occupation entered its third autumn, the energy devoted to arranging and printing Wesley Guild programmes in Jersey reflects a genuine need among Methodists for a midweek church activity that combined educational, devotional and social elements. Inevitably perhaps, the Liberation brought in its wake a decline in the Wesley Guild. Even so, in 1946 11 of the 18 churches in the circuit still maintained a Wesley Guild with a combined membership of 503.[24]

In Guernsey too the Wesley Guild proved popular with Methodists during the Occupation. As in Jersey, the majority of meetings were intended to divert attention from the privations of daily life. At the same time, gathering together on church premises was itself a small gesture of defiance against the enemy. Educational and devotional evenings afforded an opportunity to discuss issues bordering on the subversive. Wesley Guild meetings at the

Vale church in the Guernsey and Sark (French) Circuit provide a particularly noteworthy example of how midweek church activities could become a vehicle for passive resistance.[25]

Here the Wesley Guild programme for 1939 followed the safe, if undemanding, pattern of previous years. Musical evenings consisted of entertainment by soloists and groups. Literary evenings involved recitations of poetry and prose or else members prepared short talks on non-controversial subjects. At a literary evening on 'Likes and Dislikes', members declared their general contentment with life. On another occasion a number of Guild members delivered 'sermonettes', which the secretary tactfully recorded as being 'all excellent'. The remoteness of the Channel Islands from the war in Europe is reflected in a relaxed autumn programme. Barely a month after the declaration of war on Germany, the Wesley Guild evening took the form of a 'Musical Bee' in which 'the ladies beat the gentlemen by three points'.

When Wesley Guild meetings resumed in the autumn of 1940 following the usual summer break a more purposeful programme reflected the changed circumstances of enemy occupation. The autumn session began with a series of four meetings on 'How my religious beliefs help in these days'. On the first evening three members gave short talks on 'I believe in God the Father'. On the second, the subject was 'I believe in Jesus Christ'. The third evening addressed the solidly Protestant, though less creedal, theme: 'I believe in the Bible and its teaching'. Finally, the series concluded with an evening on 'Prayer'. The next series of meetings addressed 'Our Fears', during the course of which the Anglican rector spoke on 'Discipleship'. On another occasion, members considered 'The Coming of the Kingdom of God'. After sustained attention to weighty matters, the final meeting before Christmas must have come as something of a relief: members heard a talk about a motor tour through England illustrated with lanternslides.

In subsequent years the programme became overtly political as Guild members engaged with contemporary realities. A series of meetings in the autumn and winter of 1943/44 addressed the subject of 'The New World' under five headings: (1) The kind of world we hope for; (2) the way to that world; (3) the obstacles on the way; (4) the kind of peace we favour; and (5) the Christian's responsibility and opportunity, and the sphere of the Christian Church. Handbills were printed and distributed – a risky enterprise in view of German orders concerning statements against the Third Reich. The first meeting generated 'lively discussion'. According to the secretary's

VALE METHODIST CHURCH

Programme of Meetings to be held at 7.15 p.m. on alternate
Tuesdays, commencing 12th October, 1943.

" THE NEW WORLD "

1. The kind of World we hope for.
   ("The 4 Freedoms" —everyone a chance to <u>full life</u>, etc.)

2. The way to that World.
   (Remove pre-war evils, e.g. poverty; extend pre-war good, e.g. education; apply lessons of war-years, e.g. sharing; adopt new measures, e.g. Beveridge plan).

3. The obstacles on the way,
   (e.g. indifference, jealousy, worship of money, etc.)

4. The kind of Peace we favour.

5. (a) The Christian's responsibility and opportunity.
   (b) The sphere of the Christian Church,
   (Not to formulate schemes, but to stimulate the concern of its Members, maintain their ideals, foster a right attitude, etc.)

N.B. The notes in brackets are intended to indicate only a few of the possible lines of thought. Think out the subjects and come prepared to express your views.

Do not stay away on dark nights, join up with friends in your vicinity and come together !

Mr. W. J. CORBET will conduct the meetings every other Tuesday.

October 5th, 7.15 p.m., Church Anniversary Meeting.

Speaker : Rev. E. L. Frossard. Chairman : Mr. P. Le Maitre

Camp du Roi Printing Works

Figure 4.1: Wesley Guild programme, Vale church, Guernsey and Sark (French) Circuit, October 1943 (Author's Collection)

minute, 'It appeared that a certain amount of socialism was desired, that selfishness should be eliminated and that children of different countries should be able to visit other countries.' The discussion on 'The kind of peace we favour' in February 1944 reached the enlightened conclusion that 'the peace terms should be just, not vengeful and arrived at in the interests of the world in general'.

Of course, these same issues were being widely discussed in Britain and elsewhere at this time as the tide of war turned in favour of the Allies. Even so, such a bold foray into the political arena is extraordinary given the apolitical nature of life in the Channel Islands prior to the Occupation. Indeed, many islanders were indifferent to political and constitutional affairs (see Chapter 10), and there were no political parties. Such unprecedented attention to international politics in relation to the Church can only be explained as an act of passive resistance to the enemy.

Christian Endeavour was the main alternative to the Wesley Guild. As a former Primitive Methodist cause, Aquila Road church in Jersey preferred Christian Endeavour to the Wesley Guild, though the two organisations had a similar ethos and some churches ran both groups. For example, Christian Endeavour meetings at Ebenezer in the Guernsey (English) Circuit in the autumn of 1940 would have been equally at home in the Wesley Guild programme. Whilst there was one social evening, the majority of meetings featured devotional themes. Frederick Flint took prayer as his theme. Philip Romeril posed the question 'Who is this Jesus?' Another speaker introduced 'Heroes of the Faith'. The meeting due to be held on 11 November 1940 was cancelled because of uncertainty surrounding the recently announced ban on public meetings but the following week 21 people gathered to hear Flint speak on 'The Fiery Furnace', presumably with reference to the forces of evil. However, in the spring of 1941 it was decided to merge Christian Endeavour at Ebenezer and Salem with the Ebenezer Guild and a Salvation Army group in order to form a single fellowship intended primarily for young people.

Midweek meetings for women, often presided over by the minister's wife, were a feature of most Methodist churches in the 1930s. In the Channel Islands there were two kinds of women's meeting – the Sisterhood and Women's Work. An observer would have found it difficult to discern much difference between them, though Women's Work was affiliated to the Methodist Missionary Society and took an interest in its affairs. Whatever

71

their nature, women's meetings were generally held during the afternoon since at that time few married women worked outside the home. Miriam Mahy of the Vale church in the Guernsey (English) Circuit was a frequent speaker at such meetings, which usually included informal prayers, a hymn and bible reading. Speakers gave a short address on a subject of religious or topical interest.[26]

Women's meetings fulfilled a devotional and social role, whilst also providing a forum for mutual support in the challenges that the Occupation posed homemaking and caring for families. However, it would be patronising to suggest they fulfilled no other purpose. At a time when ministers and the majority of local preachers were male, a midweek meeting run by women for women was more likely to be in tune with their spiritual needs. At the same time, women's meetings were widely regarded as a means of evangelism amongst women.

For instance, the acting superintendent of the Jersey (Wesley) Circuit, Ronald South, reported in December 1943 that Wesley chapel had a vigorous Sisterhood attended by 55-60 women each week, several of whom had recently been received into membership of the church.[27] A number of other Methodist churches in Jersey started midweek women's meetings during the Occupation in response to a perceived need for fellowship and as an opportunity for evangelism. At St Martin's in the Jersey (Grove Place) Circuit a Sisterhood was formed in March 1941. Within three months attendance was reported to be 'quite good', and the venture was subsequently judged to have been worthwhile.[28]

At the annual general meeting of the Sisterhood at St Sampson's in the Guernsey (English) Circuit in October 1942 the membership was reported as 77 with an average attendance of 37. Some of the women were members of the St Sampson's corps of the Salvation Army whose own meetings were banned. The tribute paid to the recently deceased leader (the wife of Rev. Philip Romeril) confirms the evangelical purpose of women's meetings in Methodism: 'to her the Sisterhood stood as a means of grace, a stepping stone to high ideals.' Two years later, the membership had risen to 103. In June 1945 more than 300 programmes were printed for the annual Sisterhood service.[29]

Certain elements of these and other midweek church activities during the Occupation may have been diversionary; but, if so, Methodists were hardly alone in seeking respite from the drabness of daily life. Many forms of secular entertainment catered for precisely that need. In fact, midweek church activities were probably more obviously engaged with contemporary

realities than any other voluntary activity, partly because they frowned upon frivolity and partly because of their relative freedom from German scrutiny. Political discussions about the post-war world may have been the exception rather than the rule, but the devotional evenings that featured in most Wesley Guild and Christian Endeavour programmes would certainly have engaged with issues relating to the contemporary situation.

The healthy attendance recorded at midweek church activities during the Occupation confirms that these fulfilled a genuine need for fellowship and social interaction among Methodists and those on the fringes of Methodism at a time of crisis. Some midweek meetings may have offered nothing more substantial than homespun entertainment, but at least they provided a safe environment for young people. Indeed, one of the main reasons why Methodists in Jersey restarted Guild meetings during the Occupation was a concern about the undesirability of secular alternatives on offer to young people, especially 'music hall' type entertainment. In contrast, midweek church activities provided islanders with the opportunity for Christian fellowship and an edifying social life without exposure to harmful influences. Unsophisticated it may have been, but to generations of Methodists before the advent of the television era participatory entertainment of this kind was more satisfying than can readily be appreciated nowadays.

Music and Sacred Concerts

A consistent feature of island life during the Occupation was the prolific number of sacred concerts and similar forms of musical entertainment in churches of all denominations. Newspapers from the Occupation contain numerous reports of such events, and churches often placed prominent notices in the press to attract audiences. Fundraising was high on the list of objectives (see Chapter 7), though this was usually secondary to the main purpose of providing an appropriate outlet for the musical talents of church members as well as offering edifying entertainment for the general public. Even where congregations professed little aesthetic interest in music, it was commonly held that sacred concerts afforded an opportunity for evangelism, thereby legitimising the efforts of musicians and choirs.

Throughout the Occupation sacred concerts attracted large audiences from among the general public, many of whom seldom attended church services. Apart from amateur dramatic companies, churches were just about the only groups in the local community with the resources and facilities to stage concerts and the creative capacity to attract and direct the talents of

musicians and singers. In October 1944 the 'little choir' (consisting mostly of Methodists) performed to a capacity audience at Brock Road church in the Guernsey (English) Circuit. The following month the same choir performed excerpts from Handel's *Messiah*. Ord noted: 'When there is nothing for people to do it is worthwhile.'[30]

The need to provide something to alleviate a tedious existence probably explains why, even in the final weeks of the Occupation, churches of all denominations managed somehow to maintain their musical tradition despite near starvation conditions. On Good Friday 1945 St Sampson's choir in Guernsey performed 'The Passion'; at Ebenezer an augmented choir performed Wetton's 'The Fulfilment'; whilst the joint Vale and Capelles choirs led a musical service. On the evening of Easter Day a Grand Jubilee Recital took place at Les Capelles to celebrate the organist's silver jubilee in post; an 'Easter Festival' at Brock Road involved augmented choirs with violin and organ solos.[31] In Jersey the Grove Place church celebrated its 99th anniversary over the Easter weekend with special musical events. Despite extreme conditions, the church was decorated with lilies and spring flowers.[32]

The importance of the musical tradition in Methodism gave organists and church choirs a degree of prominence that frequently led to tensions with other sections of the congregation. Organists in particular were significant figures whose names often featured in newspaper advertisements for sacred concerts. There is no doubt that organists contributed a great deal to church life. In February 1945 the trustees of Brock Road church paid tribute to their organist and choirmaster, C.N. Falla, whose musicianship had 'brought the church into prominence in island life'.[33] Moreover, as a result of his efforts, the church was able to raise considerable sums of money. The profits from a single concert usually paid an organist's annual stipend.[34]

Above all, a good organist was invaluable in leading worship. The best organists were able to inspire people to sing heartily – an important consideration in a tradition that valued hymns – and probably influenced the size of the congregation. However, not everyone appreciated their attempts to raise morale through exuberant organ playing. In May 1940 the leaders' meeting at Les Capelles in the Guernsey and Sark (French) Circuit heard that certain members of the congregation were no longer attending services because of the loud way in which the organ was played.[35] The minister was given the thankless task of asking the organist to play *mezzo forte* rather than *fortissimo*.

Choirs, too, were generally regarded as an asset because most

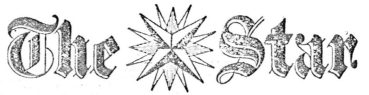

WEDNESDAY, MARCH 28. 1945

TWOPENCE

| Holy Week, Good Friday and Easter Services |

St SAMPSON'S METHODIST CHURCH

" The Passion " will be rendered by the choir on GOOD FRIDAY at 3.30 p.m,

Soloists: Tenor, Mr. Martyn Dorey ; Bass, Mr. Wilson Mahy.

EBENEZER METHODIST CHURCH

" THE FULFILMENT" by Wetton will be rendered by an augmented choir on GOOD FRIDAY at 7 p.m. Soloists include Messrs. Rex Priaulx (tenor) and Jack Ogier (baritone).

VALE METHODIST CHURCH

GOOD FRIDAY at 6.45 p.m.

MUSICAL SERVICE by joint Capelles and Vale choirs. Chairman : Rev. S. E. Beaugié, M.A. Soloists: Misses F. Martel, K. Gaudion, J. Patten : Messrs. Lloyd Mahy, John Duquemin, Wilson Mahy. Flautist : Mr. Alfred Sebire. Pianists : Miss K. Gaudion ;Messrs. E. Tostevin and W. J. Corbet.

Collection for Trust Funds.

Cycles stored under cover free of charge.

Delisles Methodist Church

GOOD FRIDAY at 6 p.m. Chapel Anniversary Service. Speaker : Mr. Alan N. Grut. Soloist : Mr. S. Ozanne

CAPELLES METHODIST CHURCH.

Grand Jubilee Recital

to commemorate Mr. Ernest Tostevin's 25th Anniversary as Organist of the above Church on

EASTER DAY, Sunday, April 1st, *at 6.45 p.m.*

Chairman : Rev. S. E. Beaugié, M.A. *Artistes :* Messrs. A. Sebire, W. W. Le Bargy, R. Le Tissier, P. J. Noyon, R. Priaulx, E. Tostevin. The Vale and Capelles Choirs are uniting in Choral Works. Soloists : Misses F. Martel and K. Gaudion.

Conductor : Mr. W. J. Corbet.

Collection for Organ Fund.

Cycles stored free under supervision.

L'ISLET METHODIST CHURCH

GOOD FRI. SERVICE, 6.30 p.m. A " Solemn Assembly—Around the Cross." EASTER SUNDAY SERVICES at 11 a.m. and 6 p.m. 2.30 p.m. A Special Service given by the Sunday School scholars. MONDAY at 6.30 p.m—MUSICAL SERVICE. Address by Mr. J. C. Langlois. A hearty invitation to all

BROCK ROAD CHURCH

SUNDAY April 1st. 6.30 p.m. Easter Festival. Augmented Choirs. Anthems with Solos. Solo Violinist: Dr. A. O. Bisson Solo Organist: Mr. E. J. Sebire

Above and overleaf, Figure 4.2 (a and b): Even in the spring of 1945 churches continued to arrange sacred concerts

Aquila Road Methodist Church

(THE CHURCH OF GOOD FELLOWSHIP)

TO-MORROW (SUNDAY)
EASTERTIDE SERVICES
(Relayed to the Hospitals)
11 a.m. and 7 p.m.

Rev. W. C. H. Fell

Morning Anthem: "Come ye Faithful"
Solo: "I know that my Redeemer liveth"
—Miss Joan Picot

Evening Anthem: "Why seek ye the
living?" (Hollings).
"The Strife is o'er." (Ley)
Solo: "The Trumpet shall sound"
—Mr. A. G. Harrison

at 7.45 p.m.
*Community Hymn Singing for
half an hour*
Join with us in this Fellowship of Praise

congregations appreciated introits and anthems. However, the tendency of choirs to become semi-independent often led to friction, especially when they made decisions without reference to others. The choir at Ebenezer in the Jersey (Grove Place) Circuit unilaterally decided the date of Choir Sunday when 'both services will be conducted by members of the choir only'. Without consulting the minister, a choir member was deputed to give the address, and several anthems were polished for the occasion.[36] In September 1942 the leaders' meeting at Les Capelles in Guernsey noted the poor attendance of choir members at services. The superintendent, Beaugié, was asked to write to all members of the choir reminding them of the importance of regular attendance at worship.[37]

As ever, the appropriateness of what choirs sang provided endless scope for dispute. In March 1941 the organist and choirmaster at Les Capelles submitted a letter to the leaders' meeting asking permission for the choir to perform a cantata at Easter. However, most of those present were against

the idea. One of the church stewards was instructed to obtain further details from the choirmaster before agreement could be given.[38] For good measure, the choirmaster was asked to choose introits and vespers for Sunday services from the *Methodist Hymn Book* so that everyone present could join in the singing – a request guaranteed to annoy any choir with a sense of its own worth.[39]

Sensitivities about the playing of music in sacred space meant that Methodist trustees were often reluctant to allow external groups (even other churches) to use their premises for concerts. In 1943 the trustees of Philadelphie chapel in the Jersey (Grove Place) Circuit, having taken the precaution of consulting Methodist regulations, turned down a request from the Anglican parish church to use the Methodist hall for a concert.[40] The trustees of the Grove Place church rejected a similar request for a sacred concert to be held on their premises on Good Friday 1943.[41]

Figure 4.3: Brock Road church, St Peter Port, photographed in 2008; the church closed for worship in 1993 (Photograph by author)

Aside from the sensitivities involved, sacred concerts during the Occupation proved popular with audiences for a variety of reasons both religious and secular. Whatever their spiritual content, concerts held on church premises acquired patriotic overtones, especially when the purpose was to raise funds for a loyal cause. In April 1942 Brock Road church hosted a sacred concert in the schoolroom in aid of the 'Help the Children Fund'. It was strictly forbidden to sing the national anthem, but at the close Ord invited the audience to go home singing it in their heart.[42] The invitation was subversive and could have landed him in trouble with the German authorities, though on this occasion there were no repercussions. It was a small gesture but still eloquent testimony to the way in which concerts on church premises could be a significant means of registering defiance of the enemy and maintaining morale amongst islanders.

Relations with other Churches

Following national trends in this pre-ecumenical era, relations between the various denominations in the Channel Islands during the German Occupation amounted to little more than peaceful co-existence with isolated examples of limited co-operation. Despite its origins in the Church of England, Methodism at this time was firmly identified with the Protestant Free Churches, who generally saw themselves as being in competition with Anglicans. There was virtually no formal contact with Roman Catholics.

In Jersey the Free Church ministers' meeting or fraternal was the principal forum for co-operation between Methodist ministers and other Nonconformist clergy. In June 1942 Walter Fell, serving for a year as honorary President of the Jersey Free Church Council, met with the Dean of Jersey and several other Church of England clergy to discuss how Nonconformists and Anglicans might work more closely together. However, even their common experience during the previous two years of enemy occupation was insufficient to overcome mutual suspicion, as Fell subsequently reported to the fraternal:

> To say the least it was a disappointing meeting. Smurthwaite [Baptist minister] had hoped to create a warmer spirit of friendship and achieve a closer cooperation between the Anglicans and ourselves. But the subsequent discussion only served to emphasise our differences. It was regretted that the friendly atmosphere prevailing a few years ago had gone with the departure from the island of several broad Churchmen.[43]

The Nonconformist clergy were alarmed at what they saw as the resurgence of Anglo-Catholicism in Jersey. In March 1944 Ronald South, acting superintendent of the Jersey (Wesley) Circuit, suggested that the paramount religious need in the island was for Methodism to recover its strength. According to South, 'The position of the Anglican Church was a queer one, the growth of Anglo-Catholicism in that Church was tremendous. If the Protestant principle is to be rallied round once again it must be done by Methodism.'[44]

Since a broad alliance involving Anglicans was out of the question, Methodist ministers in Jersey joined with their Nonconformist colleagues on issues that affected church interests during the Occupation. Regrettably, the minutes of the Free Church ministers' fraternal reflect the somewhat narrow concerns of Nonconformists at that time. In November 1942 the Free Church ministers were preoccupied with the subject of divorce. For some reason they suspected that the States of Jersey would try to rush through divorce legislation at the cessation of hostilities. Members of the fraternal saw it as their duty to oppose the introduction of divorce laws in Jersey.[45]

Preserving the sanctity of the Lord's Day was a perennial concern among Nonconformists during the Occupation. Free Church ministers in Jersey viewed with alarm the relaxation of laws controlling what activities were permissible on Sundays. In May 1944 they wrote to the Bailiff voicing concern about the increasing availability of secular entertainment on Sundays. The Bailiff assured them that existing rules controlling entertainment on Sundays were being strictly applied.[46] Occasionally, the Free Churches made representation to the civil authorities on behalf of islanders. For instance, in September 1941 long queues at the dairy for skimmed milk were causing great hardship. Two members of the fraternal were dispatched to 'interview those in control to improve conditions'.[47] But this kind of practical action was exceptional.

Figure 4.4: Rev. Ronald South, photographed in 1941 for identity card (Jersey Archive D/S/A/4/A11229 Courtesy of the Jersey Heritage Trust)

Wesley Chapel,
WESLEY STREET

To-morrow (Sunday)
11 a.m. Rev. R. E. South
7 p.m. Mr. B. C. Whiston

**TUESDAY, (17th)
at 7.30 p.m.
GUILD DEVOTIONAL MEETING**
Speaker: Pastor P. H. Hanks
All are welcome.

Above, Figure 4.5: Wesley Guild meetings were regarded as an evangelistic opportunity
Below, Figure 4.6: Young people were encouraged to give musical concerts

Methodist Church
AQUILA ROAD

TUESDAY at 7 p.m.
in the Schoolroom,

Musical Programme
by the
YOUNG PEOPLE
VOCAL and INSTRUMENTAL ITEMS.
Special Items by the Young Ladies' Choir.
President: **Mrs. A. Gore.**
Collection.

Apart from minor skirmishes with the civil authorities, practical co-operation between the Free Churches in Jersey was limited to occasional pulpit exchanges and united services. In November 1944 American prisoners of war at Fort Regent requested a Protestant Sunday service, which the German officer in charge was willing to permit at 9.30am. Since Anglican clergy found it impossible to lead worship at that time because of their own services, the Free Church ministers took it in turns to conduct a service for the American prisoners.[48]

In Guernsey, too, Methodists were aligned with other Nonconformists. As a result of transport difficulties, the Free Church ministers' fraternal ceased to meet after October 1940, though the pre-war pattern continued whereby various churches in turn hosted united services for Nonconformists on Good Friday and Christmas Day.[49] At St Andrew's Presbyterian Church in St Peter Port, where the minister died unexpectedly in September 1940, Sunday services were maintained throughout the Occupation by a voluntary rota of Free Church ministers and lay preachers. Apart from this, the most significant form of practical co-operation between the churches involved the provision of communal cooking facilities in various parts of the island (see Chapter 6).

Chapter 5

Living with the Enemy

B etween July 1940 and May 1945 the Channel Islands were obliged to play host to a German garrison whose size increased out of all proportion to the numbers required to control territory that had little, if any, strategic value. At its peak in the first half of 1943, Fortress Guernsey comprised thirteen thousand soldiers, not to mention the thousands of *OT* (*Organization Todt*) and forced labourers, mainly Russian, engaged in constructing immense concrete fortifications to repel a British invasion. In Jersey, where large numbers of *OT* and slave workers similarly laboured, the garrison alone swelled to ten thousand. The total strength of the Wehrmacht together with its auxiliaries was equivalent to more than two thirds of the civilian population – a ratio unique in German-occupied territory.[1]

In the confined space of the islands soldiers and civilians rubbed shoulders daily. Members of the armed forces were billeted in hotels and houses; fortifications sprouted close to residential areas; military traffic jostled with cyclists and pedestrians in narrow lanes; shops and cinemas served troops and islanders. Since it was impossible to avoid all contact with the occupying army, local people were obliged, individually and collectively, to develop their own code of conduct for dealing with the Germans.

For the churches there was the added complication that Christ urged his followers to love their enemies and pray for those who persecute them (Matthew 5.44). But how should Christ's teaching be interpreted in a modern war against an oppressive regime that threatened to subjugate the whole of Europe? How should congregations react if members of the occupying forces attended public worship? To what extent could a shared Christian faith be allowed to influence relations between individual islanders and German soldiers? In this chapter we investigate the way in which Methodism responded to the challenge of living with the enemy.

At first, clergy and congregations were wary of encounters with members of the German forces. Exceptionally, an enterprising Anglican priest in St Peter Port, mindful of his duty towards his new parishioners, wrote to the Commandant inviting him and his men to attend services, adding: 'We are not at all *high*, but on the "broad" side in our outlook at St James's.'[2] The Commandant, Dr Maass, politely informed him that 'The invitation and hours of services have been made known to the Troops.'[3] Probably as a result of this exchange, the church of St James the Less became established as the garrison's own church where Lutheran army chaplains conducted parade services on Sundays. St Joseph's Roman Catholic Church was used for the same purpose, as were several Anglican parish churches in the island.[4] The rector of St Sampson's, Rev. E.L. Frossard, was sometimes present at parade services in his church, though he did not take any part in them. The German flag would be laid upon the altar along with a crucifix and two lit candles. Services were well attended, and the soldiers' behaviour was impeccable. The padre brought along prayer books and hymnbooks for the men and supplied an organist.[5] A number of Methodist churches were also used for German parade services, which were usually held prior to the Sunday morning service.[6]

In Jersey, too, German padres conducted parade services in Anglican parish churches. Diarist Leslie Sinel noted the strong smell of ersatz boot polish in church afterwards.[7] In December 1940 Anglican clergy led a civic service in St Helier parish church attended by members of the civilian administration, the German Commandant and 250 soldiers.[8] A similar service was held at the Roman Catholic parish church. Whether clergy or islanders afterwards believed that it was unwise to participate in a civic service with the enemy is not known. The Germans may have felt their authority was undermined by taking part in an act of worship led by islanders. Whatever the reason, there were no more civic services of this kind involving islanders and Germans.

The most significant civic occasions of a religious nature during the Occupation were the funeral services held in Jersey and in Guernsey in November 1943 for the crew of HMS *Charybdis* whose bodies were washed ashore following a naval engagement off the Channel Islands. The sailors were buried with full German military honours at services led by island clergy. The funeral service at Guernsey's Foulon Cemetery attracted a large congregation of islanders demonstrating their loyalty to the Allied cause. Rev. Philip Romeril, superintendent of the Guernsey (English) Circuit took part in the service representing the island's Free Churches.[9]

Left, Figure 5.1: *The burial of nineteen Royal Navy ratings in Guernsey's Foulon Cemetery on 17 November 1943 was an occasion for islanders to demonstrate their loyalty to the Allied cause (GEP)*

FUNERAL CEREMONY

OF

NINETEEN NAVAL RATINGS

From " H.M.S. CHARYBDIS "

Interred at the Foulon Cemetery on
Wednesday, November 17th, 1943.

Roll of Honour

F. Booth	C. D. Lawson
F. Bradford	J. Maidment
L. L. Bunn	K. May
D. Clayton	J. R. Morgan
W. Clayton	J. D. MacDonald
W. J. Dobson	Petty Officer Murphy
J. Herbert	Clifford Ernest Roberts
T. G. Harper	H. Somers
F. Jones	T. White
	A. T. Young

GUERNSEY PRESS TYP.

Below, Figure 5.2: Rev. Philip Romeril (far left), representing the Free Churches, with other clergy looks on as the Bailiff of Guernsey, Victor Carey, lays a wreath on behalf of the island at the funeral service for nineteen Royal Navy ratings, 17 November 1943 (GEP)

84

Despite having ample opportunity to attend parade services conducted by their own padres, individual members of the occupying forces soon found their way into services of public worship in various island churches of all denominations. Ministers and congregations suspected – correctly as it turned out – that some of them were there to report anti-German statements.

On Sunday 15 September 1940, as the Battle of Britain reached its climax in the skies over Southern England, Douglas Ord in Guernsey had a new experience when what he describes as 'two plain-clothes Gestapo' attended the morning service at Brock Road church. As happened in the early Church in times of persecution, a doorkeeper was on the lookout for strangers. Recognising the pair as Blaue and Schröder, the doorkeeper politely showed them to a pew before informing Ord of their presence. During his sermon, Ord noticed 'a sort of mild grin spread over their face'; otherwise their expression was inscrutable. Afterwards he greeted them 'as if they had been islanders accustomed to visiting the church from time to time'. When he enquired, in fluent German, whether they had been able to understand the service, they assured him they had, adding 'You speak English very well.' What they meant was that Ord spoke without a Guernsey accent, which German ears found difficult to follow.

In fact, Blaue and Schröder were not Gestapo, as Ord supposed, but Feldpolizei or Secret Field Police, who also wore conspicuously plain clothes. Contrary to what was universally believed by the civilian population (a supposition the Feldpolizei did nothing to dispel), the Gestapo did not operate in the Channel Islands during the Occupation. Still, it was not unknown for the Feldpolizei to beat up troublesome suspects to secure a confession. It seems Blaue and Schröder attended the service at Brock Road as part of a German monitoring campaign to ensure clergy were heeding the warning not to make statements against the Third Reich. At least they stayed for the whole service: disconcertingly, Feldpolizei often left immediately after the sermon.[10]

But the majority of Germans attending public worship in island churches were there purely for personal reasons. As things settled down and islanders began to realise that the presence of soldiers at services did not have dire consequences, some churches made special efforts to welcome them. In the spring of 1941 the stewards at Wesley chapel in St Helier placed a notice in the porch printed in English and in German inviting members of the occupying forces to attend services. When other congregations in the Jersey (Wesley) Circuit learned about this, they asked for copies for their own use.[11]

For several reasons, Brock Road church in the Guernsey (English) Circuit

was popular with German soldiers who wanted to attend a Protestant service. Like Blaue and Schröder, they found it relatively easy to understand Ord's spoken English. Moreover, the church was unique in Channel Islands' Methodism inasmuch as the Sunday service took the liturgical form of the 'Order of Morning Prayer' from the 1936 *Book of Offices*. Having the text of prayers and congregational responses made participating in worship easier for anyone whose first language was not English. Accommodatingly, Ord conducted parts of the service in German, reading the lesson first in English then in German. He included a collect and prayers in German and pronounced the Benediction in both languages.[12] When it came to the administration of the Lord's Supper, soldiers and civilians knelt side by side at the communion rail to receive the bread and wine, Ord saying the accompanying words in English or German as appropriate. The organist and choir also contributed to the church's reputation. A soldier in St Peter Port, seeing Ord's clerical collar, volunteered the information that his church was well known among the German garrison for its music.[13]

Several entries in Ord's diary suggest that German soldiers regularly attended worship at Brock Road. In February 1942 a German soldier brought wood for the fire in the morning chapel which suggests a degree of belonging on his part.[14] The following summer Ord again observed: 'Several Germans have been attending church services regularly of late.'[15] The reasons were still the same: 'The liturgical service enables them to follow the language. They also appreciate the absence of a local dialect.'

German soldiers attended a number of other Methodist churches in Guernsey, including St Sampson's, the Vale, Les Capelles and St Andrew's. Those attending Rocquaine chapel were greeted in fluent German by George Lainé, door keeper and local preacher. Lainé, a memorable character, lost both arms in the First World War as a result of a German grenade landing in his trench. When he led services several Germans were usually among the congregation.[16]

Preaching at Les Camps in August 1940, Ord noticed two Luftwaffe men in the congregation. Characteristically, he changed the hymn after the sermon to one translated from the German *Gesangbuch*. The men knew the tune and joined in singing heartily.[17] As an experienced minister able to speak German, Ord was singularly well equipped to respond to the presence of German soldiers in worship. Less confident preachers must have felt intimidated in that situation. Leslie Roussel, a local preacher in the Guernsey and Sark (French) Circuit, was perturbed to discover a German soldier in the congregation on one occasion when he was leading worship. Talking to the

man afterwards, however, it was evident his desire to share in Christian worship was genuine.[18]

Besides members of the occupying forces, Russian labourers sometimes attended Methodist worship, though very few had any grasp of English. Once again, Ord's linguistic abilities stood him in good stead, as Ken Lewis observed at Les Camps in January 1944: 'Tonight as usual we had some Russians to chapel and Rev. Ord who was preaching said a few words to them in Russian at the end of the service; their faces lit up when they realised he was talking to them and many nodded as if to say thank you.'[19] In May Ord observed another party of Russians in the congregation and afterwards spoke with them in a mixture of Russian and German.[20]

Figure 5.3: Field hymnbook issued by the Divisional German army chaplain, Dr Ebersbach (Herbert White Collection)

Although the majority of Germans worshipping in island churches chose Anglican, Roman Catholic or Methodist services, a small number attended English-speaking Nonconformist churches, especially those close to military installations. Baptist churches were popular among evangelical German Protestants. Writing to the Commandant in September 1942, the minister of Spurgeon Memorial Baptist Church in St Peter Port, Rev. Edwin Foley, noted that:

Sometimes good Baptists come to our services, and I always give them a warm welcome in the name of our common Lord. I try to say to them in my perhaps faulty and broken German, *'wir sind Brüder in Christ'* (an expression used by one of your men to me a few Sundays ago), *'wir willkommen Sie in dem namen des Christ.'*[21]

Of course, being 'brothers in Christ' could not overcome the fact that British civilians and German soldiers were on opposite sides of the war, though since Foley's motive in writing to the Commandant was to avoid deportation to Germany (See Chapter 10) he was not inclined to see any conflict of loyalties. Given the later sensitivities surrounding relations between islanders and the occupying forces, it is necessary to consider the implications of British civilians and German soldiers worshipping together in the Channel Islands during the Occupation when their compatriots were engaged in a bitter armed conflict.

In the light of accusations by some writers that relations between British civilians and German forces in the Channel Islands strayed beyond what was appropriate between citizens of warring nations, what should we make of the fact that congregations generally accepted the presence in their midst of members of the Wehrmacht? Can clergy justifiably be accused of giving comfort to the enemy? Douglas Ord, more than anyone, was conscious of the issues at stake. His diary reveals how, intellectually and theologically, he justified his own strategy for dealing with the situation.

From his years as a prisoner of war, Ord understood the German mind better than most British people. He was acutely aware of the culture of militarism in Germany, sustained by a slavish obedience to authority that discouraged independent thought. One of his favourite aphorisms was *'on peut militariser un civil, mais on ne peut pas civiliser un militaire'*.[22] Although it would be difficult to educate the German people out of militarism, he believed that every effort had to be made if Europe was to enjoy lasting peace.

Towards the end of the Occupation, Ord reflected on the 'barrier of hatred' against Germany that would make future peace difficult to establish. He could not accept the conventional wisdom among islanders that the only good German was a dead one – an observation that contradicts claims of friendly relations between occupiers and occupied. Even in the privacy of his diary, Ord refused to demonise the enemy. The following passage is worth quoting at length:

For this military system, allied with the hateful Nazi perversion of human nature, no man can have tolerance. Nor can the world be safe while the machine continues to function and so many approve its methods. I have often expressed my feelings of anger and contempt for much that has happened in these past years at home and abroad. The sight of strutting officers or NCOs would stir anyone's indignation. Yet, when one lives among them as we, perforce, do, growing to recognize individuals and having unavoidable contacts, one is moved by the thought that for these men also Christ died. And I trust I have always made the distinction between the evil that possesses men and the men who are possessed. This I say, not from the pacifist point of view – a view I cannot accept – but because the love of Christ constrains. I hope that our people will not be so warped and embittered that in the day of liberation they may give way to undiscriminating condemnation.[23]

Ord was concerned lest the end of hostilities bring a wave of recrimination against Germany as a whole. He subscribed to the theory that a thirst for vengeance within the Allied nations led to the punitive Treaty of Versailles being imposed on Germany after the First World War resulting in the emergence of Adolf Hitler. The only hope for lasting peace in Europe depended upon Germany being reintegrated into the community of nations. This did not mean that the Nazi regime could escape the consequences of its evil actions. On the contrary, bringing war criminals to justice was compatible with Christian faith. Nevertheless, victory over Germany would bring a supreme spiritual test for the victors, who must reject the inevitable thirst for revenge.

By differentiating theologically between 'the evil that possesses men and the men who are possessed', Ord was able to look beyond the Nazi uniform to the person who wore it. Intellectually, he could see 'No inconsistency in hating National Socialism and those who exemplify its beastly features and at the same time judging every man as we find him'.[24] Thus his policy was: 'Watch every man circumspectly. Should he prove to be a decent fellow, trust him accordingly, otherwise be on your guard.' This strategy made practical sense given that some kind of accommodation with the enemy was necessary. It encouraged islanders to treat individual German soldiers with dignity, whilst warning them to be wary of the enemy.

Beyond 'judging every man as we find him', Ord believed that unquestioning patriotism was never appropriate since Christian faith demanded love even for enemies.[25] His theological account of relations between islanders and Germans within his congregation is based on the

'Peace of Christ'. According to Ord, Christians are simultaneously citizens of two kingdoms. Even if their earthly realms are at war, they may still live together in Christ's Peace as citizens of his kingdom. Analogously with the situation in Europe, where some nations stood outside the present conflict, the Church was neutral territory whose sovereignty must be respected by the belligerents. Participants in Christian worship entered into a 'neutral space' in which earthly hostilities were suspended.

As a theology of Christian relations between members of warring nations, the concept of Christ's Peace has certain weaknesses. In particular, it underestimates the conflict of loyalties that can arise between Church and state. On the whole, it is difficult to imagine an appeal to Christ's Peace being appropriate in parts of German-occupied Europe where violence was a daily reality. Nevertheless, given the calm situation in the Channel Islands, where active resistance was out of the question, describing the Church as neutral territory was a reasonable strategy since it allowed islanders and Germans temporarily to suspend their enmity without their national loyalty being called into question. So far as Ord was concerned, it enabled him to express sympathy to soldiers whose families were the victims of Allied air raids whilst remaining convinced that there was no alternative if the Nazi regime was to be defeated.

Still, appealing to the Church's neutrality was risky because it could easily be misunderstood. The Germans might conclude that Ord was more sympathetic than was the case; islanders might accuse him of giving comfort to the enemy. That neither of these things happened was due to Ord's skilful handling of delicate situations, as when the Brock Road choir performed Handel's *Messiah* to a capacity audience of islanders and Germans on Easter Day 1942. Welcoming the audience, Ord explained that they met 'on neutral territory – "Christ's Peace!" – where perchance we might forget the sword that hangs between our two nations and allow our minds to dwell on the things that belong to his Peace'.[26] Subtly, but unmistakably, Ord reminded everyone present of the boundaries to relations between islanders and the military. Whether they recognised his subtlety, the Germans present in the audience appreciated Ord's welcome. A senior Luftwaffe officer afterwards remarked to one of Ord's church members: 'This Easter Sunday will not be forgotten […] In spite of all that has happened, we feel that tonight we have been treated by your minister primarily as fellow-men and we valued the prayers in our own tongue and his words of welcome too.'[27]

Ord was sanguine about the effect of his words and actions on German troops. Shortly after the Liberation, he told a *Methodist Recorder* reporter

that many soldiers had informed him how deeply touched they were by his prayers in German. 'Who can estimate what work of grace may not have been wrought in the minds of these, our unwelcome guests, by such simple things?'[28] For Ord, this possibility amply justified his circumspect ministry to individual members of the German armed forces.

Beyond Methodism, Ord was a significant figure in the interface between the churches and the military authorities. As the only clergyman in Guernsey who spoke German, he was uniquely qualified to act as go-between. Recognising Ord's skills, in July 1940 the civilian administration invited him to become an official translator but he refused, partly because of his ministerial workload and partly because of the awkward position in which he would be placed. Shrewdly, he foresaw the possibility that the German authorities would blame mistranslation to save an embarrassing climb down when their orders turned out to be unenforceable.[29]

Unrestrained by officialdom, Ord was able to cultivate informal contacts with the occupying forces. As a result, he was almost certainly more influential in his dealings with the Germans than would otherwise have been the case. Indeed, the military authorities often made him their first port of call when it came to matters relating to the churches, irrespective of denominational niceties. For example, in July 1943 he was asked to give permission for a German suicide to be buried in Guernsey's Foulon Cemetery. As Ord admitted, it was not his decision to make but many such requests came through him because he spoke German.[30]

As the Germans must have realised, contacting Ord was probably the quickest way to secure agreement since the appropriate civil or ecclesiastical authority, supposing one could be identified, would probably procrastinate at having to make decisions that might prove unpopular. Through his knowledge of the language and the Germanic mind, Ord was able to broker deals that could not have been achieved by more bureaucratic means, though he must have known that any agreement was liable to rebound against him.

The incident over the burial of a suicide illustrates the curious mindset of German officials. When military objectives were involved they ruthlessly imposed their demands, irrespective of the feelings of civilians. Islanders were evicted from their homes and historic monuments destroyed, causing intense anger and distress. Yet, when it came to burying a German suicide in a civilian cemetery, the same officials deferred to islanders' religious sensibilities.

This double standard reflects the fact that the anti-religious Nazi party

had not been able to impose its will upon the German population in a thoroughgoing way. Christianity was tolerated (if discouraged) insofar as it motivated the German people to submissive loyalty and perseverance in the war effort. Pastors who refused to toe the line soon found themselves in prison. The Nazi leadership reasoned that, once the war had been won, the systematic destruction of the Church could begin in earnest. Meanwhile, the armed forces included in their ranks practising Roman Catholics and Protestants, as well as fervent Nazis. As a result, churches in the German-occupied territories benefited from varying degrees of religious tolerance.[31]

Christians serving in the Wehrmacht manifested the same inertia that affected anti-Nazi elements within the German population as a whole. Religious and cultural notions of obedience reinforced each other to create a powerful respect for authority which led to paralysis within the opposition to National Socialism. There was no active conspiracy against the military authorities within the German garrison stationed in the Channel Islands, though disaffected elements certainly existed.

Quite by chance, Ord established contact with a small group of disaffected Germans whose opposition to the Nazi party amounted to nothing more than listening clandestinely to the BBC and waiting for the Allies to defeat Germany or for the regime to collapse. Browsing in a bookshop in St Peter Port in September 1941, Ord was asked to help serve a German officer, who turned out to be the son of Herman Gunkel, the famous German Old Testament scholar.[32] The officer was Judge Gunkel, president of the military court, who told Ord that he was disillusioned by the dismantling of the rule of law in Germany.

Ord's encounter with Gunkel brought unexpected benefits for a member of his congregation. A few days afterwards Basil Martel was arraigned before a military court charged with insulting the German army. Martel, the victim of malicious slander, was alleged to have damaged an eiderdown in a house in which German soldiers were billeted. Ord successfully appealed to Gunkel to ensure a fair trial, and Martel was duly acquitted. Gunkel visited Ord in person to inform him of the verdict.[33]

Having established his *bona fides*, Gunkel lost no time in inviting Ord to meet the senior German army chaplain in the Channel Islands, Dr Ebersbach. However, if Gunkel had hoped to promote friendly relations between German padres and island clergy, his plans were thwarted by a frosty and unproductive meeting during which Ord robustly criticised the German forces for failing to honour their guarantees to the civilian population. Ord later confided in his diary that Ebersbach 'as a minister of God disappoints

on all counts'.[34]

When Gunkel was posted to the Russian Front a few weeks later, Ord assumed his contacts with disaffected Germans would come to an end. To his surprise, however, at the end of February 1942 Heinrich Bödeker appeared on the doorstep with an introduction from 'a mutual acquaintance' – presumably Gunkel.[35] Bödeker, a Protestant pastor, joined the navy in order to escape the attentions of the Gestapo, who were taking a close interest in his activities as one of a thousand clergy that had signed a letter of greeting to the imprisoned Martin Niemöller. Bödeker told Ord that his family at home listened to BBC broadcasts and fervently hoped for a British victory. He and his messmates in the battery also listened to the news from London.[36] Instinctively, Ord was impressed with his new contact:

> Bödeker is unlike the great majority of Germans: he does not shout when he speaks and utterly lacks that hectoring disposition characteristic of many who have acquired a little power and wish to demonstrate it. This is the more remarkable since as yet most Germans are flushed with the presumption of victory. Bödeker sees only the coming judgement in the non-too-distant future.[37]

Bödeker introduced Ord to Reinhold Zachmann, a co-conspirator from Saxony.[38] Soon the three men were holding scholarly conversations on a range of theological and political topics. Ord was encouraged to learn that they and many other Germans were disillusioned with the war.[39] Nevertheless, there was little chance that their disenchantment would lead anywhere since neither Bödeker nor Zachmann were any more ready than the rest of the German population to turn their opposition to the Nazis into active resistance.

However encouraging it was to learn of disaffection in Germany, contact with the German opposition (such as it was) was extremely risky for islanders. Had Bödeker or Zachmann been an *agent provocateur*, Ord would have been arrested and imprisoned. Utmost caution was needed by all concerned in case injudicious remarks led to disaster. The nervous strain on Ord must have been considerable, but he was never compromised.

Cloak and dagger meetings between island clergy and disaffected elements within the Wehrmacht were exceptional. Most contacts between churches and the military were conducted via bureaucratic means for more mundane purposes than conspiracy to subvert the Third Reich. Probably the most

common form of communication between churches and the German authorities took the form of applications to the censor's office for permission to hold sacred concerts and other kinds of public entertainment on church premises. The German authorities took a close interest in the content of these events. To give just one example, in June 1942 permission was given for a concert to be held in the schoolroom at Brock Road with the usual 'request' that 'the programme be submitted for approval three days in advance'.[40]

If the German censor objected to an item on the programme, permission would be refused or conditions imposed. On one occasion Ord submitted for approval a concert programme featuring Mendelssohn's *Hymn of Praise*. Since the Third Reich did not approve of music written by Jews, the item was permitted only on condition that the name of the composer was not mentioned in the programme or announced at the concert.[41]

Even an innocuous activity like carol singing in the streets required written permission from the German authorities, though consent was not usually withheld. In December 1942 Norman Grut, a local preacher in the Guernsey (English) Circuit, applied for permission for the young people at Ebenezer to go carol singing in St Peter Port on Christmas Eve and to collect donations for the Red Cross.[42] Similarly, junior members of the Wesley Guild at First Tower chapel in the Jersey (Wesley) Circuit were given permission by the German authorities to sing carols in the locality on 22 and 23 December 1943.[43]

Stage plays were another popular form of entertainment closely monitored by the German censor. In December 1942 the Wesley Guild at Georgetown in the Jersey (Grove Place) Circuit applied for permission to produce a three-act play innocently entitled *Ambrose Applejohn's Adventure*.[44] The Bailiff forwarded the application to the German authorities along with the script, recommending that the application be approved.[45] The production played to capacity audiences for three nights before transferring to another hall for a further run of three nights.[46]

Inevitably, German censorship extended to the occasional newspaper article of a religious nature. The most blatant case of censorship of this sort concerned a New Year message from the vicar of St Stephen's church in St Peter Port, Hartley Jackson, which appeared in the *Star* newspaper on 1 January 1942. As printed, the final sentence read: 'The recognition that Christ was born into the world to save the world and to bring peace on earth is the need of Britain and her Bolshevist allies.' Jackson, who had written of Christ's peace as being 'the need of the whole world', was horrified to discover that his sermon had been manipulated for ideological purposes. At least clergy

did not have to worry about their church magazines being censored in such a crude way. At the start of the Occupation, church publications were banned in order to prevent the dissemination of religious propaganda.[47]

A number of Methodists held senior posts in the civil service and administration in Guernsey and in Jersey, bringing them into daily contact with Germans. As we have already noted, John Leale was President of the Controlling Committee of the States of Guernsey between October 1940 and May 1945. The committee was established in June 1940 as a cabinet empowered to make executive decisions on behalf of the more unwieldy States of Guernsey. That Methodists held four of the eight cabinet posts reflects the influence of Methodism in Guernsey. Besides Leale, Sir Abraham Lainé was Vice-President in charge of essential commodities; Raymond Falla held the agriculture portfolio; and Richard Johns was responsible for labour. The States of Jersey set up a Superior Council along similar lines to the Controlling Committee in Guernsey. Methodists held two of the eleven

DEATH OF SIR JOHN LEALE

IT is with deep regret that the "Evening Press" records the death, at the age of 77, of Sir John Leale — a man who, in the course of a remarkable and lengthy career, gave notable service to his island as a statesman and in many other capacities, and also was a leading figure in the business life of the community. He died yesterday afternoon at the Royal Hotel, where he had a suite.

A Methodist minister, a knight, a diplomat and a business man — such were the facets in John Leale's remarkable career.

The son of a well-known St Sampson's business man, the late Jurat John Leale, he was born on January 15, 1892, and was at Elizabeth College from 1900 to 1907, when he continued his education at Jesus College, Cambridge. He gained the degree of Master of Arts and became a Methodist minister.

During the First World War, John Leale was commissioned in the Royal Guernsey Light Infantry, but resigned, owing to ill-health, in 1918.

CONSEILLER

On his return to his birthplace, Sir John was elected a people's deputy in 1930, a position he held until 1934, when he was elected a jurat. He continued to be a member of the States and was elected conseiller in 1948, one of the first to

MASTERLY ADDRESS

Sir John's address to the States, shortly after Liberation, was such a masterly document that it was reprinted in booklet form. He was the author, too, of something totally different — a little volume entitled "The Saint and the Boy," which came out several years ago.

The late Alan and Mary Wood, in their book, "Islands in Danger," wrote thus of John Leale: "As president of the Controlling Committee, Leale kept absolute integrity . . . He did not even claim privileges to which his position clearly entitled him, like the use of a car.

"Every morning he walked the two miles from his home at St Sampson's to his office at St Peter Port, and every evening he walked the two miles back again. If Sherwill had the virtues of a soldier, John Leale had some of the virtues of an ascetic, and he proved the Germans could have respect for both . . .

Sir John Leale.

Figure 5.4: Press announcement of the death of Rev. John Leale , 21 July 1969 (GEP)

cabinet posts: Cecil Harrison was Solicitor General; Jurat P.E. Brée (a local preacher) was responsible for Public Instruction.

The actions of Methodists serving in a private capacity as government officials belong to a general history of the Occupation and therefore need not be investigated here. However, we shall briefly consider how Leale's Christian convictions may have influenced his strategy for dealing with the Germans which has been criticised in some quarters for being acquiescent and unpatriotic.

From time to time lurid accusations surface in British newspapers and books that islanders, individually or collectively, collaborated with the occupying forces. Often these stories are based on evidence that is easily discredited. A serious study of the subject is hampered by the fact that 'collaboration' is a notoriously slippery term with different shades of meaning. Moreover, it is misleading to compare the situation in the Channel Islands with what happened in European countries such as France or Norway where the occupying forces established collaborationist administrations.

Paul Sanders in his magisterial study of the German Occupation of the Channel Islands offers a penetrating analysis of relations between the civilian administrations and the military authorities. Drawing on the 'menu' of different types of collaboration proposed by Peter Davies, Sanders concludes that 'there is no evidence of heart-and-soul collaboration, wait-and-see collaboration or conditional collaboration, the last because the Channel Islands administrations were in no position to impose conditions'.[48] According to Sanders, the dominant attitude amongst civilian leaders in the islands was one of 'submission on the grounds of superior force' interspersed with elements of 'shield philosophy' and 'tactical collaboration'. Essentially, 'shield philosophy' denotes the strategy of acting as a buffer between the military and islanders; 'tactical collaboration' refers to the policy of bargaining with the German authorities in certain matters in order to gain concessions in the overall interests of the civilian population.

In Sanders' estimation, the Bailiff of Jersey, Alexander Coutanche, exercised decisive leadership in comparison with the 'dysfunctional Guernsey triumvirate' of Victor Carey (Bailiff), Ambrose Sherwill (Attorney General) and John Leale. Moreover, 'It is one of the open secrets of the Occupation that Guernsey travelled somewhat further down the slope of collaboration than did her sister island.'[49] Whilst both sets of leaders followed a policy that involved tactical collaboration with the enemy, Sanders detects a difference in rhetoric. According to Sanders, a speech

delivered by John Leale shortly before the Occupation reflects the 'very patronising and disenfranchising tone in Guernsey':

> Should the Germans decide to occupy this Island, we must accept the position. There must be no thought of any kind of resistance, we can only expect that the more dire punishment will be meted. I say this, the man who even contemplates resistance should the Germans come is the most dangerous man in the Island and its most bitter enemy. The military have gone. We are civilians.[50]

Certainly, labelling as an enemy of Guernsey anyone 'who even contemplates resistance' was unlikely to gain Leale credit for patriotism. Yet Sanders does not give sufficient attention to the way in which Leale linked his rejection of all forms of resistance with his policy of citing the Hague Convention as the benchmark for relations with the occupying power. In his report to the States of Guernsey submitted shortly after the Liberation in May 1945 Leale acknowledged that his critics on occasion may have doubted his patriotism: 'But in the long run I have no doubt whatever that our right and interests as British people were best safeguarded by sticking to International Law through thick and thin [...] We followed the example of those who take partners for life. We espoused the Hague Convention "for better for worse".'[51]

These last two sentences in particular (not cited by Sanders) with their reference to the marriage service are essential in understanding the mindset of a politician who was also a Methodist minister. For Leale, the Hague Convention was not so much a convenient political tool as a pseudo-religious covenant analogous to marriage. It was a tenet of his 'faith' in the Hague Convention that the welfare of the population depended upon their adhering strictly to its terms and conditions as a matter of principle and not just in order to avoid furnishing the occupying forces with an excuse to impose excessive demands. Any resistance on the part of the population would seriously undermine attempts by the Controlling Committee to hold the Germans to the terms of the Convention. Being wedded to the Hague Convention 'for better for worse' meant accepting its obligations towards the occupying power – against the grain of patriotism – in pursuit of strategically more important goals in the best interests of the population. That is why he could describe as 'enemies' of Guernsey those islanders that might contemplate resistance.

The contrasting personality of the two principals also helps explain the

difference in rhetoric. Alan Wood and Mary Seaton Wood accurately describe Coutanche as 'something of a thruster and a showman', whereas Leale was 'quiet, studious and ascetic'.[52] It was in keeping with Leale's asceticism and his 'equally characteristic single-mindedness' that he should disregard the painful side effects of his strategy in pursuit of its central objective.[53] If paternalism was necessary in order to achieve his objective – and unpopularity the consequence – then so be it.

Sanders accepts that hitching the fortunes of islanders to the Hague Convention was an 'honourable' strategy, though he doesn't fully appreciate its connection with Leale's stance against resistance. Whilst the Hague Convention was drawn up in deliberately vague terms that did not specify the protection afforded to civilians in occupied territories, at least it gave islanders a measure of security (and their leaders a degree of leverage with the occupying forces) that would otherwise have been denied them. The vagueness of the convention permitted the legal officers in Guernsey and Jersey to spar with their German counterparts, whose bureaucratic nature relished the opportunity for debate.

Although very different in temperament, Leale and Coutanche were both shrewd politicians, skilfully playing what few cards were available to them in the best interests of their people. Though he tended to keep his political and religious roles separate, Leale was undoubtedly influenced by his Christian convictions, as Alan Wood and Mary Seaton Wood acknowledge in their description of him as manifesting 'the occasional Christian guile whereby Methodists are characterized'.[54] Quite what they meant by this is not clear, though it may be an oblique reference to the pragmatism that allows Methodists to shift positions in response to changing circumstances. If Sanders is correct in stating that Guernsey and Jersey diverged in their relations with the occupying forces, it would be unfair to single out Leale for blame in this regard. In his own way he was as formidable a negotiator as Coutanche, though hampered by the fact that he lacked the status of Bailiff.

Chapter 6

Daily Life

A study of Methodism during the German Occupation of the Channel Islands must take account of the impact of deteriorating social conditions on the daily life of islanders. Despite strenuous efforts by the civil authorities to maintain food supplies, increasingly severe rationing for all but the very young led to widespread malnutrition. Only the arrival of limited relief via the International Red Cross from January 1945 saved the civilian population from starvation. Moving accounts have been published of how islanders coped with the situation, but the effects of prolonged deprivation and hardship on the churches and those who sustained them have not been explored.

Contemporary records provide only rare glimpses into the conditions under which Methodists gathered for worship or for one of the business meetings that feature in the life of any organisation. Reading these documents nowadays in the comfort of island archives it is easy to forget how religious activities were sustained by people who were constantly hungry and exhausted, operating in draughty and cold premises. For clergy, there was the added burden of stress caused by being a conduit for islanders' frustrations and the constant fear of being denounced by informers.

In the present chapter we investigate how Methodism was affected by the main hardships suffered on a daily basis by islanders during the Occupation. The topics that will be considered are fuel shortages and heating, food rationing and the black market, communal cooking facilities, wireless offences, and the psychological impact on clergy of living under extreme conditions over an extended period of time.

Fuel and Heating

From the outset of the Occupation, churches recognised that the cost and availability of fuel posed a threat to their activities. If nothing else, cash-strapped churches would have to find the wherewithal to pay increased

energy bills since the coal needed to supply gas and electricity to their premises and power their boilers would have to be imported from France under wartime conditions. Realistically, the civil authorities could be expected to impose fuel rationing, and no one could tell where churches would rank in the order of priorities.

Prompted by these concerns, early in September 1940 one of the circuit stewards in Guernsey wrote to the Controlling Committee on behalf of Methodism enquiring whether evening services and midweek activities would be permitted in the autumn and winter. The Controlling Committee recognised the serious economic and social implications at a time when its Essential Commodities Committee was working assiduously to reduce consumption by a mixture of regulation and appeals for voluntary economies. Aware that the churches constituted a sizeable lobby, the Controlling Committee devoted a large part of one of its regular meetings to considering the matter.

The eight members of the Controlling Committee were divided. One felt that evening services should be prohibited in order to conserve light and heat for more essential purposes. By the same token, there was also a strong case for banning midweek church activities during the hours of darkness – a restriction that would effectively close churches during the winter. But why single out churches when other community groups were also energy consumers? Aware of the consequences that a wholesale ban would have on the morale of the civilian population (as well as the difficulty of enforcement), John Leale proposed that voluntary groups be permitted to continue their activities. But would the population accept a ban on evening services or would public pressure force an embarrassing climb down? The official minute is a classic example of bureaucratic indecision: 'After discussion it was agreed to reply to Mr Collas that it was not possible to give a definite ruling; the committee considered, however, that Sunday evening services should not be permitted during the winter months in order to save lighting and heating, but that the reasonable activities of the community should not be curtailed on week nights, subject to the least expenditure on lighting and heating.'[1] What constituted 'reasonable activities' was open to interpretation.

In Jersey the authorities tried to be more decisive but in the end backed down. In September 1940 the Superior Council agreed that 'supplies of gas or fuel for heating purposes to churches, chapels and places of entertainment' would be discontinued with immediate effect.[2] The Essential Commodities Committee duly wrote to churches informing them of the decision, which

meant no electric light for evening activities and, for the majority of churches, no heating either.[3]

There must have been a strong reaction from churches, though no correspondence on the subject is extant. At all events, six weeks later the Superior Council 'agreed the recommendation of the Department of Essential Services, that having regard to the rationing of electricity and gas, places of worship should be placed on the same footing as other consumers'.[4] This would allow them to consume two thirds of the energy they had used in 1939. A revised rationing scheme was introduced in the middle of 1943 because of further shortages. Eventually, consumers experienced severe disruption in the supply of gas and electricity but, for the time being at least, church activities would be able to continue during the winter.

In the first winter of the Occupation when the population was still relatively well fed a lack of heating in churches was not a serious problem. In December 1940 attendance at Brock Road in the Guernsey (English) Circuit was still good despite icy weather.[5] A 'marvellous congregation' at the carol service huddled together wrapped in blankets, which provided cover for the romantically inclined to hold hands.[6]

The novelty of a cold church soon wore off, however. In January 1942 a woman fainted in church and was found to be icy cold.[7] In December 1942 Ambrose Robin noted that the church was 'far too cold and draughty'.[8] The following winter was even worse: 'Very cold in church, a miserable place'.[9] By the summer of 1944 the population was physically weaker as a result of the constant shortage of food with the result that cases of fainting were common. Members of the St John's Ambulance Brigade were reported to be attending church services in case they were needed to give First Aid.[10]

In Jersey, when the fuel shortage began to bite, a number of churches sought alternative ways of heating their premises. In January 1942 the trustees of Grove Place church sought advice from the manager of the Jersey Gas Company, who recommended installing wood-burning stoves that would provide modest heat as long as firewood was available. The cost of installation would be £57. After careful deliberation, the trustees decided to proceed with the scheme in the knowledge that a donor had already promised £5.[11]

The lack of fuel for heating also made church premises difficult to clean since hot water was no longer readily available. Some trustees were critical of the performance of chapel keepers in this regard and insisted on improvements. Whilst a few employees may have been remiss, the fact was that maintaining buildings to pre-war standards of cleanliness was

No. **15358**   Date of Issue **1 · 10 · 40**

CLOTHING & FOOTWEAR CARD

MALE (14 and over)

Holder's Name _Sidney E. Beaugie_

Address _St Michael's Rectory_
Vale

This card is valid until September 30th, 1941. It is not transferable. Misuse of this card renders you liable to a penalty.

If any part of this card becomes detached from the whole, the coupons are useless.

The coupons on this card are only valid for the articles mentioned in Page 2.

You are informed the number of coupons required for each article.

If found, please return to Controller of Clothing and Footwear, Ladies' College, Guernsey.

Figure 6.1: Clothing and Footware ration card belonging to Rev. Sidney Beaugié (Herbert White Collection)

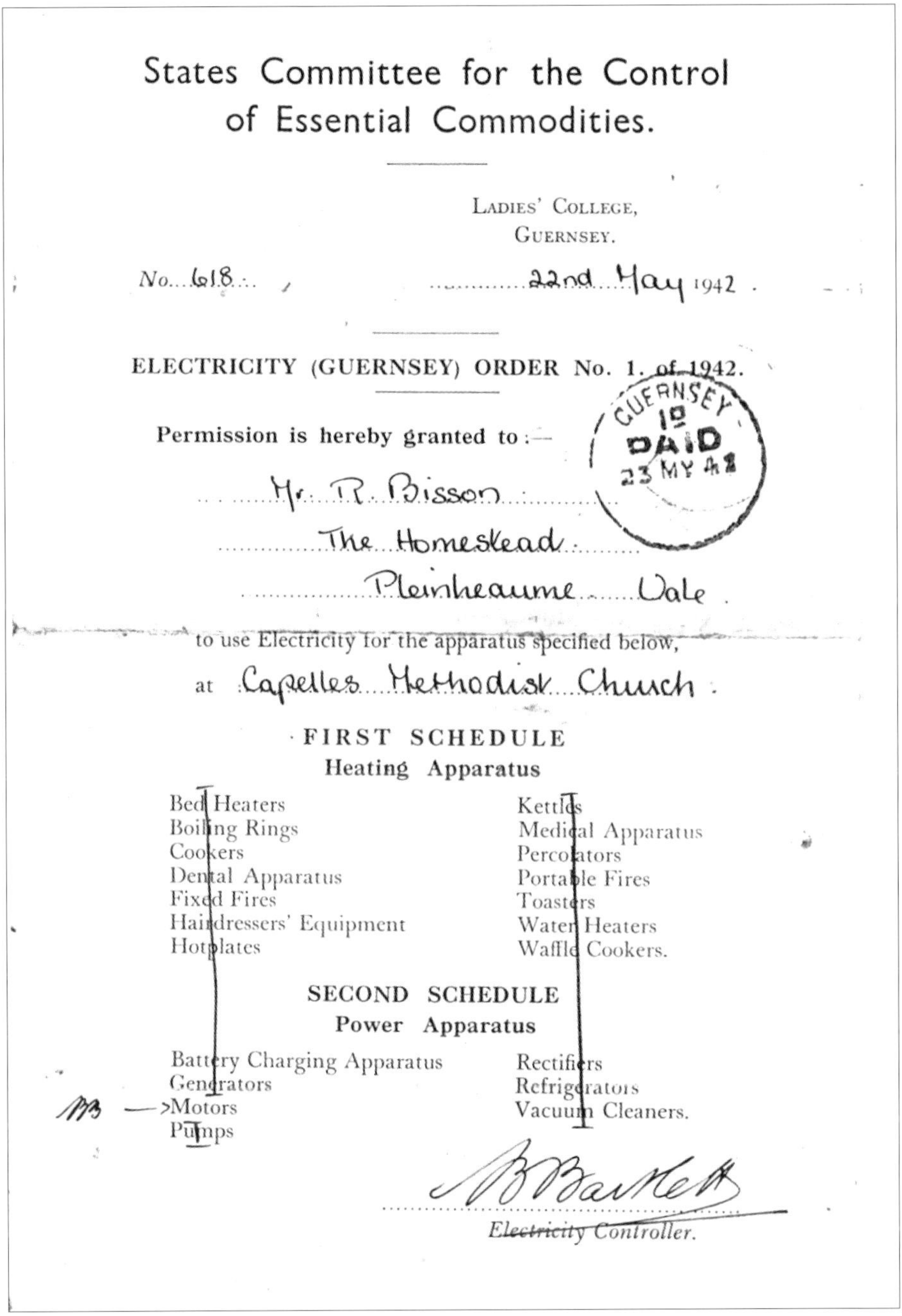

States Committee for the Control of Essential Commodities.

LADIES' COLLEGE,
GUERNSEY.

No. 618 22nd May 1942.

ELECTRICITY (GUERNSEY) ORDER No. 1. of 1942.

GUERNSEY 1d PAID 23 MY 42

Permission is hereby granted to :—

Mr. R. Bisson
The Homestead
Pleinheaume Vale

to use Electricity for the apparatus specified below,

at Capelles Methodist Church.

FIRST SCHEDULE
Heating Apparatus

Bed Heaters
Boiling Rings
Cookers
Dental Apparatus
Fixed Fires
Hairdressers' Equipment
Hotplates
Kettles
Medical Apparatus
Percolators
Portable Fires
Toasters
Water Heaters
Waffle Cookers.

SECOND SCHEDULE
Power Apparatus

Battery Charging Apparatus
Generators
MB —>Motors
Pumps
Rectifiers
Refrigerators
Vacuum Cleaners.

Electricity Controller.

Figure 6.2: Permit for use of electricity for the organ at Les Capelles church, Guernsey (Herbert White Collection)

impossible. When the members of Georgetown in the Jersey (Grove Place) Circuit wanted to spring clean the premises in May 1942 they had to resort to heating buckets of water on a wood fire outside and carrying them indoors. Cleaning materials were begged from the Essential Commodities Committee.[12] Even so, despite special efforts from time to time, churches assumed the air of grubbiness that characterised public buildings during the Occupation.

As people became increasingly undernourished, their ability to withstand low temperatures was reduced. On winter days Ord sat in his cold study huddled under layers of clothing unable to concentrate.[13] He was amazed that people continued to attend worship even in icy weather.[14] Yet there were limits to what people could withstand. On 14 January 1945, the coldest day that Ord could remember in Guernsey, the congregation at Brock Road was the smallest of the entire Occupation. The length of the service was cut to the shortest possible.[15] As a result of the intense cold, on the last Sunday in January 1945 only three children turned up for Sunday school at Bethlehem chapel in the Jersey (Grove Place) Circuit. Nan Le Ruez gave the lesson to the children before deciding that the Sunday school would not meet in February.[16] Another winter under siege would have made it even more difficult for the churches to sustain worship and midweek activities.

Food Rationing and the Black Market

In peacetime the Channel Islands imported most of their food from England so could not possibly be self-sustaining during the Occupation. With German approval, Guernsey and Jersey dispatched purchasing commissions to France armed with huge amounts of cash and instructions to import whatever they could obtain. In each of the main islands an Essential Commodities Committee had the unenviable task of ensuring that scarce food supplies were distributed equitably. Though there were constant shortages, the rationing system coped remarkably well until the Allied invasion of Normandy in June 1944 severed links with the outside world.

Even before the siege of 1944-45 and despite the best endeavours of the civil authorities, there was never sufficient food for an adequate diet. By accepting hospitality from members of the congregation, preachers were unwittingly contributing to their hardship. For families would often go short of food during the week in order to be able to provide appropriate hospitality to preachers, who were regarded as honoured guests. From July 1942 the preaching plan published by the Guernsey and Sark (French) Circuit carried the announcement (in English): 'Preachers who are planned out for the day

would be thankful for hospitality – but ONLY on condition that they are treated as one of the family.' This notice disappeared after 1943 because of the difficulty in providing any kind of hospitality for preachers. Revealingly, in October 1943 Ord recorded being grateful to receive a loaf of bread 21 days old.[17] Whether circumstances in the sister island were a little easier, in the summer of 1944 the Jersey (Grove Place) Circuit still hoped that preachers would be given hospitality by members of the congregation.[18]

Towards the end of the Occupation, islanders had to rely mainly on their own efforts at growing whatever food they could in the limited space available. However, many residents of St Helier and St Peter Port lacked the skills necessary to become successful smallholders, and some did not possess gardens. Even where householders were able to grow food, the resulting diet was a curious mixture. In July 1944 Ord's 'watery' diet consisted mainly of tomatoes, cucumbers, melons, lettuce and a few garden vegetables.[19] The final winter of the Occupation saw near starvation conditions alleviated only by occasional food parcels from the International Red Cross in Lisbon. In February 1945 Ord met a man in a state of collapse through hunger, but there was nothing he could do because there was no food to share.[20]

Yet, even at this late stage of the Occupation, the situation in the country parishes was not as bad as in St Peter Port. That same month Ord told the congregation at a country chapel about the plight of those living in St Peter Port. After the service a man came into the vestry to ask if what Ord had said was really true since he rarely went into town and was unaware of conditions there.[21] Despite the small size of the island, this may well have been the case. Certainly, it is true to say that no two islanders experienced the Occupation in quite the same way because of the wide variation in personal circumstances.

Inevitably, as in other occupied territories, those closest to the source of production (farmers, commercial growers and fishermen) generally had greater opportunity to obtain non-rationed food for personal consumption, albeit at the expense of the rationing system. This of course created a moral dilemma for islanders. As with other aspects of the Occupation, it is difficult now to judge the actions of islanders under circumstances that would challenge the moral code of any society.

Like virtually every islander, Douglas Ord was an occasional beneficiary of locally produced food that had not been declared to the authorities for rationing purposes. In April 1941 he and his wife stayed with friends for a long overdue weekend on leave. This particular friend was 'a principal

wholesaler and retail butcher' who therefore had 'ways and means' when it came to putting food on the table. However, Ord took little pleasure in what for him was a rare experience of a full plate. His wife 'found it rich fare and was ill'.[22] That same month Ord accompanied Beaugié to tea at the home of a farmer prior to a Sunday preaching appointment. Whilst Beaugié (a widower) gratefully accepted the hospitality offered, Ord found it difficult to eat knowing that his wife was at home with only a morsel of food.[23] Ord's discomfort at receiving non-rationed food was exceptional. Many regarded bending the rules as a harmless deception that benefited islanders whilst depriving the Germans.

Appropriating food at its source for the benefit of family and friends was one thing; selling food at inflated prices on the black market was a different matter. Ord was critical of farmers who illegally sold milk and other produce to members of the German forces. Besides being greedy and unpatriotic, such activity showed scant regard for fellow islanders. Aware that some of the culprits attended church, he shared the 'bitter but just criticism' that was being voiced by many islanders.[24]

Rev. Clement Mylne, imprisoned in Jersey for a wireless offence, witnessed a great deal of black market activity as fellow prisoners paid out vast sums to supplement meagre rations. His prison notes include a scribbled selection of black market prices current in December 1943: eggs at £3 per dozen; tea at 10s per ounce; $\frac{1}{2}$lb sugar for 17s/6d; 1lb salt for 12s/6d; 1lb pork at 22s/6d; and pork brawn at 8s/6d per lb. Cigarettes – a universal currency – could be obtained at 6RM for 20. Turkeys ranged in price from £10 to £18. Only a very few could afford to pay the asking price of £80 for an out of season fig. Half a dozen Christmas roses were available at 5s and chrysanthemums at 1s/6d per stem. Single bars of Lifebuoy soap were on sale for 5s/6d.[25]

Of course, black market prices were far beyond the means of a Methodist minister: Mylne's annual stipend was only £260. He and his wife survived in prison largely because of the generosity of Methodists who brought food at considerable sacrifice to themselves. Whilst the black market may have benefited a small section of the population, simple economics indicate that clergy could not have been amongst them unless they had substantial private means. In fact, most clergy were probably worse off than the majority of their parishioners not only financially but also because of their lack of access to family-based networks that were the gateway to non-rationed sources of food

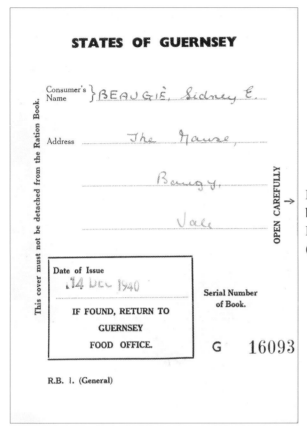

Figure 6.3: Food ration
book belonging to
Rev. Sidney Beaugié
(Herbert White Collection)

Communal Cooking Facilities

From the outset of the Occupation, concerns in Guernsey about the shortage of fuel prompted ideas for setting up facilities that would provide nourishing meals for the civilian population at reasonable cost. In July 1940 John Leale arranged for bakers to make their ovens available for cooking dishes supplied by customers. Using bakers' ovens, he suggested, was a public-spirited action that saved fuel.[26] Guessing that his suggestion would meet with little enthusiasm, Leale appealed to island tradition: previous generations of islanders took 'bean jars' (a type of vegetable casserole) and similar meals to their local baker to be cooked. However, in the summer of 1940 few islanders were willing to embrace the idea. Undeterred, in September 1940 Leale invited a number of Anglican clergy, along with Sidney Beaugié representing Methodism, to attend a meeting to discuss the possibility of establishing 'soup kitchens' staffed by volunteers from the churches.[27]

The first such facility opened for business in October 1940 operating from the premises of Les Capelles church in the Guernsey and Sark (French) Circuit. For a modest outlay of £10 the States of Guernsey provided cooking equipment. The potato board supplied potatoes and vegetables at cost price. After the first month, one of the organisers was reporting excellent progress.[28] In a single day 300 pints of soup were sold to local residents at 2d per pint. So successful was the venture that demand exceeded supply. The same organiser enthusiastically informed Leale: 'Certainly the idea of communal cooking has appealed to the people of L'Islet, and all classes of families come to buy.'

Encouraged by this early success and aware of the need to do something to alleviate the effect of a reduction in the bread ration, in March 1941 Leale wrote to the Dean of Guernsey and the parish rectors asking them to consider setting up 'communal cooking centres' that would serve hot meals.[29] Given the nature of island society, only the Anglican clergy could provide the lead required to mobilise the voluntary sector. Philip Romeril, a minister in the Guernsey (English) Circuit who worked part-time for the Labour Office, was deputed to make the necessary arrangements on behalf of the States of Guernsey.[30]

Reactions to the idea were mixed, though the rector of St Sampson's was one who responded enthusiastically. He promised to organise a 'canteen' providing bean jars, stews and, when obtainable, fish dishes. Meals would be priced at 4d and staff paid in order to give them a financial stake in the 'restaurant'. A system of coupons would be required so that no one received more than one meal

Figure 6.4: Rev. Philip Romeril, photographed in 1941 for identity card
(Courtesy of Island Archives, Guernsey)

per day. All this was offered on the condition that the States would provide the financial outlay and supply vegetables at cost price so that meals could be provided economically.[31]

In contrast, the rector of St John's church in St Peter Port saw 'no great demand' for a canteen or even a soup kitchen in his locality. Pointedly, he suggested that 'the clergy are not the best folk to commence organising such matters', adding that a soup kitchen previously operating in the church hall was run by teachers at Amhurst School. 'While I am ready to give such assistance to the project as is within my power at the same time I do not feel myself capable of undertaking the initial responsibility and would be obliged if you would look to some one else.'[32]

The rector of Torteval replied cautiously. Admittedly, there was an island-wide shortage of potatoes and vegetables 'but most of our country folk have a plentiful supply'. A communal canteen would not be needed in the coming months since islanders would be able to cook outdoors using gorse for fuel. Furthermore, suitable buildings and cooking facilities did not exist in his parish, though the Methodist schoolroom could perhaps be used if a suitable kitchen range was available. His inclination was to wait and see. 'All things considered, therefore, I do not feel that there is any real demand for these centres in this part of the island *at the moment*. What may be necessary later on depends on how things develop.'[33] The situation did not improve, and at the end of August 1941 he signalled his willingness to set up a communal canteen.[34]

In the course of the next few months volunteers from the churches established six 'communal kitchens' in Guernsey: two in St Peter Port (one of them for single working men); two in Castel (at Les Capelles and Delisle Methodist churches); one at Cobo; one in St Martin's; and a 'soup kitchen' at St Peter in the Wood.[35] The communal kitchen at Delisle opened in February 1941 in the schoolroom. The venture was headed by the wife of the local Anglican rector but the success of the scheme was due to the efforts of the Methodist congregation.[36]

The communal kitchen in St Martin's opened in 1941 and later found a permanent home in the schoolroom at Les Camps in the Guernsey and Sark (French) Circuit. By July 1944 the facility was experiencing 'a falling off in numbers and consequently a lack of funds'. Anxious to avoid liability for a trading deficit, the organisers sought advice from Leale. His reply was unequivocal: 'My own view is that this kitchen has served and should continue to serve an ever increasing need and that every effort should be made to continue it.'[37] He suggested that 6d per meal was too cheap since

109

other facilities charged 9d. The organisers should therefore increase the price of meals to cover costs. The following month he wrote again, recommending a further price increase since meals in St Peter Port now cost a shilling. At the same time, he had words of warning for the trustees at Les Camps: 'In view of the fact that the premises now in use belong to a religious body, it is felt that they should not wish to make any money out of the letting of the premises.'[38]

In the final days of the Occupation the shortage of food made it impossible for the communal kitchens to operate. The facility in St Peter Port for single working men was eventually obliged to close on 1 May 1945 because vegetables were unobtainable. Nevertheless, it had served its purpose and had been able to keep going to within just a few days of the Liberation.

After a hesitant start, the communal kitchens run by volunteers from the churches eventually played a crucial role in helping feed the civilian population in Guernsey during the Occupation. After the first soup kitchen opened, a St Peter Port resident wrote to Leale appealing for a similar facility in her neighbourhood. When she returned home from work she could not cook a hot meal because there was no gas or electricity in the evenings, and oil and paraffin were unobtainable. The few commercial restaurants still operating in St Peter Port were heavily over subscribed, and there was nowhere to purchase a hot meal at reasonable cost during the lunch hour.[39] She was typical of the many islanders who benefitted from the practical co-operation between island churches and the States of Guernsey in providing hot meals for the local community.

In Jersey the first communal restaurant opened in St Helier in October 1940 under the aegis of the States. For a shilling customers could purchase a two-course hot meal. Eventually, there were seven communal restaurants in Jersey. However, it was not until the summer of 1944 that these facilities came into their own when the Allied invasion of Normandy led to severe fuel rationing in the island.

With its larger commercial and public sectors, Jersey was better equipped than Guernsey to devise and run a scheme for producing a substantial number of meals without recourse to the voluntary sector. When the public gas supply eventually ceased in Jersey in August 1944 because of the Allied blockade, 42 bakers' ovens were immediately pressed into service alongside the existing communal centres to provide hot meals for the civilian population. At a cost of 3d, islanders could take their own food in a container to their nearest baker and have it cooked.[40] In April 1945 the civilian authorities estimated that a total of 1,150,000 hot meals had been provided

in this way. It was noted that about 30 percent of the meals were potato based (the potato ration was then just about exhausted), whilst 70 percent were 'bean crocks, milk or batter puddings, pastries, pies and cakes of various description'. Overall, the scheme was judged a huge success with just 125 complaints.[41]

The contrasting policy of the civil authorities towards mobilising the voluntary sector reflects the different circumstances of the two islands, the availability of suitable infrastructure, and the personalities of the principal leaders. The fact that Leale was a clergyman may also have made a difference in Guernsey. Having served in the Manchester and Salford Mission at the end of the First World War, Leale knew the capacity of the churches to engage in social work and was sufficiently bold to draw upon their resources of people and buildings. Romeril, too, was the ideal person to organise this voluntary work on behalf of the States of Guernsey.

Wireless Offences

Besides coping with shortages, islanders risked fines and imprisonment for contravening German orders. Common offences were the failure to produce identity cards on demand, infringement of the blackout, breaking the curfew, and the illegal possession of radios. Anyone violating the blackout was fined, though army patrols sometimes executed summary justice by shooting out lights.[42] Those breaking the curfew could expect to spend a night in the cells followed by a fine. The possession of radios after these were prohibited was a more serious offence leading to a substantial fine and sometimes imprisonment. What made matters worse for those convicted of a 'wireless offence' was the knowledge that their arrest by the German police usually followed an anonymous tip-off from a fellow islander bearing a grudge.

One of the most serious cases of imprisonment for the illegal possession of a radio concerned Clement Mylne, superintendent of the Jersey (Great Union Road) Circuit.[43] In January 1943 Mylne's 21 year-old daughter, Vivienne, joined the teaching staff at the island's prestigious Girls' College.[44] According to Mylne, certain individuals felt aggrieved that such a coveted position had not gone to an island-born person. Three weeks after she took up her post, members of the Secret Field Police (like everyone else at the time Mylne refers to them as Gestapo) arrived at the manse to arrest Vivienne for distributing war news. Anticipating that the house would be searched, Mylne showed them a broken radio, which he knew could not be made to work. A working radio was safely stashed beyond reach. Unfortunately, a search of the house turned up an overlooked camera belonging to Vivienne,

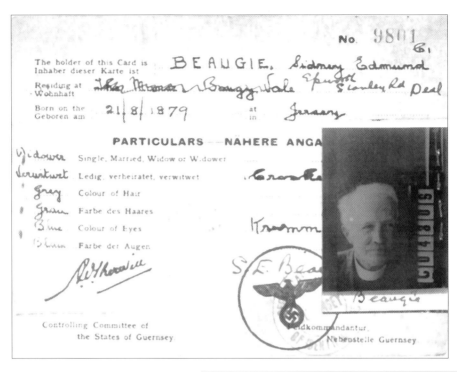

No. 9801

The holder of this Card is
Inhaber dieser Karte ist   B E A U G I E, *Sidney Edmund*

Residing at
Wohnhaft

Born on the
Geboren am   21/8/1879   at
in   *Jersey*

PARTICULARS — NÄHERE ANGA

Widower   Single, Married, Widow or Widower

verwitwet   Ledig, verheiratet, verwitwet

grey   Colour of Hair

grün   Farbe des Haares

Blue   Colour of Eyes

Blau   Farbe der Augen

Controlling Committee of
the States of Guernsey

Feldkommandantur,
Nebenstelle Guernsey

Above, Figure 6.5: Identity card belonging to Rev. Sidney Beaugié
(Richard Heaume)

Right, Figure 6.6: Rev. Clement Mylne, photographed in 1941 for identity card (Jersey Archive D/S/A/4/A8631
Courtesy of the Jersey Heritage Trust)

who was arrested and questioned at German police headquarters. Bravely, she stood her ground, refused to admit any offence and challenged her inquisitors to produce evidence of wrongdoing. After a gruelling week of interrogation, she was released without charge.

A few days later, Mylne and his wife were summoned for further questioning about their illegal possession of a radio. Mylne admitted as much but pointed out that, since the Field Police had failed to make the radio work, his offence was a technicality. Nevertheless, his interrogators persisted, presenting Mylne with a list of his circuit officials and threatening him with the death penalty unless he revealed the names of those who possessed radios. Denying all knowledge of clandestine radios, Mylne was eventually released to appear before a court martial. Hurriedly, he tipped off several Methodists who might be at risk of arrest.

The court martial was a travesty of justice: Mylne was not informed what the charge was; there was no defence counsel; and no witnesses were called. Proceedings were entirely in German, and it was evident that the interpreter was terrified of the judge. Had Vivienne, the judge wanted to know, spoken about Stalingrad? Admitting she had, Vivienne spiritedly pointed out that thousands of islanders were guilty of the same offence (Stalingrad was currently dominating the war news). The trial lasted twenty minutes. At the end the judge read the guilty verdict and sentence from a sheet brought into court before the trial began.

The sentence was severe even for a wireless offence. Mylne and his wife were fined £30 each and given a three-year prison sentence. Vivienne was to serve two years in prison. Mylne promptly appealed against the sentence. Cynically, German courts in the Channel Islands regularly imposed heavy sentences, which were then usually reduced on appeal to show leniency. The court adjourned briefly before the judge returned to announce revised sentences, which were still harsh. Mylne and his wife were to serve twelve months in prison in Jersey; Vivienne was to serve ten months in a French prison.

It seems the Mylnes were victims of an unfortunate combination of circumstances. To begin with, the usual military judge was out of the island on leave. Earlier in his career he had served as German consul in Australia and spoke fluent English. Islanders sensed that he reduced sentences as much as he dared in order to avoid reprisals after the war. His replacement came from Paris where his most recent case was to try Frenchmen accused of murdering German soldiers. More used to the hostile conditions of occupied France, he was not inclined to treat islanders leniently. Another

factor was the news from the Russian Front, where events had turned against Germany. With German forces now on the defensive, wireless offences were regarded particularly seriously. Making an example of a clergyman and his family sent a powerful signal to the population.[45]

Beyond all these reasons, the Mylne family were harshly treated mainly because they refused to co-operate with the German authorities by implicating others. The Germans correctly supposed that Mylne knew a great deal about Jersey Methodists, and they leaned upon him to provide incriminating evidence. However, they mistook their man. Ministers with experience of overseas missions tend to be single-minded characters, and Mylne was no exception. His obdurate stance saved a number of Methodists but consigned himself and his family to the ordeal of imprisonment. He later learned with a great deal of satisfaction that his name was passed to the authorities in Berlin as an enemy of the German Reich.

Mylne subsequently interpreted his imprisonment as an act of aggression against an island community that could offer no resistance. The Germans were acting as if they were in the most hostile war zone whereas the population of the Channel Islands was peaceable. He was also critical of the moral cowardice of those Germans who, though disapproving of Nazism, offered no resistance. At the root of the problem lay a false patriotism towards Germany that allowed its leaders to act brutally without serious internal challenge – a diagnosis largely shared by Ord.

Psychological Effects

The remorseless strain of living under conditions of enemy occupation produced physical and psychological effects upon the civilian population ranging from mild depression and increased susceptibility to minor ailments such as colds to more serious cases of mental and physical breakdown. Ambrose Robin spoke for many islanders when he declared in November 1943: 'We are all tired of this miserable existence and long for the end of German domination.'[46] At times, even his attendance at church brought little relief, though his faith remained undiminished. The following passage from his diary is worth quoting at length as it reveals Robin's thoughtful and well informed intellect:

> Church and church services are not very inspiring these days [...] For some time past my old attraction for church and church services has been withering – whether this is right or wrong I am not quite sure. My thoughts and feelings are somewhat those of Thos. Carlyle as

represented by J.A. Froude. To Carlyle, God's existence was not an arguable probability, a fact dependable for its certainty on Church authority or on Apostolic succession etc. but an awful reality to which the fate of nations, the fate of each individual man, bore perpetual witness. We were to do our work, not because it would prove expedient and we should be rewarded for doing it, *but because we were bound to do it by our Master's orders* [...] We were to be just and true, because God abhorred wrong and hated lies, and because an account of our deeds and words was literally demanded and exacted from us. And the lesson came from one who seemed 'to speak with Authority and not as the scribes' as if [what] he said was absolute certainty beyond question or cavil. Religious teachers say the same thing but stifle the practical bearing of their creed under their doctrines and traditions that honest men find a difficulty in listening to them.[47]

Clergy felt intensely the burden of leadership. Ord's diary provides a rare glimpse into the stress endured by ministers through having to preach and exercise pastoral care among islanders whose morale and faith was often at a low ebb. He laboured painfully to prepare sermons, conscious that 'Brain work is difficult because of the lack of food.' At times he found it difficult to retain his train of thought. Before he could type his sermon outline, he had forgotten some of the points to be included.[48]

Between January and April 1942 Ord lost two stones in weight, partly because of a shortage of food and partly because of the intense pressure under which he was living. Preaching was a great strain, and he sometimes felt faint in the pulpit, especially after cycling a long distance.[49] After Flint was deported in September 1942, he found himself ministering over 'an impossibly wide area'.[50] In November of that year he noticed how sermon preparation took longer than usual. Later he realised just how close he was to suffering a nervous breakdown in the autumn of 1942.[51] Even without the burden of ministerial responsibilities, the dreariness of daily life reminded Ord of his time as a prisoner of war.[52]

As a result of the psychological and physical burden, most of the Methodist ministers in the Channel Islands experienced extended periods of sick leave during the Occupation.[53] Ord's recognition that he had been close to a nervous breakdown was unusually frank but one consistent with the honesty that pervades his diary.

To make matters worse, ministerial workloads increased considerably during the Occupation, partly as a result of covering for colleagues absent

on sick leave or through deportation and partly because of pressing pastoral needs relating to illness and death. As a result of a significant increase in the death rate, especially during the winter, clergy were conducting many more funerals than normal. In the second winter of the Occupation Ord noted that the number of funerals he was taking had increased considerably.[54] In January and February 1944 he conducted at least two funerals every week. Within eight weeks, he buried three members of one family. In each case starvation was to blame.[55] Anglican clergy were even busier: the Dean of Guernsey once conducted four funerals in a single day.[56]

Some idea of the death rate during the winter can be gleaned from the fact that on 26 March 1944, Ord was issued with the 200th burial permit of that year. This compares with a total of 460 recorded deaths in Guernsey in 1943 (two percent of the civilian population). In Jersey there were 719 deaths in the same year. The situation worsened in the final winter of the Occupation. In November 1944 Ord's wife suggested he take his bed down to the cemetery to save energy and shoe leather.[57] On 3 January 1945 he received burial permit number 16.[58] Overall, the number of civilian deaths in the Channel Islands during the Occupation was not excessive in the circumstances, but a shortage of clergy after the deportations of 1942 and 1943 created more work for those remaining.

The industry of death was just the most visible aspect of the pastoral ministry, a ministry that involved giving comfort and encouragement to disconsolate and vulnerable people. Responding to personal traumas and crises of faith would test the pastoral skills of even the most resourceful of ministers. Tired, hungry and emotionally drained, ministers were nevertheless expected to radiate unshakeable confidence in the Gospel whilst managing to convey the impression they were immune to the fears that haunted others. In ordinary circumstances clergy often have to bear the brunt of their congregation's frustrations, displaced anger and self-deceptions. In the circumstances of the Occupation, experiences of this kind must have been greatly magnified. The enduring personal cost to island clergy cannot readily be imagined, though the number of clergy forced to retire early through ill health tells its own story.

Chapter 7

'Follow the Money'

Methodism, unlike the Church of England, has no historic endowments of land and property that provide the wherewithal to sustain its activities. The burden of financing Methodism in the Channel Islands fell almost entirely upon the shoulders of local Methodists. Besides the cost of maintaining church buildings and manses, ministerial stipends constituted the single largest item of expenditure. Raising sufficient money to cover costs was a constant headache for all circuits and churches. In the years leading up to the Second World War there were three main sources of income in Methodism: collections at services of public worship; occasional fundraising events in the shape of bazaars, sacred concerts, gift days and sales of work; and pew rents.

In the 1970s Watergate scandal in the United States the investigative journalists Woodward and Bernstein were advised by their informant to 'follow the money'. Whilst there is no suggestion of scandal in church finances during the German Occupation of the Channel Islands, 'following the money' in Methodism provides an insight into how islanders reacted to the situation. In a way that has not been fully appreciated by historians of the Occupation, financing the churches (especially Nonconformist churches) and their objectives provided an outlet for passive resistance, one of the few means by which islanders could register their defiance of the enemy in a tangible way that staked a claim for the future.

In June 1940 the expected arrival of German forces in the Channel Islands prompted urgent action to safeguard the assets of individuals and organisations, including the churches. Some hastily transferred their valuables to England for safekeeping, whilst others buried property deeds and other legal documents in secret locations.[1] Churches transferred their funds to London, where on 1 July the clearing banks froze all accounts accessible in the Channel Islands in order to thwart German attempts to

seize financial assets.[2] Once communication with the islands was cut off, those whose income came from employers or pension funds in Britain would be in financial difficulty. Anglican clergy, for instance, would no longer be able to receive their stipend from the Ecclesiastical Commissioners.

Alarmed at the devastating effect this would have on clergy and their churches, the Dean of Guernsey, Agnew Giffard, approached the Controlling Committee shortly before the Occupation asking that the States of Guernsey take responsibility for paying clergy stipends in the event that communication with the mainland was severed. In return, the Ecclesiastical Commissioners would pay an equivalent sum into a States of Guernsey account at one of the London clearing banks. Leale accepted the proposal on behalf of the Controlling Committee but declined to guarantee the level of stipends in case 'circumstances might arise in which we should be forced to ask the incumbents to accept lesser sums than those to which they are entitled'.[3] In fact, the administration was already envisaging that public sector pay would have to be reduced should the island be occupied.

In July, following the arrival of German forces, Leale informed the Dean that clergy stipends would be reduced under the pay formula currently being used to cut the salary of civil servants. Under this formula, clergy would have a basic stipend of £100 plus half the difference between their normal stipend and the basic. Special cases would be considered individually on their merits. To forestall argument, he added: 'I fancy that you will agree that it would be undesirable for the clergy to be in a privileged position vis-à-vis the rest of the island.'[4]

The Dean pondered this development for two weeks before writing a carefully worded appeal for special treatment: 'The clergy being compelled to reside in the Parsonage and in most cases to keep up a garden for its produce makes it necessary that they should be treated on rather different lines to civil servants, though in the spirit of their treatment as far as possible.' Taking this to be a request for the full stipend, Leale countered by suggesting it would be 'invidious' for clergy to be treated differently to civil servants. Nevertheless, recognising the relatively low remuneration of clergy in comparison with civil servants, he proposed an adjustment to the pay formula. Clergy would receive a basic stipend of £150 plus half the difference between their normal stipend and the basic.[5] Honour satisfied on both sides, the deal was struck, and the States of Guernsey paid Anglican clergy stipends at the agreed rate throughout the Occupation.[6] Similar arrangements were put in place in Jersey.

In contrast to the system of central payments in the Church of England,

Figure 7.1: German currency circulated in the Channel Islands during the Occupation (Author's Collection)

the stipend of Methodist ministers was solely the responsibility of their circuit. As long as circuit income during the Occupation continued at pre-war levels, there would be no problem in paying stipends. But the evacuation of a substantial number of islanders in June 1940 coupled with the collapse of trade and the capping of wages led to a financial crisis in Methodism because of the likely impact on Sunday collections – by far the largest source of income.

In Guernsey, where almost half the population evacuated, the situation was particularly acute. The crisis meeting involving ministers and circuit officials on 26 June (see Chapter 2) was driven mainly by financial considerations. Already, the English circuit was feeling the effect of evacuation more than the French circuit because most Methodists born outside the island worshipped in one of its churches. Understandably, island-born Methodists were more reluctant to abandon their homes, though no one could reasonably predict how many might eventually decide to leave rather than live under enemy occupation. Thus the decision to reduce the ministerial staff by two was prompted mainly by financial considerations.

In Jersey, where the evacuation was on a smaller scale, circuits still felt the financial effects because of the reduction in wage levels. At the crisis meeting on 28 June, the Chairman of the District, Frederick Flint, passed on

an assurance from the stationing committee in London that a special fund would be established to support those circuits in south-east England and the Channel Islands which might be adversely affected by the evacuation of civilians. Noting that no money from central finances was being promised, the meeting responded cautiously to the news: 'it does not need much imagination, in these times, to envisage difficulties in raising a substantial fund for the purpose, and it is not wise, therefore, to place too much reliance on this.'[7] Whilst the mood of those present was that ministers should remain in post irrespective of any financial implications, the final decision was postponed pending consultation with churches. But German forces occupied the island before the meeting could re-convene.

As a result of the evacuation, Methodism commenced the Occupation in financial turmoil. On paper, church membership figures remained unchanged since Flint gave instructions that evacuees and those serving in the armed forces should continue to be counted. But the stark reality was that in Guernsey and, to a lesser extent, in Jersey there were fewer Methodists in the pews to contribute towards the maintenance of what was still a substantial ecclesial infrastructure. Moreover, given the unprecedented economic situation caused by isolation from the outside world, circuit treasurers could not predict with any confidence what the future held so far as church finances were concerned, though peacetime experience in Methodism did not inspire optimism.

According to conventional wisdom, in places where the numerical strength of Methodist congregations declined, the level of financial giving invariably followed suit, with the result that circuits were obliged to cut costs by reducing their ministerial staff, thereby initiating a spiral of decline. The annual re-invitation system provided a mechanism for circuits to review staffing levels in the light of finances, placing ministers in a somewhat precarious position. But shedding ministers was no longer an option in the Channel Islands once communication with England was interrupted.

Thus the most urgent challenge facing Methodism at the beginning of the Occupation was to reduce expenditure in order to stabilise finances. On 2 July ministers and officials in the Jersey (Wesley) Circuit set up a finance board to oversee all circuit income and expenditure. Church treasurers were asked to place their assets at the disposal of the board in the interest of carrying on Methodist work more effectively. The quarterly meeting retrospectively approved this radical course of action, though not without complaints at such lese-majesty towards the Methodist constitution. In consultation with other Jersey circuits it was agreed that the annual levy

imposed on circuits by the Conference in order to fund central activities would unilaterally be suspended during the Occupation to help reduce costs.[8] Within a few months the finance board had gained control of all funds in the circuit which it continued to administer for the remainder of the Occupation. In December 1944 the board was judged a success exceeding all expectations.[9]

A key task for the finance board was to negotiate the level of stipend that would be paid to ministers during the period of 'closed economy' caused by the Occupation. It was estimated that the circuit's annual expenditure would be in the region of £700, of which by far the largest element was stipends. The annual assessment or quota levied on churches in order to cover circuit expenditure was judged about right, but in some cases this had only been met in previous years through special fundraising efforts or, in one case, by means of a bank overdraft. In view of the uncertain finances of the churches, the circuit could not guarantee to pay ministerial stipends at the normal level. Bowing to the inevitable, Stuart and South 'graciously agreed' to accept the minimum stipend set by Conference in 1937 (£260 for superintendents and £160 for probationers), though even this was 'in the nature of an understanding and not a guarantee'.[10]

The other Jersey circuits were also obliged to reduce clergy stipends in order to relieve the financial pressure on churches. After agreeing a revised stipend with Mylne, in September 1940 the Jersey (Great Union Road) Circuit announced significant reductions in the annual levy on churches: Great Union Road £220 (previously £290); Royal Crescent £208 (down from £267); and Les Landes £36 (reduced from £44).[11] Ministerial stipends in the Jersey (Grove Place) Circuit were similarly reduced in line with other circuits.

In Guernsey ministers and officials of the two circuits met together in July 1940 to review the financial situation. Despite the reduction in ministerial staff by three, there was still acute anxiety. It was agreed that, in order to reduce expenditure, ministers would have to take a cut in stipend in line with the reduction in civil service pay.[12] Correspondingly, the annual levy on churches was reduced to two thirds of the pre-war level.[13] But whether this would be sufficient to stabilise finances remained to be seen.

In fact, despite initial fears, the financial crisis caused by the evacuation was generally short-lived, relieved partly by cutting ministerial stipends and partly because Methodists responded by giving substantially more in Sunday collections and at other events. Within two years ministerial stipends had been increased, and in spring 1944 were restored to the full amount.[14] This pattern of increased giving is so consistent as to require explanation,

especially since it bucked peacetime trends in British Methodism. Not only was this level of giving sustained throughout the Occupation but, as we shall see, it also increased in response to appeals for specific purposes both internal and external to Methodism.

In Jersey the financial situation stabilised fairly quickly. By March 1941 finances in the Jersey (Aquila Road) Circuit were regarded as 'very satisfactory indeed', though of course there was only one church.[15] By September 1941 finances in the Jersey (Grove Place) Circuit were judged 'satisfactory at this difficult time', and thereafter the situation remained unchanged.[16] Even the Jersey (Wesley) Circuit, hardest hit by the evacuation, managed to end the Occupation in a healthy financial position. In March 1945 the quarterly meeting heard that 'all trusts are in credit for the first time for many years'.[17]

In Guernsey, Methodist finances also recovered more swiftly than might have been expected. Presenting their accounts for 1940, several church treasurers commented that, although income was generally down in the second half of the year, the financial situation was still satisfactory. As early as August 1940, weekly collections at Les Capelles, the largest church in the Guernsey and Sark (French) Circuit, were considered 'very satisfactory'.[18] In December the income for the previous quarter was down £18 against the same quarter in 1939 and down £100 on the year – overall a far better position than had been predicted and 'quite satisfactory' in the circumstances.[19] To a greater or lesser degree, other Methodist churches in Guernsey experienced a similar financial recovery. In June 1943 all churches in the Guernsey and Sark (French) Circuit reported an increased income.[20]

In fact, by the end of the Occupation some of the smaller churches had substantially more financial assets than before the war. At St Martin's Mission in the Guernsey (English) Circuit income rose steadily year after year, enabling the trustees to improve facilities.[21] In February 1944 the trustees thanked seventeen members for taking turns at blowing the organ, promising to install an electric motor 'at the first opportunity'. Relief eventually came in February 1946 when an electric blower was installed at a cost of £50, expenditure only made possible by the funds accrued during the Occupation.[22]

In theory, Brock Road church in the same circuit was the poor relation. At the end of 1940 the debt on the trust funds amounted to £176/9s/10d, but even here the 'finances of [the] church were being satisfactorily maintained' since the Occupation began.[23] A gift day was expected to reduce the deficit, though in response to a letter from the organist lamenting the

poor state of the organ, the trustees could offer only 'friendly consultations' instead of commitments to further expenditure. Encouraged by the excellent response to the gift day held in 1941, in February 1943 the trustees proposed another gift day to coincide with Pentecost. 'It was felt that every effort to clear the accounts should be made during the present situation, so that, by way of thanksgiving for the release for which all hearts yearned, the question of the heating system might be tackled.'[24] By the end of 1943 the trust fund showed a balance in hand of £39/12s/11d thanks to the generosity of the congregation and an unnamed 'special donor'.[25] What is more, substantial repairs to the church roof were also undertaken and paid for in the same period.

The desire of the Brock Road trustees to install an improved heating system might appear self-indulgent in the midst of a European war but linked, as it was, with the Liberation (still a distant prospect in February 1943), it manifests confidence in future deliverance in a manner reminiscent of the prophet Jeremiah, who invested in a field near Jerusalem at a time when the city was besieged (Jeremiah 32). The same confidence in the future is reflected in the trustees' decision to alter 'the eastern end' of the church (choir stalls, pulpit and communion area), the work to begin 'as soon as the island is at liberty'. In February 1945 the 'reconstruction fund' stood at £353, an impressive total in the circumstances.[26] Evidently, the Liberation deprived the scheme of much of its impetus: two years later the balance of the fund had increased only by the interest accrued, which tends to confirm that the main appeal of the project was as an expression of passive resistance to the German Occupation.

Financial Statement for Quarter ending MARCH, 1942.

Places.	Circuit Assessment.			General Assessment.			Income.				Expenditure.			
	£	s.	d.	£	s.	d.		£	s.	d.		£	s.	d.
EBENEZER	82	5	0	16	0	0	Ebenezer	50	0	0	Ministerial Allowances	158	15	0
BROCK ROAD	73	15	0	13	0	0	Brock Road	50	0	0	Children's Fund	13	13	0
SALEM	67	10	0	6	5	0	Salem	—	—	—	Fire Insurances	6	18	3
ST. SAMPSON'S	102	10	0	18	5	0	St. Sampson's	75	0	0	Guernsey Gas Light A/c.	1	1	0
MORLEY	5	0	0	1	5	0	Morley	—	—	—	States Water Board A/c.	2	12	10
ROHAIS	7	0	0	2	0	0	Rohais	6	0	0	Furnishings A/c.	2	3	3
ST. MARTIN'S	5	5	0	1	15	0	St. Martin's	4	13	4	Repairs A/c.	4	17	4
BAILIFF'S CROSS	3	10	0	0	15	0	Bailiff's Cross	2	16	8	Sundries A/c.	6	6	0
L'ISLET	10	0	0	1	5	0	L'Islet	7	10	0	States Telephone A/c.	4	2	9
BORDEAUX	7	0	0	2	0	0	Bordeaux	6	0	0	Rates and Taxes A/c.	6	0	0
								202	0	0		206	9	5
	£363	15	0	£62	10	0	Grant from French Circuit, December Quarter	50	0	0	Balance in Bank—			
							Insurance repaid from Rohais	2	5	0	March Deposit A/c.	301	18	8
							Bank Interest	1	18	8	„ Current A/c.	79	7	11
							Balance in Bank— December Deposit A/c.	360	0	0				
							„ Current A/c.	31	12	4				
								£587	16	0		£587	16	0

Figure 7.2: Quarterly financial statements were printed in the Guernsey (English) Circuit preaching plan (Author's Collection)

Additional Sources of Income

Bazaars and sales of work were a useful supplementary source of income for churches in the years prior to the Second World War, and Methodists were skilled practitioners at the art of selling. A lavish coronation bazaar at Victoria Road church in the Guernsey and Sark (French) Circuit in 1937 drew large crowds, including the Lieutenant Governor and other civic dignitaries.[27]

The outbreak of war in 1939 brought this form of fundraising to an abrupt end, though not without the risk of offending those whose religious interests lay chiefly in organising such events. In October 1939 the leaders of Rohais church in the Guernsey (English) Circuit wrote to the bazaar committee tentatively recommending that: 'The present situation of war made it advisable to postpone the forthcoming bazaar to a more opportune period.'[28] Instead, cash-strapped churches would have to rely on appeals to the generosity of their members through gift days (when thanksgiving offerings were sought). In January 1941 the Jersey (Aquila Road) Circuit held a gift evening instead of the usual bazaar.[29]

That stalwart of the Methodist calendar the sale of harvest produce created an acute dilemma for churches during the Occupation. In peacetime auctioning harvest gifts to the highest bidder was an innocuous source of income. Under food rationing, however, an auction sale was uncomfortably close to black marketeering and therefore morally dubious if not actually illegal. To avoid breaking the law, churches sold foodstuff at controlled prices after giving some of it to the poor, any loss of revenue being made up by the auction of other goods. A harvest sale at St Martin's in the Jersey (Grove Place) Circuit in September 1943 raised a large sum towards the annual circuit levy.[30] A similar event at La Moye in the Guernsey and Sark (French) Circuit saw high prices paid for goods such as carrageen moss, useful for making blancmange. A member of the congregation later recalled that nothing was auctioned until harvest goods had been freely distributed to the poor and sick.[31] All the same, since these would presumably have benefited from receiving goods that were subsequently sold, delicate decisions were involved as to what was held over for sale or auction.

Despite the hazards of selling goods, harvest festival continued to provide a useful source of income during the Occupation, though not everyone was content that Methodism should be the main beneficiary. Harvest festival in Sark in 1943 raised a record sum of nearly £100. Although the church was sorely in need of funds to replace lighting batteries commandeered by the Germans, the leaders' meeting felt it expedient to donate £20 to the Red

Cross in appreciation of the help given to Sark families deported to Germany after the Commando raid earlier in the year – 'this suggestion arising from an oft-repeated expression of the public that some part of the Harvest proceeds be donated to charity'.[32] The following year £15 was donated to the Red Cross even though harvest festival raised only £43. The leaders' meeting justified retaining £28 for church funds 'mainly because of the rather large sum required to replace the lighting batteries'.[33]

Figure 7.3: The harvest sale of produce was a traditional means of fundraising in Methodism (Jersey Evening Post)

When church finances were tight, arranging musical concerts was another tried and tested means of fundraising which was put to effective use during the Occupation. In the first half of 1941 the Jersey (Aquila Road) Circuit held a series of monthly concerts, partly to maintain morale and partly to restore depleted finances.[34] In 1942 Grove Place church held a series of concerts to raise funds in order to pay its levy to the circuit.[35] In 1943 Royal Crescent church in the Jersey (Great Union Road) Circuit hosted a concert to clear the deficit on its finances.[36] A hymn recital at Ebenezer in the

Guernsey (English) Circuit in August 1943 in aid of trust funds attracted a capacity audience of a thousand who gave generously.[37]

Figure 7.4: Concerts on church premises were a valuable source of income during the Occupation (GEP)

Pew rents, another mainstay of fundraising in pre-war years, continued to provide a useful source of income for Methodism during the Occupation. Whilst the idea of reserving seats in church offends modern sensibilities, pew rents were an easy way to generate a regular income with minimal administration required. One of the sidesmen's tasks before services was to steer visitors towards unreserved seating.

Wesley chapel in St Helier recorded its income from pew rents in a 'seat rent ledger' supplied by the Methodist Publishing House. Income was recorded quarterly – at Midsummer, Michaelmas, Christmas and Lady Day (so it is not quite true to say that Methodists have never acknowledged a Marian festival). Seats were available at 2s or 1s/6d per quarter, though it is not clear what benefit members of the congregation received by paying an extra 6d.[38] At Tabor chapel in the Jersey (Grove Place) Circuit, seats could

be rented for a modest 3s or 2s/6d per year, a price that had increased by only 6d since 1875. At St Aubin's, pew rents were 1s/6d per quarter, netting an average annual income of £7. Here pew rents continued until December 1963.

The size of the congregation in some of the larger churches made renting pews a worthwhile investment, though latecomers could not always be assured of finding their seat unoccupied. In June 1944 members of the Jersey (Aquila Road) Circuit discussed the difficulty of reserving seats on certain Sundays when large congregations were expected. Despite the difficulties facing sidesmen on such occasions, 'It was felt to be inadvisable to dispense with pew rents.' Since there was no obvious solution to the problem, the minister was deputed to ask 'seat holders to be patient and sympathetic towards the sidesmen who are doing their best and will continue to do so'.[39]

In Guernsey, too, pew rents were an established part of the Methodist economy. In 1939 Salem in the Guernsey (English) Circuit raised £21/18s/9d from seat rents, sufficient to pay the organist's annual honorarium, though down from £23/5s/9d the previous year.[40] The pulpit notices book at St Andrew's in the Guernsey and Sark (French) Circuit contains little beyond bald announcements naming the preachers appointed to lead worship on the following Sunday and the sum raised by collections on the previous Sunday. A notable exception occurred on the first two Sundays of the calendar year when the preacher was asked to announce: 'Will friends please note that pew rents are now due and will be received by the stewards.'[41]

After the Liberation, pew rents swiftly became a casualty of egalitarian social norms that may have been hastened by the Occupation but were probably inevitable in any case. The records of Brock Road church for 1946 reflect the demise of pew rents in post-war Methodism:

> It was agreed that the names of pew-holders should be removed as all seats are [now] free. An announcement, to the effect that those who desired still to occupy seats to which they had long been accustomed should be in their places a few minutes before the beginning of the service, was ordered to be made. After that time it was agreed that the seats should be available for anyone, though the sidesmen were requested to avoid as far as possible introducing others to such pews.[42]

A few churches continued to raise money from pew rents for several more years before the practice eventually died out. All the same,

possessiveness towards pews lingered for many years afterwards and not just in the Channel Islands. Every Methodist church has apocryphal stories of visitors who never returned having been rebuked for unwittingly occupying someone else's seat.

The Poor Fund

As well as funding ministry and maintaining church buildings, Methodist finances were also used to provide welfare payments for necessitous members and adherents through what was called the Poor Fund. Administered by the minister in conjunction with a layperson known as the Poor steward, the fund was financed from a second collection taken during the administration of Holy Communion. Nowadays called the Benevolent Fund, its purpose remains unaltered, though the increased level of social security in the post-war state has greatly reduced the need for additional welfare provision by the churches.

Since the principal form of pre-war social security in the Channel Islands was a rudimentary system of poor relief administered by parish officials, the Methodist Poor Fund constituted an internal means of addressing the problems of members and adherents in financial straits. During the Occupation, churches continued to draw on the Poor Fund in cases of hardship, either in the form of a one-off payment or else as a regular allowance. For instance, at St Sampson's in the Guernsey (English) Circuit in October 1940 the Poor Fund was used to pay a doctor's bill, and a number of people were awarded a quarterly allowance of £1.[43] Since disbursements were usually approved by the leaders' meeting, the names of recipients were semi-public. Whilst the lack of privacy would nowadays be considered poor pastoral practice, at least it meant that congregations were aware of particular needs so that individuals could offer additional help and support.

The importance of the Poor Fund increased as the effects of the Occupation began to be felt. In November 1940 'a little amount' of the Poor Fund at Grove Place church in Jersey was made available at the minister's discretion 'for a few people he knew were deserving of a little help in these times'. By the middle of 1942 several people were receiving 'monthly pay' from the Poor Fund. Moreover, calls upon the fund grew to such an extent that a committee was set up to consider ways of boosting income. Attempts to raise additional income proved successful, and by May 1945 the amount available in the Poor Fund stood at £42 as against just £9 in 1940.[44]

In both main islands calls upon the Poor Fund were greater in some parishes than in others. The Guernsey and Sark (French) Circuit invited

donations from churches which it then redistributed to others where there was insufficient money in the Poor Fund to meet local needs.[45] Tabor chapel in the Jersey (Grove Place) Circuit made only one modest grant to a church member in 1943 and in 1944 there were judged to be no necessitous cases.[46] In November 1944 Carmel chapel donated its Poor Fund to Georgetown 'for the poor in that district'.[47] Here collections on Good Friday and Easter Day were allocated to the Poor Fund in addition to the regular collections at services of Holy Communion, which suggests that the number of necessitous cases was higher than elsewhere.[48] The same was true of St Martin's where the Christmas Day collection in 1941 was for 'the poor of the parish'.[49] In March 1942 the church gave a grant of £1 to each of two families; in November a grant of £2 was awarded to a member who was sick.[50] Family support was still being given in 1943.

Occasionally, congregations had to be reminded of their obligation to contribute to the Poor Fund. In Jersey the Aquila Road church eventually decided that collections for the Poor Fund would be announced during the service so that 'friends will not pass unheeded the poor box in the vestibule'.[51] Evidently, this had the desired effect since in March 1943 the Poor Fund stood at a record £45/15s/10d even though £20/5s/4d had recently been spent on Christmas gifts for the sick and needy. The congregation was informed that more money was needed 'so that regular payments could be paid to certain aged recipients'.[52]

The importance of poor relief in Methodism's pastoral ministry can be gauged by the fact that even the Sark chapel (with just 20 members) maintained a Poor Fund. In February 1940 the leaders' meeting approved a grant of £1 to a church member living in Guernsey. In April 1941 the Poor steward reported that collections for the Poor Fund since the beginning of the Occupation amounted to just 7s/4d: 'This small amount is due to the absence of Communion Services; since the occupation by German forces the visit[s] of our ministers from Guernsey have ceased through the uncertain navigation between the two islands.' The amount available in the fund was currently less than £2. Fortunately, in December the fund received an injection of £5 from the proceeds of a 'carol party' arranged by the proprietor of the Dixcart Hotel.[53] When the lay pastor was authorised to celebrate the Lord's Supper in January 1942 the number of collections for the Poor Fund increased. In the twelve months to May 1944 a total of £4/4s/3d was disbursed, leaving a balance of £3/17s/11d. When the Poor steward was deported to Germany another was immediately appointed in his stead, confirming that the role was too important to be left unfilled for any length

of time.[54]

Although the Poor Fund was intended for the benefit of church members and adherents, occasionally it was used to support charitable causes beyond Methodism. At Samarès chapel in the Jersey (Grove Place) Circuit there were no calls on the Poor Fund in the first two years of the Occupation; so in December 1942 £2 was donated to the *Evening Post* Winter Relief Fund.[55]

Rather than draw on the Poor Fund for external purposes, churches held special collections from time to time in aid of particular causes. For instance, in September 1940 churches in the Jersey (Grove Place) Circuit held a retiring collection for the Jersey Dispensary.[56] After public collections of money were prohibited in 1943 the churches were the only place where islanders were able to respond to financial appeals on behalf of charitable causes. As a result, in the final months of the Occupation Methodist churches in company with others raised a considerable sum of money for the International Red Cross, which was supplying food parcels to the civilian population. In Guernsey the first Sunday in 1945 was designated 'Thanksgiving Sunday' in response to the first distribution of Red Cross food parcels a few days earlier. Collections for the Red Cross were launched in all Methodist churches.[57] St Andrew's raised £37 on the first day (15 times the usual total) and the final total was in excess of £70.[58] Elsewhere the response was equally spectacular. Les Camps raised £64 on the first day, Les Capelles £140, and the Vale church a staggering £209.[59] The Sark chapel had already allocated £15 to the Red Cross from harvest proceeds but here too a special collection was organised.[60] In the Jersey (Grove Place) Circuit a collection for the Red Cross at Pentecost 1945 raised £1,137.[61] All this money came from additional giving on top of contributions to church finances. By acting as a financial channel in support of a patriotic cause, island churches again provided a means of passive resistance to the enemy.

Overseas Missions

The annual cycle of denominational festivals in Methodism was principally concerned with raising funds for mission in one form or another. Despite the economic situation, Methodists in the Channel Islands continued to raise a substantial sum of money during the Occupation in support of British Methodism, most especially for overseas missions. In March 1941 the superintendent of the Jersey (Grove Place) Circuit, William Ward, appealed for continuing financial support for overseas missions: 'It is impossible for an Overseas Missionary Deputation from the Mainland to serve us this year [...] but we must do all we can to see to it that the funds of this excellent

cause do not suffer. Owing to world conditions, help was never more needed than now. Let us bear in mind the explicit teaching of Our Master (Matt. 28.19-20) and support all the services as arranged.'[62]

In fact, Ward need not have feared that fundraising would suffer. The popularity of overseas missions in the Methodist psyche was undiminished during the Occupation, as local church records confirm. The priorities of the average Methodist congregation at this time are clearly reflected in the Sunday collections at Galaad in the Jersey (Grove Place) Circuit. Over three consecutive weeks in February 1942 the amounts raised were: 12s/1d for circuit funds; £1/4s/8d for local trust funds; and £4/11s/1d for overseas missions.[63]

When communication with the mainland was restored in May 1945 Methodist leaders in Britain were surprised to receive significant donations from the Channel Islands towards overseas missions. For instance, in June 1945 Women's Work in Jersey sent £631/2s/3d raised by women's meetings for overseas missions during the Occupation. The letter acknowledging receipt hints at the reason why Methodists in the Channel Islands contributed so generously to appeals for overseas missions at a time when they were unable to forward the money raised: 'It is wonderful to think that whilst you had the enemy so close at hand, obtruding in every walk of your life, you all had vision to see people thousands of miles away and to enter into their needs with love and understanding and sympathy.'[64] By continuing to devote time and energy to fundraising for overseas missions during the Occupation, Methodism in the Channel Islands discouraged introversion and instead encouraged islanders to see themselves positively as being in a relatively privileged position in which they were able to do something for others. As a result, between 1942 and 1944 the amount raised by the Channel Islands District for overseas missions actually increased as a result of buoyant fundraising in the islands and donations from Channel Island Methodists temporarily resident in Britain.

At the end of the Occupation the financial situation of Methodism was healthier than anyone could have predicted in June 1940. In some cases debts had been cleared and considerable sums spent on property maintenance. In May 1946 the District Synod, meeting for the first time since 1940, noted with satisfaction 'the healthy condition of all the Trusts in the District'.[65] It was also a matter for thanksgiving that church premises were generally in good condition.

Confounding peacetime trends, Methodists had responded to the

Great Union Road Methodist Church

SUNDAY, August 29th.

11 a.m.—MR. R. H. FORD.

7 p.m.—MR. J. C. PALLOT.

Overseas Missions

The ANNUAL PUBLIC MEETING

will be held on

MONDAY, August 30th

at 7.30 p.m.

Speaker: REV. W. J. WARD (formerly of Africa).

Chairman: MR. J. LUCAS.

Soloist: MISS M. BUNTING.

A cordial invitation is extended to all.

Figure 7.5: Methodists continued to raise funds for Overseas Missions during the Occupation (JEP)

financial crisis of June 1940 by significantly increasing their financial contributions. The response of the congregation at Tabor chapel in the Jersey (Grove Place) Circuit was typical of the way in which Methodists reacted to the situation. In May 1941 the minister, John Scott, circulated a letter to everyone associated with the church seeking help in clearing a debt of £40. He challenged the congregation to raise a further £20 for roof repairs as 'a practical way of expressing thanks to God who giveth all things richly to enjoy'. In the event, the appeal raised £80 which Scott described as 'a credit to all concerned'.[66] That the accumulated debts of peacetime were paid off during the Occupation is remarkable. It was the same story in other Methodist churches as congregations seized the opportunity to defy the enemy and demonstrate their confidence in future victory.

Chapter 8

Watching over one another in love

John Wesley's description of Methodist discipline as 'watching over one another in love' is enshrined in a legal constitution that provides for various ecclesiastical courts to oversee church affairs. Although the principle of subsidiarity provides a degree of local autonomy, there is a clearly defined 'connexional' (as against a congregational) structure that makes churches, circuits and districts mutually dependent. The highest court in British Methodism is the annual Conference, which comprises mostly representatives elected by the District Synods. In the 1940s, besides the Conference, the principal courts in Methodism were the circuit quarterly meeting, the circuit local preachers' meeting, as well as the leaders' and trustees' meetings in each local church. The Chairman of the District was responsible for ministerial discipline; superintendents were charged with upholding the authority of the Conference in their circuit.

Whilst the Methodist constitution was intended to cope with every conceivable eventuality, those who drafted it could hardly have foreseen the situation created by the German Occupation of the Channel Islands which prevented circuits from communicating with the Conference. In this unprecedented situation Methodists in the islands could only uphold the constitution as best they could, where necessary relying on the Chairman of the District to assume in person the authority of the Conference. In the present chapter we investigate how Methodists continued to 'watch over one another in love' during the Occupation, with particular reference to presidency at the Lord's Supper, discipline among local preachers and ministers, and church membership.

Presidency at the Lord's Supper

In Methodist polity only ordained ministers preside at the Lord's Supper in normal circumstances. However, in situations where Methodists would otherwise be deprived of the sacrament because of a shortage of ministers,

the Conference may authorise named lay people to preside at the Lord's Supper in a particular circuit for a specified period. In 1939 there were considered to be sufficient ordained ministers in the Channel Islands not to require special 'dispensations' for lay presidency. During the Occupation, however, an acute shortage of ministers deprived several congregations of receiving the sacrament reasonably frequently, prompting the Chairman of the District to act *ultra vires* in order to resolve the problem.

The first case of deprivation arose in the summer of 1940 when ministers in the Guernsey and Sark (French) Circuit were refused permission to cross over to Sark. Eventually, on 10 November 1940 the superintendent, Sidney Beaugié, was finally allowed to relieve the lay pastor so that Methodists on Sark could receive the sacrament for the first time since Bunting died in May. However, he was not permitted to visit Sark again until March 1941, and no one could tell how long it would be before his next visit. The following month the Sark leaders' meeting noted that the reduction in the number of communion services was having an adverse impact on the Poor Fund.[1]

Soon afterwards the leaders' meeting wrote to the District Chairman, Frederick Flint, seeking permission for the lay pastor to celebrate the Lord's Supper. In due course the meeting noted 'the kindness of Rev. F. Flint for having given permission to our much esteemed Mr Tardif to administer Holy Communion'.[2] Acknowledging their letter of thanks, Flint wrote: 'It has been a matter of regret that you have not been able to receive the Holy Communion for so long a period. Under the unusual conditions of our work at present there was no other course but to give Mr Tardif the requisite authority for its administration.' Beaugié visited Sark twice in 1942 and thereafter annually to relieve Tardif and to celebrate the Lord's Supper. Otherwise, the lay pastor celebrated the Lord's Supper twice a quarter between June 1942 and September 1945.[3]

The situation on Sark may have been unique because of its isolated location but after Rev. Henry Foss was deported to Germany in February 1943 Beaugié was left in sole pastoral charge of fourteen churches in the Guernsey and Sark (French) Circuit. The ministers of the Guernsey (English) Circuit were already lending assistance, but Flint's deportation in October 1942 left only Romeril and Ord to look after ten churches. Faced with an acute shortage of ministers, in February 1943 Beaugié appointed two senior and widely respected local preachers, J. Allés Simon and Edwin Langlois, as lay pastors for Foss's churches with authority to preside at the Lord's Supper.[4] One or other of them presided at the sacrament in each church at

The Daffodils,
Doyle Road,
Guernsey.
13th. Feb.1942.

Dear Mr. Carre,

It was a great pleasure to receive your letter.
It has been a matter of regret that you have not been able to
receive the Holy Communion for so long a period. Under the
unusual conditions of our work at present there was no other course
but to give Mr Tardif the requisite authority for its administration.

I am glad to note your expression of esteem for
Mr . Tardif. It was a relief to secure his services and I trust the
work under his leadership will prosper and be a blessing to all
your people and to the community.

I wonder when I shall be privileged to see your
lovely island again I know that my wife who is away will be often
recalling the many happy days we spent there.

With kindest greetings to yourself and all
friends,
Most sincerely yours,

Figure 8.1: Letter from Rev. Frederick Flint to the Sark Methodists, 13 February 1942 (Courtesy of Island Archives, Guernsey)

least once every quarter from April 1943 until the end of the Occupation.[5]

In Jersey there were two cases of lay people being authorised to celebrate the Lord's Supper. The first of these arose in the Jersey (Great Union Road) Circuit in 1943 when Clement Mylne was imprisoned by the Germans for ten months. The Acting Chairman of the District, Walter Fell, authorised one of the local preachers, W.F. Chapman, to celebrate the Lord's Supper until Mylne was able to resume his duties.[6] In the second case the acting superintendent of the Jersey (Wesley) Circuit, Ronald South, reported to the quarterly meeting in June 1944 his difficulty in arranging services of Holy Communion. The meeting agreed that he should approach the Acting

Chairman of the District seeking permission for one of the senior local preachers to celebrate the Lord's Supper.[7]

The procedure followed in these situations preserved the connexional nature of Methodism as far as was possible in the circumstances. In three out of the four cases surviving records indicate that circuits sought permission from the District Chairman for a named lay person to preside at the Lord's Supper. Whilst there are no records extant in the fourth case, it is reasonable to suppose that the same procedure was followed. It is a reflection on Methodism's sense of discipline that, even in the circumstances created by the Occupation, there was no recourse to a congregational polity whereby local churches felt free to make their own decisions of this kind.

Of course, as everyone involved must have been aware, the Chairman of the District did not possess the authority to grant permission for lay people to celebrate the Lord's Supper. Yet it was commonly accepted that he embodied the authority of the Conference and should therefore act in its stead until communication with the mainland was restored. Therefore, with the consent of circuits and churches, the District Chairman exercised the authority of the Conference in what he perceived to be the best interests of Methodism.

Local Preachers

The circuit local preachers' meeting, usually held once in each quarter, was responsible for the preachers' discipline, moral character and fidelity to Methodist doctrine. In the Jersey (Wesley) Circuit a serious dispute about the suitability of a particular group of preachers led to a crisis that threatened to destabilise Methodism.

At the height of the evacuation in June 1940, the superintendent, Donald Stuart, informed the Jersey (Wesley) Circuit advisory committee of his plans to create 'a band of temporary preachers to tide over the present shortage of local preachers owing to the emergency'.[8] Where these preachers were to come from is not recorded. The following month, however, he advised the Free Church ministers' meeting that a number of conscientious objectors (sent to Jersey as agricultural labour) had been left stranded in the island when the Germans arrived: 'some of them were willing and able to undertake services as lay preachers.'[9] In September he informed the local preachers' meeting that a dozen lay preachers from various denominations – presumably the same conscientious objectors – were 'temporarily resident' in Jersey. They had already taken a number of preaching appointments in the circuit which could not otherwise have been filled. At Stuart's bidding,

their names were added to the list of preachers on the quarterly preaching plan without anything to indicate that they were not fully accredited Methodist local preachers.[10]

Stuart's unconstitutional *imprimatur* of 'temporary preachers' who were not members of the Methodist Church was unwise despite accredited local preachers being in short supply. If these had proved acceptable in the pulpit, then Stuart's irregular action may not have had any more adverse consequences than a few ruffled feathers amongst the accredited preachers. However, within the circuit there were strong objections to several temporary preachers on doctrinal or moral grounds. There were also widespread doubts about their loyalty to Britain.[11]

In March 1941 Stuart's colleague, Ronald South, proposed to the quarterly meeting that preachers be listed on the circuit plan in the conventional arrangement of ministers, accredited preachers, preachers on trial, then 'exhorters and helpers'.[12] The real significance of this proposal was that the temporary preachers would be required to submit to Methodist discipline as preachers on trial or else be listed as auxiliaries. Either way, they would be subject to examination by the local preachers' meeting and could more easily be excluded from Methodist pulpits if their preaching attracted complaints.

As may well have been South's intention, this proposal brought discontent into the open. Concern was voiced about 'the standing and character' of 'certain preachers'. Stuart repudiated the charge that they had been added to the circuit plan without being examined as to their character and doctrine. He had examined the preachers himself and was entirely satisfied with their answers. He warned of the 'possible consequences' of making allegations about preachers but did not specify what these might be. After heated debate, South's proposal was carried.

This contretemps reveals a superintendent at loggerheads with his ministerial colleague and local preachers. A few weeks before, an accredited local preacher and two preachers on trial had transferred to the Jersey (Grove Place) Circuit.[13] At this juncture, such an unusual occurrence can only have been in reaction to the introduction of temporary preachers. Even in the unprecedented circumstances created by the Occupation, Stuart was naïve to imagine he could carry the day without the co-operation of his ministerial colleague and the local preachers.

Why was Stuart so determined to accept temporary preachers without their being examined by the local preachers? Stuart must have known or else strongly suspected that the conscientious objectors would not satisfy

the accredited local preachers in an oral examination. Whereas Stuart believed this was due to prejudice, the accredited preachers no doubt felt justified in wanting to sift the conscientious objectors in order to weed out troublemakers and draft dodgers. Stuart's Pacifism may not have been the issue so much as his inability to realise that not every conscientious objector claiming to be a preacher was a high-minded idealist and suitable candidate to conduct worship and preach in Methodist churches.

The imbroglio in the Jersey (Wesley) Circuit caused by the temporary preachers continued after Stuart's abrupt departure from the circuit at the end of May 1941 (see below). The following September, the Jersey (Aquila Road) Circuit agreed that in view of the 'exceptional difficulties' in the Jersey (Wesley) Circuit, Fell would offer two preaching appointments in the following quarter.[14] In December 1941 South met with three preachers who were causing concern in order 'to talk over Methodist doctrine, and discipline, and endeavour to clear up any misunderstanding in respect of the same'.[15] Whilst it cannot be established with certainty that these were temporary preachers, the particular form of words used in the minutes suggests that this was the case since accredited local preachers were unlikely to misunderstand Methodist doctrine and discipline.

Aside from problems relating to temporary preachers, there were two disciplinary cases in the Jersey (Wesley) Circuit during the Occupation involving accredited preachers. The local preachers' meeting removed the name of one person from the list of accredited preachers because he had ceased to be a member of any church in the circuit.[16] Another, who for two years refused to accept preaching appointments, was warned in writing that his peers were 'very dissatisfied' with his conduct and that a formal charge would be brought against him unless he was 'reconciled to the meeting'. After hearing his written response, the meeting upheld a formal charge against him of 'not conforming to the ruling of the local preachers' meeting'. His name was removed from the quarterly preaching plan, thereby withdrawing his status as a Methodist local preacher.[17]

In comparison, the affairs of the Jersey (Grove Place) Circuit were less turbulent, though not entirely without incident. In 1942 the superintendent interviewed a local preacher who was judged to be in an 'anomalous position' due to his employment, which prevented him from accepting preaching appointments or attending worship. The local preachers decided he must resign.[18] Concern was expressed about another preacher's fidelity to Methodist doctrine. The superintendent wrote to him seeking assurance on several matters. After receiving his written reply, the local preachers

concluded that it would be in the best interests of the Methodist Church for him to cease preaching. His name was duly removed from the preaching plan.[19]

Two other disciplinary cases in the Jersey (Grove Place) Circuit illustrate how preachers' moral character was also subject to scrutiny. The first concerned a local preacher who appeared in court as a defendant. Although acquitted of all charges, nevertheless he was interviewed by fellow preachers, who 'after a full, frank and withal brotherly discussion [...] warmly and sympathetically decided to affirm [their] fullest confidence' in him. The second case concerned a local preacher suspended in 1937 as a result of bankruptcy. In 1943 the suspension was lifted and he was permitted to resume preaching. The reasons for lifting the suspension are detailed: (1) he had already been suspended for a period of six years; (2) he had won the confidence of people as a result of which he had recently been appointed cemetery supervisor; (3) his largest creditor now had 'a kindly regard' for him; (4) he had continued to support his local church, where he was secretary to the trustees, Sunday school superintendent and an assistant steward; and (5) his interview with fellow preachers was positive.

Besides illustrating how seriously Methodism approached the discipline of preachers, these cases confirm just how controversial was Stuart's attempt to introduce temporary preachers whose credentials were not established to the satisfaction of the local preachers' meeting. If a man found innocent in a court of law must still account for his behaviour to fellow preachers, it was small wonder that Stuart was criticised for asserting the *bona fides* of temporary preachers on the basis of his private examination of their character and doctrine.

Of course, not all discipline exercised by local preachers' meetings in Jersey during the Occupation was punitive. There were preachers on trial to be examined and admitted as accredited preachers. In May 1941 Nan Le Ruez in the Jersey (Grove Place) Circuit began training as a local preacher. In August 1942 her performance at a written examination in Scripture knowledge was 'highly satisfactory'. The following December she successfully conducted a final trial service and was accepted as an accredited local preacher.[20]

Even the troubled Jersey (Wesley) Circuit managed to recruit and train new preachers. In September 1944 the local preachers' meeting received a 'very satisfactory' report concerning a preacher on trial, Elsie du Feu, who dealt 'quite efficiently' with a written examination set by the acting superintendent. The meeting accepted her as an accredited local preacher and arranged for a recognition service to be held at Wesley chapel.[21]

W. J. WARD, 22 Vauxhall Street.
A. T. SKYRME, 6, St. Mark's Crescent.
D. L. COLLINGS, O.H.M.S.
J. W. J. SCOTT, Craig Choyl, Old Beaumont Hill.
P. H. HANKS, 9 Ryburn Avenue.
THOMAS LE RUEZ, Homestead, St. Pierre   1880
JOHN MAUGER, Rosehill, Trinité.   1885
PHILIP A. HUELIN, 27, Garden Lane   1888
JOHN DE LA HAYE, Fernleigh, Grouville   1888
PHILIP E. BREE, Hesket, Grouville   1890
FRANCIS E. DU FEU, Oakleigh, St.-Ouen   1890
NICHOLAS GALLIENNE, 13 Parade Road
PHILIP J. SARRE, Le Pout, St. John
JOHN B. LE QUESNE, 45 St. Mark's Road   1902
P. N. GALLICHAN, Villa Memphis,
                            Mont a l'abbe.   1908
E. P. AHIER, 1 Montrose Villas, Millbrook.   1908
A. DE B. BRETON, 1, Yaralla, 1st Tower.   1905
THOMAS RENOUF, Clos Fallu, St. Martin.   1919
EMILE SIOUVILLE, Oakborne, Grouville   1920
ARTHUR C. QUEREE, Lake Vale, St. Ouen   1920
PHILIP C. PALLOT, Riva Bella, Roseville St.   1924
WALTER QUEREE, Le Rocher, St. Lawrence.   1924
WILFRED E. MOURANT, Longueville.   1928
ENID LE FEUVRE, Somerleigh, St.-Pierre.   1929
P. E. NOEL, 71, Rouge Bouillon.   1929
EDWARD LE FEUVRE, Les Augerez, St. Pierre 1929
R. K. HARRIS, 5, Beach Road.
E. J. AHIER, 27, Duhamel Place.
P. LE RUEZ, Dielament Manor, Trinity   1932
H. W. MAILLARD, Blanche Pierre, St. Lawrence.
M. A. WARD, 22, Vauxhall Street.
E. C. A. LE CORNU, 78 Stopford Road.
AUBREY L. ROBSON, 84, Stopford Road.
CHARLES A. GOODSMAN 17, Trinity Road.
REGINALD R. JEUNE, 1, Peirson Place, Bagot.
A. M. LE RUEZ, The Homestead, St. Peter.
DONALD E. PICOT, 25 St. Clement's Gardens (O.H.M.S.)
A. M. FREEMAN, 28, St. Mark's Road.

SOUS EPREUVE.

DENNIS W. LAIDLAW, 27, St. Mark's Road. (O.H.M.S
R. A. FOSTER, Avoca, Tabor, St. Brelade's (O.H.M.S.)
NORMAN LE BROCQ. 21, Stopford Road.
R. DE GRUCHY, 2, Clubley Estate.

Figure 8.2: Ministers and Local Preachers listed in the Jersey (Grove Place) Circuit preaching plan, January 1943 (Author's Collection)

141

Whether or not Methodists in Guernsey were aware of the problems in the Jersey (Wesley) Circuit, they adopted a more cautious approach to the use of unaccredited preachers. In 1942 the Guernsey and Sark (French) Circuit introduced a new category of 'auxiliary preacher'. Men (*sic*) not less than forty years of age with suitable experience, for example as Sunday school teachers, and who were actively involved in their local church would be permitted to preach as auxiliaries. They would be members of the local preachers' meeting and therefore subject to its discipline but would not have the status of accredited preachers. One man was immediately accepted as an auxiliary preacher but otherwise the category does not seem to have been used. A handful of Salvation Army preachers were permitted to preach in Methodist churches as accredited preachers of another denomination.

Nine preachers on trial became accredited local preachers in the Guernsey and Sark (French) Circuit during the Occupation, though in some cases the customary presentation of a bible at the recognition service had to wait until after the Liberation as these became scarce.[22] In the Guernsey (English) Circuit four preachers on trial became accredited local preachers, though a recognition service was postponed until after the Liberation.[23]

Surprisingly, in view of events in Jersey, there are no recorded disciplinary cases amongst accredited local preachers in Guernsey during the Occupation, though this may have been due to a rigorous examination of preachers on trial. Whilst the majority of those on trial successfully completed their period of training, a few either withdrew or else were discontinued by the local preachers' meeting. In one case local preachers in the Guernsey and Sark (French) Circuit decided that the spirit shown by a particular preacher on trial 'would not justify the meeting in accepting him as a prospective local preacher for the time being'.[24]

Conditions during the Occupation made the process of becoming a local preacher even more daunting than normal. Roy Rabey in the Guernsey and Sark (French) Circuit led his first service as a preacher on trial in the winter of 1941 aged just 19. As he walked to Wesley church it started snowing. Because there was no heating, the building was freezing cold, and the congregation of five sat huddled in the back row of pews. At his 'trial service', the congregation at St Andrew's was augmented by two local preachers deputed to report on him, plus three German military police officers taking copious notes. After an oral examination at the next local preachers' meeting, he was accepted as an accredited local preacher. He subsequently became a Methodist minister.[25]

Preaching during the Occupation also tested preachers' faith as they faced

PASTEURS ET PRÉDICATEURS
LOCAUX.

Sidney E. Beaugié, The Manse, Baugy, Vale
Henry J. Foss, La Viltole, Plienmont. Tel. 3394

———

A. E. Tardif, Rosebud Cottage, Sark.

———

Sous Epreuv

William Corbet, Hermon. Le Valle   1885
Walter Coles, West Ways, Doyle Rd.   1894
Alfred F. Roussel, Grove Dale Le Valle   1896
Walter H. Rabey, Elmsleigh St. Martin   1898
George A. Rabey, 17, Havilland Street.   1898
J. Allés Simon, Les Rouvets, St. Sauveur 1900
James McKane, Epworth, Torteval   1900
John Gilroy, Pleinheaume Le Valle   1905
E W. Langlois La Pallotterie St. Pierre   1906
Peter Corbet, Brookland, Robergerie, S.S. 1907
Julius Touzeau, Brookfield, St. Samson   1909
T. Lainé, Le Bourg, La Forêt.   1911
C. M. Gaudion, Mont Morin.   1911
F. W. Martin, Les Vallettes St. Sauveur   1912
Edwin Falla, Bon Air, Le Valle   1914
Thomas Remphry, Sercq   1914
Alfred R. Tostevin, King's Mills Le Catel 1914
Cecil J. Le Pelley, Dolce Huis, Brock Road.1918
Geo. H. Lainé, Grande Lande, St. Sauveur 1914
Arthur F. Robin, Les Fontaines, Castel.   1921
J.C. Langlois, Collings Rd. St. Pierre-Port 1924
John R. Allez, Les Corbinez, S'Pierre.   1926
F. Renouf, Les Naftiaux, St André   1928
E. J Brehaut, La Mare, St. Peter's.   1932
A. E- Heaume, Les Boulains, Castel   1932
O. Falla, Brincliffe, Vale.   1932
Leslie Roussel, Longue Rue, Vale   1933
A C Le Tocq, Passée, St. Sampson's   1934
Ernest Jehan, La Marette, S'Saviours   1934
W Bourgaise, Vimy Ridge, St. Peters   1934
W. Giffard, Les Lauriers, Sark
Stanley Ozanne, King's Mills, Castel   1935
B. P. Brebaut. Rue des Landes. Forest.   1935
Jas Le Page, Roc Poisson, S'Pierre   1939
G. Roussel, Rosewood, Vale   1941

SOUS ÉPREUVE

F. Bourgaize, Seaview, Torteval   1912
J. H. Jenkins, La Forge, Sark
J. De La Mare, La Rocque, S'Peters.   1942

AUXILIAIRES.

W. J. Corbet. Balmoral, Vale.

Figure 8.3: Ministers and Local Preachers listed in the Guernsey and Sark (French) Circuit preaching plan, October 1942 (Author's Collection)

LOCAL PREACHERS.

Approved

Year	Name	Address
1896	T. A. Gosselin	La Couture, St. Martin's
1896	T. Ozanne	Bordeaux
1897	T. C. Huxster	Grasmere, Brock Road.
1900	E. W. Saunders	Marlborough, Braye Road
1902	W. Hill	Contrée Mansell
1902	F. H. Bragg	Nursteed, Canichers
1906	A. J. Pattimore	Nicoya, Fosse André
1907	L. Ozanne	Eatonhurst, Canichers
1908	H. Plummer	12, Havilland Street
1911	W. H. Marquis	Grovehurst, 14, Mount Row
1912	F. L. Dorey	Duncreggan, Delancey
1913	F. Johns	Brierton, Vale Avenue
1916	W. Hamlin	Fermaina, Fort Road
1919	S. J. Bragg	Roseneath, L'Islet
1923	W. F. Hamlin	3, Carmel Cottages, St. Martin's
1923	H. Bowles	Bordeaux Villa, Vale
1923	A. Nicolle	The Haven, La Moye, Vale
1923	W. Renouf	King's Road
1924	S. W. Falla	1, Davenport Villas, St. Martin's
1925	A. E. Tardif	Eyam Glen, Havilland Road
1932	P. Plummer, M.A.—	12, Havilland Street
1933	D. Plummer, B.A., B.Sc.—	12, Havilland Street
1935	F. Queripel	6, Gibauderie.
1941	A. H. Green	Friends' House, Hauteville

ON TRIAL.

M. Plummer, B.A., Somerville House, Mount Row.

T. Robinson, Greenwood, Rohais Road

Y. Paine, New York Vineries, Coutanchez.

A. Grut, Myosotis, Green Lanes

E. Rabey, 17, Havilland Street.

ON NOTE.
Supply "A"

Mission Band Leader: Mr. R. Bragg.

Figure 8.4: Local Preachers listed in the Guernsey (English) Circuit preaching plan, July 1942 (Author's Collection)

the same trials as fellow islanders. Leslie Roussel was a local preacher in the Guernsey and Sark (French) Circuit. The Occupation brought his horticultural business to a complete standstill, and his home was requisitioned by the Germans. His young wife of two years died in 1941 leaving him with a seven-month-old baby son to care for; and his father died later that same year. Yet he continued to lead up to twelve services a quarter throughout the Occupation. [26] That the majority of local preachers faithfully carried out their duties should not be overshadowed by the small number of cases where individuals failed to live up to their calling.

Ministers

Short of initiating a formal charge on doctrinal or moral grounds, declining to extend a minister's appointment was the only avenue open to circuits dissatisfied with his performance. Fortunately, most ministers enjoyed an amicable relationship with their circuit during the Occupation, and their re-invitation to serve was often accompanied by expressions of gratitude.[27] This was just as well since there was no possibility of ministers transferring to another appointment elsewhere. The only serious dispute between a circuit and one of its ministers occurred in Jersey.

As noted in Chapter 2, the superintendent of the Jersey (Wesley) Circuit, Donald Stuart, arrived in 1939 with his wife and daughter. In March 1940 the quarterly meeting confirmed his appointment for the ensuing year, and Stuart commented 'how happy he and his family were in the island'.[28] However, the Occupation produced a set of circumstances that were to drive a wedge between Stuart and many in the circuit.

The root of the problem lay in Stuart's Pacifism, an honourable stance adopted by a number of his ministerial contemporaries who had witnessed the horrors of the First World War but one that Stuart held with a passion that led him to make a series of misjudgements. A member of the executive committee of the national Peace Fellowship, he was deeply committed to the cause of Pacifism and found it difficult to understand how Christians could adopt any other position. In peacetime his ardent Pacifism would have been controversial enough; under enemy occupation it was bound to lead to confrontation with a significant number of Methodists who fervently prayed for the speedy victory of British armed forces.

In February 1941 the Jersey (Wesley) Circuit advisory committee met to discuss various matters, including recommendations to the quarterly meeting about ministerial appointments for the next year. The timing could not have been worse for Stuart: the row over the temporary preachers was

in full swing. Stuart reported to the meeting that he had received a letter from the circuit stewards informing him they were unable to recommend he continue in his appointment. What was more, 'in view of the lack of confidence between the minister and circuit officials' they felt it would be impossible for them to continue in post should their advice be rejected. At least one of those present felt Stuart was being judged 'on the Pacifist issue alone' but others insisted this was not the case. The vote to recommend that the quarterly meeting extend his appointment for a further twelve months was evenly divided.[29]

The quarterly meeting a few days later was acrimonious. The circuit stewards proposed that, in the best interests of the circuit, Stuart not be invited to serve as superintendent beyond September 1941 because of his 'pulpit and pastoral work and also administrative difficulties between the minister concerned and his officials'. They specifically 'repudiated the suggestion that the objection was based on the Pacifist convictions of Mr Stuart but rather on his mishandling of the difficult situation bound to arise where such views held prominence'.[30] Stuart vigorously defended himself, insisting that the real objection to his ministry lay in his Pacifism and accusing the circuit stewards of obstructing his ministry. The proposal that he continue to serve as superintendent for a further twelve months was carried by a small majority with several abstentions. Ignoring this less than ringing endorsement, Stuart indicated his intention to remain as superintendent whereupon the circuit stewards resigned.

At this juncture, the Chairman of the District intervened. Flint was given exceptional permission by the German authorities to visit Jersey, where he met with the ministers and circuit stewards in an attempt to resolve the conflict. It was agreed that Stuart should take sick leave at least until September because he was in need of rest and a complete change. Stuart expressed his hope that 'the separation might make each love the other more'; but it was not to be.

In May 1941 Stuart left Jersey to reside in Guernsey (where his wife had a property), leaving behind another problem.[31] Three days after his departure, South convened an emergency meeting of the circuit manse trustees to report that Stuart was proposing to install a Mr Green in the manse as resident caretaker – probably he was one of the conscientious objectors known to Stuart. Several of the trustees objected to the proposed tenant but Stuart was insistent that the arrangement stand. The secretary to the trustees (correctly) explained that legally the manse was their responsibility. A minister had use of the manse exclusively for his personal

use whilst he remained in office. If Stuart and his family left for an indefinite period, it was the trustees' duty to make arrangements for the safe custody of the house and its contents. Accordingly, it was decided to let the manse to a member of the congregation at Wesley chapel – a commercial traveller from Bournemouth who was in the island on business when the Germans arrived.[32]

Flint visited the troubled Jersey (Wesley) Circuit again in June, this time to chair the quarterly meeting. He explained that Stuart's sick leave would be extended to Christmas, and even then it might not be possible for him to return to work. For the time being, he would undertake light duties in Guernsey but, since finance was a problem in that island, Jersey would have to help out. The meeting left the matter of Stuart's eventual return with Flint, promising to consider any financial assistance that might be required. Meanwhile, South would carry out the duties of superintendent with the help of ministers and local preachers from other circuits.[33]

Surprisingly, in March 1942 Stuart wrote to South stating his intention to resume his ministry in Jersey after Easter. The quarterly meeting promptly vetoed this proposal, appealing to Flint 'under the present abnormal conditions to use his powers as Chairman and personal representative of the Conference to meet the wishes of the circuit' by appointing South as acting superintendent. The circuit was willing to grant Stuart use of the manse and a pension but could not permit him to resume his ministerial duties.[34] In the event, Stuart did not stay long in Jersey. In October 1942 he returned to Guernsey and was immediately deported to Germany (see Chapter 10).

Whilst some in the circuit may well have been ill disposed towards him because of his Pacifism, Stuart cannot escape a share of the blame for the breakdown in relations. Rashly, he misjudged the level of opposition to the use of temporary preachers whose credentials were suspect. Attempting to impose a settlement on the manse was also an error of judgement. At the same time, he was the victim of a set of circumstances that no one could have envisaged when he arrived in Jersey in 1939. For an ardent Pacifist to minister in a circuit where Methodists were obliged to live under enemy occupation required more grace and mutual understanding than either side was able to muster. The use of conscientious objectors as temporary preachers merely ignited an already explosive situation.

Church Membership

Reflecting the societal origins of Methodism, in the 1930s suitable candidates for admission into membership of the Methodist Church were received by a vote at the leaders' meeting of their local church. There was no liturgical rite of confirmation, though the *Book of Offices* (1936) provided an optional service for the 'recognition' of new members. Apart from having been baptised (and most recruits to Methodism would have been baptised as infants), the criterion for church membership was regular attendance at worship, so that anyone deliberately absenting themselves from services was eventually removed from the list of members for having 'ceased to meet'. Those who attended Methodist worship reasonably frequently but were unwilling to become church members were known as 'adherents'.

In every Methodist church it was the task of the leaders' meeting to 'watch over' the congregation in conjunction with the minister in pastoral charge. This involved regularly reviewing the membership list, making pastoral enquiry of anyone no longer attending worship, adding new members and removing the names of those who had died, transferred to another church or else ceased to meet. Methodists whose names were recorded on the official membership list were issued annually (or in some cases quarterly) with a 'ticket' of membership confirming their status as such.

Some churches zealously pruned the membership list, but the majority preferred to wait and see – sometimes for years – whether members might resume their involvement in the life of the church. For this reason the church membership figure is not always a reliable guide as to the size of the congregation since it did not count adherents but did include others whose attendance was infrequent. Nevertheless, since the size of membership was used to determine the financial levy on churches, there had to be some correlation with the strength of the congregation. Accordingly, in the absence of any more reliable indicator, church membership figures for this period provide a rule of thumb as to the relative size of congregations. As noted in Chapter 2, the overall Methodist membership in the Channel Islands on the eve of the Occupation was more modest than the number and size of the buildings might indicate.

During the Occupation, the leaders' meeting in each local church diligently continued to watch over the Methodist community by annually reviewing the membership list. Since church membership tickets could no longer be obtained from Britain, these were printed locally each year between 1941 and 1945. Given the pressing need to reduce costs, this commitment to expenditure indicates the importance attached to maintaining Methodist

discipline concerning membership.

Figure 8.5: Ticket of church membership 1941 belonging to Enid Foss, daughter of Rev. Henry Foss (Herbert White Collection)

The statistics that can be pieced together from contemporary records suggest that Methodism in the Channel Islands just about managed to avoid a decline in church membership between 1940 and 1945. However, the downward trend in the recruitment of church members from among the older Sunday school scholars (see Chapter 9) reveals signs of institutional decline.

Surprisingly perhaps, membership in the Jersey (Wesley) Circuit remained fairly stable during the Occupation despite the controversy surrounding Stuart and the temporary preachers. Table 8.1 compares church membership figures in the circuit in 1936 and 1944.[35]

Table 8.1 Church Membership in the Jersey (Wesley) Circuit

CHURCH	1936	1944
Wesley	143	133
St Aubin	58	59
First Tower	29	53
Gorey	32	25
Samarès	13	35
Seaton Place	47	20
TOTAL	**322**	**325**

The circuit continued to recruit new members during the Occupation. In the autumn of 1943 eight new members were received at St Aubin, where there were also a number of 'enquirers' as well as 'borderline' candidates for membership.[36] Yet the total number of members in the circuit hardly changed between 1936 and 1944 – decline at Wesley chapel and Seaton Place cancelling out growth at Samarès and First Tower. Whilst the turmoil in the circuit in 1941 may have contributed to the decline at Wesley, the reality was that, even in the favourable spiritual climate created by the Occupation, Methodism found it difficult to maintain its ground let alone expand. When South informed the quarterly meeting in March 1944 that 'this circuit has ten or twenty years' hard work in front of it for the extension of Methodism on the Island' he may have intended to inject a note of realism into the perennial Nonconformist hope that revival was just around the corner. However, even this sober estimate began to look wildly optimistic in the post-war period.

Confounding a straightforward diagnosis of institutional decline, the Jersey (Grove Place) Circuit recorded a modest increase in church membership during the Occupation. Table 8.2 shows the annual membership figures for the circuit between 1941 and 1945.[37]

Table 8.2: Church Membership in the Jersey (Grove Place) Circuit 1941-1945

Date	Full Members	On Trial	Junior Members
1941 (6 March)	890	28	97
1942 (4 June)	882	48	106
1943 (9 December)	913	34	99
1945 (8 March)	925	62	94
1945 (14 June)	924	62	70

In December 1941 membership in the circuit stood at a total of 900, a figure considered 'very satisfactory in these difficult times'. After falling back in 1942, membership picked up again in 1943 and remained buoyant for the rest of the Occupation. However, these figures must be treated with caution since they include some who had evacuated from the island in June 1940. Realistically, few of these were expected to resume their involvement with Methodism on their return to Jersey.

Figures from the Jersey (Aquila Road) Circuit illustrate just how much absentee members could inflate the membership. In March 1941 the quarterly meeting recorded 232 members in the circuit (an increase of 11 since the

previous year). In December 1943 the circuit membership stood at 250, with 215 described as 'resident', 9 'On His Majesty's Service' and 26 'evacuated'. On the face of it, these figures show an encouraging increase, though the number of absentee members (14 percent) suggests the actual strength of the church was lower. In the Jersey (Wesley) Circuit the number of absentee members was even higher – 57 members (17 percent).[38]

In Guernsey membership figures were similarly inflated by the inclusion of absentee members, especially in the Guernsey (English) Circuit, though no reliable figures have survived to indicate the precise number. On the eve of the Occupation there were 933 members in the Guernsey (English) Circuit and 1,243 in the Guernsey and Sark (French) Circuit.[39] A lack of circuit records for the Guernsey (English) Circuit makes it possible to reconstruct only a partial picture of fluctuations in membership during the Occupation. Membership figures that were already in decline before the outbreak of the Second World War showed little or no sign of improvement during the course of the Occupation. Even Brock Road church, which enjoyed a high public profile due to its strong musical tradition, did not buck the trend. In January 1940 there were 151 members, a total that remained unchanged for the next five years.[40]

St Sampson's church in the Guernsey (English) Circuit illustrates a trend that was becoming increasingly commonplace in British Methodism in the twentieth century. In October 1940 there were 187 church members, 32 of whom (17 percent) were resident in England following the evacuation in June 1940. By the end of the Occupation, however, the total had declined to 152, mainly as a result of the widening gap between the number of young people being received into church membership and the number of deaths in an ageing community.[41]

Membership in the Guernsey and Sark (French) Circuit appears to have remained virtually unchanged throughout the Occupation, though the figures have to be treated with caution. Table 8.3 shows the membership of churches in the Guernsey and Sark (French) Circuit between June 1940 and June 1945. Between October 1941 and July 1944 no change in membership was recorded which tends to suggest that the circuit ceased compiling accurate figures from the information supplied by local churches.

Table 8.3 Church Membership in the Guernsey and Sark (French) Circuit 1940-1945

Church	June 1940	Oct. 1941	July 1944	June 1945
Victoria Road	79	91	91	91
Wesley	53	53	53	48
Les Camps	124	124	124	124
Forest	53	53	53	53
Sion	57	57	57	50
Torteval	49	49	49	57
Les Adams	45	45	45	44
Rocquaine	25	25	25	29
Carmel	44	44	44	37
St Andrew	82	82	82	82
Castel	84	84	84	79
Galaad	59	59	59	54
Les Capelles	229	229	229	213
Vale	197	197	197	208
La Moye	55	55	55	52
Sark	20	20	20	22
TOTAL	**1,255**	**1,267**	**1,267**	**1,243**

Only four churches registered an increase in membership between 1940 and 1945; the rest show slight decline. In the case of Victoria Road and Forest churches the membership figure merely denotes a book entry since both closed in July 1940 for the duration of the Occupation, their members dispersed to neighbouring churches. Again, the inclusion of absentee members means that these figures have to be adjusted downwards to provide a more realistic indication of the actual size of congregations. By a strange quirk, the total membership in June 1945 was exactly the same as that reported in May 1940, which confirms the overall impression of stagnation. In December 1945 the membership was reported as 1,144.[42]

The plain fact is that, as elsewhere in the British Isles, by the 1940s the era of Methodist expansion in the Channel Islands was a rapidly fading memory. Even in the unique religious climate created by the Occupation, when it is reasonable to suppose that spiritual concerns were more prominent in the mind of the civilian population than in peacetime, Methodism was still unable substantially to increase its membership. Whilst a significant number of islanders may well have turned to the churches for spiritual consolation at some point during the Occupation, so far as Methodism is concerned there was no religious awakening or revival that translated into

a commitment to church membership.

A detailed comparison with the other denominations must await further research, though the task is made difficult by the fact that few churches record their membership statistics with as much forthrightness as Methodism. On the whole, there is little reason to suppose that the experience of other denominations during the Occupation was significantly different from that of Methodism, though the Liberation saw a bulge in the number of people being confirmed as Anglican and Roman Catholic bishops visited the Channel Islands to deal with the backlog (see Chapter 11).

Chapter 9

Children and Young People

In 1901 Wesleyan Methodism in the Channel Islands reported having 48 Sunday schools with a total of 1,345 teachers and 5,146 pupils on the register.[1] Forty years later, work with children and young people was still the most successful aspect of Methodism in the islands. On the eve of the Second World War, every Methodist church in Jersey and Guernsey invested heavily in its Sunday school, and even if the number of children attending was not usually as high as popular memory often supposes, Methodist children's work reached widely into the local community to the envy of other denominations.

Like everything else in Methodism, Sunday schools were highly organised in the interests of efficiency and evangelism. In each church the leaders' meeting was responsible for appointing a Sunday school superintendent in overall charge, assisted by a secretary and sufficient staff to teach groups of children according to age and gender. The circuit's close supervision of Sunday schools reflects the high priority Methodism attached to work among children and young people. The circuit Sunday school council, chaired by the superintendent minister or one of his ministerial colleagues, arranged periodic inspections of schools. Although training for teachers was minimal, teaching notes were available from connexional headquarters.

Besides meeting in class each week, Sunday schools led 'anniversary' services in church, usually twice each year. These were regarded as evangelistic opportunities since parents were specially invited to attend in order to see their children take part. The Sunday school council was responsible for determining the dates of anniversary services which were then published on the quarterly preaching plan. As surviving orders of service confirm, these occasions were principally children's festivals, featuring singing by junior choirs and the recitation of edifying poems and devotional material.[2] Sometimes anniversaries took the form of a 'flower

service' where children brought along bunches of flowers, which were later distributed to the sick.

The strong cult of the child in Methodism ensured that Sunday school anniversary services were important occasions in the cycle of worship, though ingrained attitudes towards the social order often meant that the place of children in church life was a source of tension within congregations. Since Methodism's work among children during the Occupation fared differently in each island, we shall consider Jersey and Guernsey separately.

Jersey

On the eve of the Occupation, Sunday schools in Jersey were in a strong position. In February 1940 the Sunday school council in the Jersey (Grove Place) Circuit reviewed the schedules completed by each church for 1939. These schedules, summarised below in Table 9.1, provide a detailed picture of Sunday schools in the island's largest circuit six months before the Occupation.[3] The average weekly attendance was 628 children and 138 teachers. Given that the numerical strength of the circuit was just under 900 members, these figures suggest that the number of children attending Sunday school was probably not far short of the number of adults attending worship. This helps explain why Sunday schools were so important for Methodism and why circuits took a keen interest in their affairs.

Table 9.1 Jersey (Grove Place) Circuit Sunday School Teachers and Children

	1939	1938
Total Number of Teachers	294	298
Of these, the number who are Members of the Church	206	203
Average attendance of teachers in morning Sunday schools	117	127
Average attendance of teachers in afternoon Sunday schools	21	22
Sunday School Children		
Under 8 years of age	327	326
9-11 years of age	264	246
12-14 years of age	226	199
15+ years of age	58	93
Total number of children	**875**	**864**
Average attendance of children in morning Sunday schools	542	562
Average attendance of children in afternoon Sunday schools	86	84

Overall, the position in 1939 was little changed from the previous year except that there were noticeably fewer children aged 15 and above registered with Sunday schools. The Sunday school council identified a problem in retaining children beyond the age of 14 and a corresponding need for a strategy to reverse the trend. Noting that nine Sunday schools in the circuit had branches of the International Bible Readers' Association, the council recommended that other churches follow their example in order to encourage bible reading among children. The number of additional children enrolled in Sunday schools during the course of 1939 was 97 as compared with 118 in the previous year. Although this was a slight decrease, the number of infants baptised in 1939 was 210 as compared with 165 the previous year. Thus the future prospects for Sunday schools in the circuit looked healthy.

The impact of the evacuation on Sunday schools in the Jersey (Grove Place) Circuit in June 1940 was not as great as was feared beforehand, though the weekly attendance dropped slightly. The following September the Sunday school council heard about the difficulty of arranging visits of inspection to Sunday schools because of the upheaval caused by the evacuation and the prohibition on private transport, though as yet no one expressed concerns about attendance. Looking to the future, it was felt that teachers would find it difficult to plan their lessons in 1941 without access to the teaching notes published annually by the Methodist Church.[4]

By the end of 1940 things had settled down. In January 1941 the Sunday school council again appointed visitors to schools 'to act if opportunity arose'. Teachers were instructed to prepare lessons using the bible readings from the lectionary printed on the preaching plan, and teaching notes dating from 1936 were dug out to assist. The shortage of blank schedules posed a problem in compiling Sunday school returns for the previous year. So, on behalf of all the circuits, the council arranged for a stock of schedules to be printed locally, the cost to be apportioned according to the number of schools in each circuit. This commitment to additional expenditure in the prevailing climate of belt-tightening confirms that the efficient administration of Sunday schools was a high priority. Hence the council's relief that children's work was not prohibited. A note in the minutes records 'thankfulness to Almighty God for the way in which the Sunday School workers had been permitted to continue teaching the great truths of Christianity to the young people in this national emergency'.[5]

The Sunday school council had good reason to be relieved that children's work was allowed to continue. The Third Reich was hostile to organisations that might compete with the Hitler Youth for the hearts and minds of children

and young people. Scouts, Girl Guides, the Boys' Brigade and the Girls' Life Brigade were among the groups banned by the German authorities in the Channel Islands. This reduced the number and variety of church-based activities available to children and young people. As a result, churches found it even more difficult to retain the interest of older children. Fortunately for Methodism, however, the Third Reich did not consider Sunday schools a threat. For a regime ideologically opposed to the Church, this was a costly error. Besides instilling Christianity in children, there was a strategic reason why the effectiveness of Sunday schools continued to be important to Methodism in the Channel Islands during the Occupation. Quite simply, Sunday schools constituted the most significant recruiting ground for new church members.

In 1941 the Sunday school council in the Jersey (Grove Place) Circuit reminded churches of the 'importance of establishing junior classes for those scholars who have signified their willingness to become junior members by signing the decision card on Children's Sunday; the class being led by some older teacher and to meet as often as practical in order to prepare these scholars for full membership of the Methodist Church'.[6] Junior members were catechumens undergoing instruction in the faith. After a period of preparation that included studying the Methodist catechism, junior members would be accepted as full members of the Methodist Church. The pivotal role of junior membership classes in recruiting new church members explains why the decrease in children aged 15 and above on the books of Sunday schools was considered a problem requiring a fresh strategy.

If not reversed, a decrease in the number of junior members would result in a fall in the number of adult members in the circuit. In March 1941 the quarterly meeting recorded 890 members with a further 28 undergoing membership training and 97 junior members.[7] The fact that the number of junior members was equivalent to around ten percent of the circuit membership provided ample justification for the allocation of resources to Sunday schools. To a large extent, the future of Methodism lay in the hands of those responsible for its Sunday schools.

So far as the Jersey (Grove Place) Circuit was concerned, its investment in Sunday schools continued to bring returns during the Occupation. Reviewing the completed schedules for 1941, the Sunday school council noted that new recruits exceeded the number of scholars who left the island in the evacuation.[8] By March 1944 there were 888 scholars on the books (a slight increase over the previous year) and 269 teachers (11 more than in the previous year).[9] In March 1945 the quarterly meeting recorded 94 junior

members, a figure that had remained fairly constant during the Occupation, though in June 1945 it dipped to 70.[10]

Whilst the vital importance of children's work necessitated a serious approach, not every Sunday school was as strict as that at Ebenezer. In October 1944 the Sunday school superintendent reminded teachers to take particular care when marking children's merit books (a reward scheme culminating in the annual prize giving). Before awarding merits, teachers were to take careful note of children's punctuality and whether they arrived for class having read and learned the bible lesson for the day. But what was to be done in the case of persistent offenders? 'After some discussion it was decided to ask the parents of various scholars to co-operate with the officials of the school by seeing to it that their children learnt their lessons before they left home for Sunday school.' Whether this strategy had the desired effect is not clear, though it reminds us that Sunday school scholars in the 1940s were probably not so very different from the children of today.[11] For the mostly untrained Sunday school staff, maintaining effective control of children must have been far from easy.

Judging by the numerous reported resignations among Sunday school teachers in the Jersey (Grove Place) Circuit, recruiting and retaining staff was a constant headache for church leaders. No reasons are recorded for the high turnover among Sunday school staff but a lack of training must have been a factor in disillusioning those who signed up for duty oblivious to the challenge that an average group of children poses to the unwary adult. It can hardly have helped matters that many Sunday school teachers were themselves young people only slightly older than the children they taught. Aside from any behavioural problems to contend with, once the novelty of being responsible for a group of children wore off, many young Sunday school teachers would have found the regular commitment difficult to sustain. On the whole, the popular image of the dedicated Sunday school teacher is not borne out by the high turnover of teachers in the Channel Islands, though there is no reason to suppose they were unique in this regard.

The large number of teachers required to maintain Sunday schools in the Jersey (Grove Place) Circuit created a constant need for recruitment. However, with a pool of around 900 church members to fill nearly 300 teaching posts, simple arithmetic dictated that staff would have to be recruited from outside the ranks of committed Methodists. This was undesirable not only for reasons of accountability but also because allowing adherents to engage in children's work undermined the status of church membership, especially in the eyes of junior members. Perhaps with these

reasons in mind, in 1942 the Sunday school council recommended that churches encourage all teachers to become members of the Methodist Church. What the response was to this appeal is impossible now to establish but it was unlikely to have had the desired effect. Given the shortage of staff, churches were hardly in a position to impose conditions on volunteers. Most churches were just grateful to have anyone who was willing to work with children.

Figure 9.1: Book prizes for regular attendance at Sunday school were a common feature in Methodism (Author's Collection)

Recognising the challenges faced by Sunday school teachers, the Jersey (Grove Place) Circuit made some attempt during the Occupation to provide training. In 1943 the Sunday school council arranged a convention for teachers to consider: '(1) Should children take a full part in the Sunday School Anniversary? (2) Should the catechism be re-introduced after the Occupation? (3) The problem of the intractable child.'[12] The reasons for selecting these particular themes can only be surmised, but presumably they reflect contemporary concerns. No doubt the real value in arranging a convention lay in bringing together Sunday school teachers from around the circuit for mutual encouragement and support.

That the 1943 Sunday school convention was judged a success may be deduced from the fact that another was held in May 1944 using the same

format. This time the subjects for discussion were: '(1) The usefulness of Scripture examinations; (2) Sunday observance; and (3) how to make the best use of Children's Sunday.' Presumably, making the best use of Children's Sunday meant increasing the number of youngsters who became junior members. The 1945 convention was postponed because of the Liberation. When eventually it went ahead in November the subject was the Methodist Youth Movement, a topic which probably reflects a universal concern for young people in the post-war world.

Looking back on the Occupation in September 1945, the Sunday school council recorded 'its gratitude to Almighty God for the manifold blessings bestowed on Sunday School work in the circuit during the past five years of German Occupation and increasing difficulties and restrictions and looks forward to a new era of increased service by officials and teachers of all schools in gratitude for our preservation'.[13] In the circumstances the circuit had just cause for satisfaction. The total number of Sunday school scholars peaked at 888 in 1944 and in December 1945 there were still 815 scholars on the books, though by the end of 1946 this had fallen back to 758.[14]

The Jersey (Wesley) Circuit was more seriously affected by the evacuation of civilians in 1940 than the other circuits in the island. In June 1942 Ronald South, acting superintendent, summarised the current state of Sunday schools in the circuit. Out of a combined total of 431 children, 125 (29 percent) had evacuated along with 13 teachers (out of a total of 38). Nevertheless, some lost ground had been made up in the previous two years as a result of new recruitment so that the combined total was now 212 (49 percent of the number reported in 1939). Furthermore, there were 37 teachers – one short of the total in 1940. Remarkably, the average weekly attendance at Sunday school in 1941 was 193 compared with 195 in 1940, and this despite a number of schools switching from Sunday mornings to afternoons. However, as in the Jersey (Grove Place) Circuit, fewer children above 14 years of age were attending Sunday school.[15]

Table 9.2 below shows the total number of Sunday school children in the Jersey (Wesley) Circuit between 1939 and 1946.[16] The effect of the evacuation can be seen in the reduction in the number of Sunday school scholars by almost half. Recovery was slow, and by the end of 1946 the combined strength of the Sunday schools was still only two thirds of the pre-war level.

Table 9.2 Jersey (Wesley) Circuit Sunday School Children 1939-1946

YEAR	1939	1940	1941	1942	1943	1944	1946
Number of children	431	237	212	230	241	289	282

Table 9.3 below shows the distribution of Sunday school scholars among the churches in the Jersey (Wesley) Circuit in 1943 and 1944.[17] Three of the five Sunday schools recorded a significant increase in the number of scholars in 1944, though children's work at Wesley chapel continued to struggle. An increase of 26 children at Samarès confirms the picture of a thriving congregation outgrowing its premises.

Table 9.3 Jersey (Wesley) Circuit Sunday School Children 1943-1944

Church	1943 Average Attendance		1944 Average Attendance	
	Morning	Afternoon	Morning	Afternoon
Wesley	62	56	12	37
First Tower	51	69	45	-
Samarès	60	86	-	50
St Aubin's	31	40	27	-
Gorey (No Return)	(37)	(38)	?	?

Even before the Occupation, Jersey Methodism struggled to retain its young people when they became too old for Sunday school. In some cases this may have been due in part to the attitude of an older generation, who sometimes failed to understand the needs of young people. In March 1939 the leaders' meeting at St Martin's in the Jersey (Grove Place) Circuit heard complaints about 'the behaviour of certain young people (notably talking before the service)'. The minister was asked to arrange for two appropriately worded notices to be printed, one to be displayed in the porch, the other in the choir vestry.[18] It obviously never occurred to those who complained that their attitude may have encouraged young people to leave the church. Still, it would be wrong to imagine that the majority of church members were unsympathetic towards young people. On the contrary, many were keen to support their young people and did their best to dispel criticism of them.

Social conditions during the Occupation did little to help churches recruit and retain young people. The superintendent of the Jersey (Aquila Road) Circuit, Walter Fell, blamed the loss of young people on wartime

conditions, in particular the 'desecration' of Sundays through 'music hall' entertainment that lured youngsters away. A scarcity of materials also made it difficult to organise suitable activities for them. Altogether, he believed the Occupation was a challenging time for Methodist work with children and young people. Urging 'utmost keenness', he could only 'plead for greater devotion on the part of all our workers in church, school, choir and Christian Endeavour'.[19]

In the face of increased competition from secular alternatives, the Methodist calendar provided a traditional means of evangelising young people. In addition to Children's Sunday and Sunday school anniversary services there was also Young People's Sunday. Announcing that the first Young People's Sunday of the Occupation would be held on 20 October 1940, Donald Stuart, superintendent of the Jersey (Wesley) Circuit, asked that 'prayerful efforts should be made to win all our Young People for Christ. Preachers are affectionately urged to give appropriate messages on that day.'[20] But by the 1940s relying on preachers to offer 'appropriate messages' was no longer an effective means of drawing young people into church membership. What was needed instead was some form of activity that was likely to appeal to a younger generation.

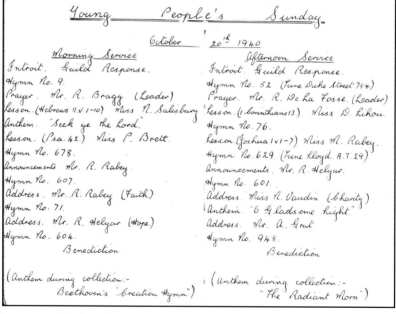

Figure 9.2: Order of Service for Young People's Sunday 1940, from the preaching diary of J. Allés Simon (Courtesy of Island Archives, Guernsey)

The solution lay in adapting a long-established tool in the arsenal of revivalism. The circuit rally was a large-scale event that brought together several congregations for an uplifting time of hymn singing and an inspiring address. A rally specifically for young people in the Jersey (Grove Place) Circuit was held on Whit Monday 1943, prompting a small group of them to re-open the Wesley Guild at Bethlehem chapel in the autumn (See Chapter 4). Following the success of this event, another rally for young people was held on Whit Monday 1944.[21]

Beyond these occasional rallies, the Wesley Guild and Christian Endeavour meetings were the principal midweek activities for young people in both Jersey and Guernsey during the Occupation. Surviving church records contain numerous references to young people organising and taking part in such meetings. For instance, in the autumn of 1943 between 20 and 25 young people regularly attended the Wesley Guild at St Aubin.[22] One of the driving forces behind the re-opening of Wesley Guilds in Jersey during the Occupation was the need to provide a safe environment for young people. For this reason, Royal Crescent church in the Jersey (Great Union Road) Circuit organised a Wesley Guild specifically for young people as early as July 1940.[23]

The concerns expressed during the Occupation about the future of Methodism's work among children and young people in Jersey need to be seen in the context of a movement that was still vigorous. Despite the various challenges posed by the Occupation, Methodist Sunday schools in Jersey were undoubtedly in a healthy position at the Liberation in 1945, and significant numbers of young people continued to be involved in Methodism. Yet there were also a few dark clouds on the horizon. In 1946 the Jersey (Grove Place) Circuit recorded just 35 young people received into membership – a little over a third of the number registered as junior members in 1945. Only two young people were received into membership in the Jersey (Aquila Road) Circuit and none at all in either of the other circuits.[24] But, outwardly at least, Methodist children's work showed promising signs of recovery as uniformed groups restarted and the Methodist Association of Youth Clubs provided a new model for engaging with young people.

A visit to Jersey from the Vice-President of the Methodist Conference in September 1948 was reported on the front page of the *Evening Post* under the banner headline 'Methodists Show Their Strength'.[25] More than 800 Methodist Sunday school scholars paraded through St Helier led by the Salvation Army band. There was also a sizeable contingent of young people from the various Methodist youth organisations, including Scouts, Boys'

Brigade and Girls' Life Brigade. A service held at Grove Place church was attended by 1,500 Methodists. The presence at the service of the Lt Governor of Jersey and the Permanent Under-Secretary of State at the Home Office reflects the continuing importance of Methodism in island life in the post-war period.

Figure 9.3: Rev. George Whitley with King George V inspecting Boy Scouts in Guernsey (1921) (Herbert White Collection)

Guernsey

Methodist Sunday schools in Guernsey were no less healthy than their Jersey counterparts in the years immediately prior to the Second World War. In May 1940 the Sunday school council in the Guernsey (English) Circuit analysed the annual schedules returned by Sunday schools in the circuit. Despite wartime conditions, the figures were considered very satisfactory; overall the number of scholars had increased by more than 70 since the previous year. The greatest challenge lay in recruiting sufficient teachers. At St Sampson's a shortage of teachers meant that children above the age of eight were meeting together in a single group.[26] Whilst this was unsatisfactory, there was no alternative if the school was to remain open.

The mass evacuation of Guernsey schoolchildren in June 1940 had a devastating effect on Methodist Sunday schools. The States of Guernsey calculated there were only 1,051 children of school age left in the island.[27]

What happened at Les Camps in the Guernsey and Sark (French) Circuit illustrates the impact of the evacuation and the slow process of rebuilding children's work during the Occupation.

On 28 April 1940 the Les Camps Sunday school held the first of its anniversary services for the year. During the service, the congregation reflected on the upheaval and unrest in Britain and Europe caused by the war, little realising the fate that lay ahead of them.[28] On Sunday 16 June 51 children attended classes as normal. However, in the course of that week the majority left the island with their day schools. The following Sunday the Sunday school superintendent and secretary, accompanied by Rev. George Whitley, waited to see if any children turned up for classes. When none did, the three men prayed together then went home. Later that same week, Whitley evacuated to England. It was later established that nine children on the Sunday school register were still in the island but this number did not make it viable to resume classes.

Twelve months later, however, the Sunday school re-opened to cater for a number of families that had recently moved into St Martin's from neighbouring parishes. On 20 July 1941 nineteen children attended the first meeting of the newly re-opened Sunday school.[29] Flint greeted them and encouraged each to bring along a friend who did not already attend Sunday school. Gradually, the number of scholars increased. In October Ken Lewis, one of the teachers, counted 32 children present and noted that the Sunday school had 'grown considerably in the past 14 weeks'.[30]

Despite the encouraging increase in the number of children, circumstances remained difficult. The staff struggled to prepare lessons without the aid of teaching notes. In winter there were frequent absences because of a shortage of children's footwear and clothing.[31] In January 1942 it snowed so heavily one Sunday afternoon that none of the children arrived for class.[32] There were further setbacks, notably when a number of children were deported with their parents to Germany in September 1942. Nevertheless, by May 1943 30 children were attending Sunday school regularly, and anniversary services were resumed.[33] By October 1944 there were 60 children on the register, though the weekly attendance was nearer 45.[34] The annual prize giving for attendance was able to continue through the generosity of members of the congregation who donated second-hand books for presentation to the children.[35]

Elsewhere in the Guernsey and Sark (French) Circuit the evacuation of schoolchildren had a similar effect on children's work. The Sunday school at Les Capelles was the largest in the circuit but in August 1940 the staff

Figure 9.4: Les Camps Methodist Church, St Martin's, in the Guernsey and Sark (French) Circuit (Photographed by author)

had to restructure classes because only 14 scholars were still in the island. Instead of four classes – beginners, primary, juniors and seniors – there would be just two. The beginners and primary classes would meet together, as would the juniors and seniors. Sunday school anniversaries were cancelled for the foreseeable future.[36] However, by the end of 1943 the situation was looking a little better: 17 children on the roll of the beginners/primary class with an average weekly attendance of 9; and 29 children on the roll of the juniors/seniors class with an average weekly attendance of 18. Moreover, there were now 33 infants on the baptismal roll (9 of whom had been added in the course of the previous year). By the middle of 1944 the number of scholars had again increased.[37] However, only following the Liberation and the return of evacuees were Sunday school activities restored to something approaching their pre-war level.

Churches in the Guernsey (English) Circuit fared no better. At Brock Road only four or five children on the register did not evacuate but it was decided

nevertheless to keep the Sunday school going. An advertisement was placed in the newspaper announcing that the Sunday school would re-open on Sunday 7 July 1940: 'Any children from other Schools now temporarily closed will be welcomed.'[38] Gradually, the Sunday school increased in size. Ambrose Robin noted two or three dozen children taking part in the Sunday school anniversary service in July 1943, all of them between the ages of 4 and 7. There were very few children between the ages of 7 and 17.[39]

St Sampson's church was one of the largest in the circuit but its Sunday school closed in the summer of 1940 following the evacuation of schoolchildren. However, in April 1942 the leaders' meeting decided to resume children's work. The minister's wife was asked to approach the local rector and day school seeking their support in gathering children together.[40] A small Sunday school continued to function for the remainder of the Occupation.

At St Martin's Mission, Sunday school attendance in July 1939 averaged 26 children in the morning (an increase of two from the previous year) and 35 in the afternoon (an increase of one). In May 1940 the situation remained unchanged, despite the fact that the assistant Sunday school secretary had been called up for military service.[41] Following the evacuation, however, only a handful of children on the register remained in the island. According to Douglas Ord:

> We held the remaining four scholars for the summer months of 1940 by an afternoon Bible class [...] This also was helpful to the teachers and a few members of the congregation but in common with the rest of the island, the longer evenings and lack of heating called for afternoon services instead of evening ones and caused the school activities automatically to cease.[42]

The following summer the few remaining children were encouraged to attend the re-opened Sunday school at nearby Les Camps. Contrary to fears expressed by some teachers, this did not lead to the permanent demise of children's work at the Mission. Following the Liberation, in June 1945 the teachers decided to reopen the Sunday school. An advertisement was placed in the local press, and by December 1945 there were 34 children on the books.[43]

Aware of various initiatives in children's work in the circuit, in September 1942 the Sunday school council wrote to churches seeking information about the present state of Sunday schools: '(1) What numbers of scholars on the

books before the German Occupation still attend? (2) Have you been able to gain any new recruits since June 1940? (3) What number of teachers have you now? How many then? (4) We are anxious to learn if you have tried any new methods under the present circumstances.'[44] Whilst the responses to these questions have not survived (except in the case of St Martin's Mission), the fact that they were posed demonstrates a continuing commitment to children's work despite the difficult circumstances of the Occupation.

It would be useful to be able to compare how Methodism's work with young people in Guernsey fared in comparison to the situation in Jersey. Unfortunately, however, any statistics that were compiled by Guernsey Methodism during and immediately after the Occupation have not survived. On the whole, it is reasonable to suppose that Methodism's work with young people suffered as a result of the evacuation, though spirited individuals did their best to provide other church-based activities for the remaining young people in addition to the opportunities for joining the Wesley Guild.

For example, Leslie Roussel was among those who recognised the need for young people to be allowed to entertain themselves on church premises without an overtly religious purpose. With Beaugié's agreement, the trustees at Les Capelles allowed him to organise concerts and games evenings exclusively for young people. He even turned a blind eye to the dancing that occasionally went on during the course of such events. A modest entry charge raised a considerable sum which was divided between the church (to provide more facilities) and local charities.[45] It was to all intents and purposes a prototype of the open youth clubs that would become a characteristic feature of Methodism in the post-war period.

Though he could not have known it, Roussel's efforts to cater for young people were in tune with developments in British Methodism during the war. The Methodist Association of Youth Clubs (MAYC) was founded in 1943 in response to the increasingly distinctive needs of young people. In the immediate post-war period one of the key objectives of Methodism in the Channel Islands was to establish the work of MAYC. Encouraged by the newly arrived ministers, in the autumn of 1945 Methodist youngsters eagerly began renovating dilapidated church premises in order to provide a suitable venue for a youth club. Eventually, MAYC proved highly successful in maintaining Methodist work among young people in the Channel Islands.

The baptism registers of Methodist churches in the Channel Islands during the Occupation reveal another post-war challenge facing Methodist children's work. Whilst incomplete records provide only a partial picture,

GREAT UNION ROAD
METHODIST CHURCH

TO-MORROW'S SERVICES

11 a.m. Rev. C. N. MYLNE
6.30 p.m. Mr. GEO. WATSON

School sessions : 10 a.m. & 2.30 p.m.

THE SCHOOL ANNIVERSARY takes place
on SUNDAY, April 22nd, Tuesday,
April 24th, and Thursday, April 26th
Special Hymns, part songs and Choral
Marches by the children with full choir
in support. Conductor: Mr. J. de-L. Le Montais
Note the dates and come with friends; it
will cheer you up!

Above, Figure 9.5: Sunday school anniversary services were important occasions in the Methodist calendar

Left, Figure 9.6: St Aubin's Wesleyan Sunday School (Jersey Methodist Circuit)

the decrease in the birth rate during the Occupation had a consequential effect upon the number of baptisms in Methodist churches. Table 9.4 shows the number of baptisms between 1939 and 1946 in two typical churches, the Vale in the Guernsey and Sark (French) Circuit and Wesley in the Jersey (Wesley) Circuit.[46] Even in 1939 few baptisms were recorded. During the Occupation, the figures shrank even further.

Table 9.4: Baptism Figures between 1939 and 1946

	1939	1940	1941	1942	1943	1944	1945	1946
Vale	7	2	1	0	2	9	4	?
Wesley	3	5	0	1	1	1	1	3

It is customary in Methodism to enter the names of baptised infants onto a baptismal roll until they reach an age when they are eligible to join the Sunday school. Baptismal roll figures for Jersey reported in 1946 reveal a mixed outlook. Promisingly, the Jersey (Grove Place) Circuit recorded a total of 210 infants on the baptismal roll, though that was across 18 churches. In the whole of the Jersey (Wesley) Circuit there were only 12 children on the baptismal roll. The Jersey (Great Union Road) Circuit counted 13 children on the baptismal roll, as did the Jersey (Aquila Road) Circuit. Unfortunately, comparative figures are not available for Guernsey but the evidence of the Vale church suggests the position was similar. The implications of a shrinking baptismal roll for the future of children's work were plain to see.

If children's work after the Liberation was not to experience significant decline as a result of the fall in the number of baptisms during the Occupation, churches would have to hope that a high proportion of returning evacuees would resume their previous involvement in Methodism. But the children would be five years older, and it did not require much imagination to realise that their experience of life in Britain would make it difficult to reintegrate them into church life. For congregations, as much as for the wider community, the task of reintegrating homecoming evacuees would be the most challenging legacy of the Occupation.

Chapter 10

Evacuation and Deportation

The evacuation of thousands of civilians from the Channel Islands in June 1940 shortly before the arrival of German forces was traumatic and demoralising for all concerned. The individual decision whether or not to leave was agonising, even though in Guernsey the civil authorities encouraged the evacuation of schoolchildren.

Sister Edith Clark, a Wesley deaconess, taught at Vauvert Primary School, St Peter Port.[1] Her experience of the evacuation is typical of many. Along with fellow staff and pupils, she arrived at school at 3am on 20 June bearing a single suitcase. Two hours later, a long column of adults and children began snaking its way towards the harbour, though it was not until midday that the evacuation boat finally departed after its passengers had been kept waiting on the quayside for six hours without food or water. The crossing to Southampton took eleven hours, during which time many children were seasick. Arriving late at night, they were subjected to a medical examination before being transferred to the railway station to continue their journey. Eventually, more than 36 hours after leaving home, they arrived in Glasgow, which was to become their new home. Apart from a short stop at Preston for tea and sandwiches, there had been no food or rest en route.

In most cases the evacuation of schoolchildren meant the separation of families. For twelve-year-old Lois Brehaut, life revolved around the family home (where Guernsey French was the first language), the Ladies' College and Forest church in the Guernsey and Sark (French) Circuit. The offer of evacuation threw the family into turmoil. After much heart searching, it was agreed that the children would leave with their schools whilst their parents remained in the island in order to supervise the family business. Lois, along with her brother and 800 other children, embarked on a foul smelling cattle boat for the slow crossing to Weymouth before being put on a train for Rochdale, Lancashire, where she was billeted with a local family.[2]

The arrival in Britain of several thousand Channel Islanders added

another strain to the exotic mix of European refugees fleeing the advancing Nazis. For islanders, many of whom had never previously left their tightly-knit communities, Britain was just as much a foreign country. They would have to establish a whole new way of life in employment or at school until such time as they were able to return home. That most of the children had left their parents behind added to the sense of bereavement. Women waited anxiously for husbands to join them, but the possibility of leaving the islands was soon foreclosed. None of the Channel Island refugees could have imagined their exile in Britain would last for five long years.

Given the strength of Methodism in the Channel Islands it was inevitable that a sizeable proportion of refugees had some kind of link with one of its churches, Sunday schools or midweek activities. But how could they be encouraged to maintain their link with Methodism in new and strange surroundings? Stranded in London just before the Occupation, Rev. Douglas Moore developed a unique mission to Channel Island refugees in Britain. With the assistance of Rev. George Whitley, who pitched up in London at about the same time, Moore established an office at Westminster Central Hall from where he set about establishing contact with as many Channel Island refugees as he could trace.[3] The weekly *Methodist Recorder*, avidly read by a large number of laypeople and ministers, provided a ready means of communication that proved highly effective in profiling the plight of Channel Island refugees and marshalling support among British Methodists.

In what became a regular column Moore appealed to readers to let him know the whereabouts of Channel Islanders with Methodist connections so that he could get in touch.[4] Around 10,000 islanders, mostly children, were now believed to be living in Lancashire, Cheshire and West Yorkshire, with a further 3,000 in Glasgow.[5] Others were scattered around the country, some in Bristol and the southwest of England. Whilst the total number of Channel Islanders registered under the evacuation scheme was later put at 14,228, Moore estimated that a further 13,000 arrived on evacuation boats or else paid for their passage on scheduled services by sea and air.[6]

As a result of his appeal, Moore was able to establish a nationwide network of Channel Island refugees with some Methodist link. Besides helping to maintain morale by sharing information, he hoped to strengthen their Methodist identity. At a practical level, a network of contacts would facilitate the distribution of financial and other forms of assistance that he was already soliciting from Methodists in Britain.

In the summer of 1940 the most immediate need among refugees was for

news of fellow islanders. In his *Methodist Recorder* column Moore published several lists containing the names of Channel Islanders who were now in Britain.[7] Since keeping tabs on a mobile population was far from easy, he resorted to a simple marketing technique that would encourage refugees to provide a current address. Thanks to a private sponsor, a free copy of Moffatt's translation of the New Testament was available to every Channel Island refugee who volunteered an address.[8]

In the course of the next 12 months Moore and Whitley distributed more than 900 bibles on their frequent visits to areas of Britain where Channel Island refugees were located in significant numbers.[9] By today's standards the inscription printed inside the front cover sounds sentimental but it was intended to offer comfort:

> FOR TODAY, to remind you of the infinite love watching over our loved ones and ourselves, to acknowledge with thanksgiving that we have found kindly friends as well as hardship in our time of exile. FOR THE COMING DAYS the remembrance that even this time of distress has brought its own enriching experience, not yet to be measured or understood. THIS BOOK... is sent to bring to you its own word of strength, and 'Grace to help in time of need.'

Eventually, Moore was in touch with some 1,100 adults and 900 children, less than 15 percent of the Channel Island refugees in Britain but still a considerable private network of contacts.[10]

Employment for refugees was another pressing need in which Moore took a keen interest. When *Methodist Recorder* readers learned about the arrival in Britain of a large number of Channel Islanders offers of employment poured into his office. A married couple were needed as caretakers in return for a house, coal, light and 20s weekly.[11] There were numerous opportunities for housekeepers, domestic helps and cooks. Agricultural workers were also in demand. August 1940 was the busiest month for Moore's recruitment agency with 'many openings available in various kinds of domestic service'.[12] Such was the high demand for domestic servants that, by the end of the month, he was obliged to decline further offers of employment: 'Please don't write any more asking for domestic servants. I simply haven't any. But if some of our refugees (mother and child) are still available to take work as housekeepers, I have a fine list of comfortable homes waiting for them.'[13] For prosperous British householders, the influx of Channel Islanders provided an ideal opportunity to overcome

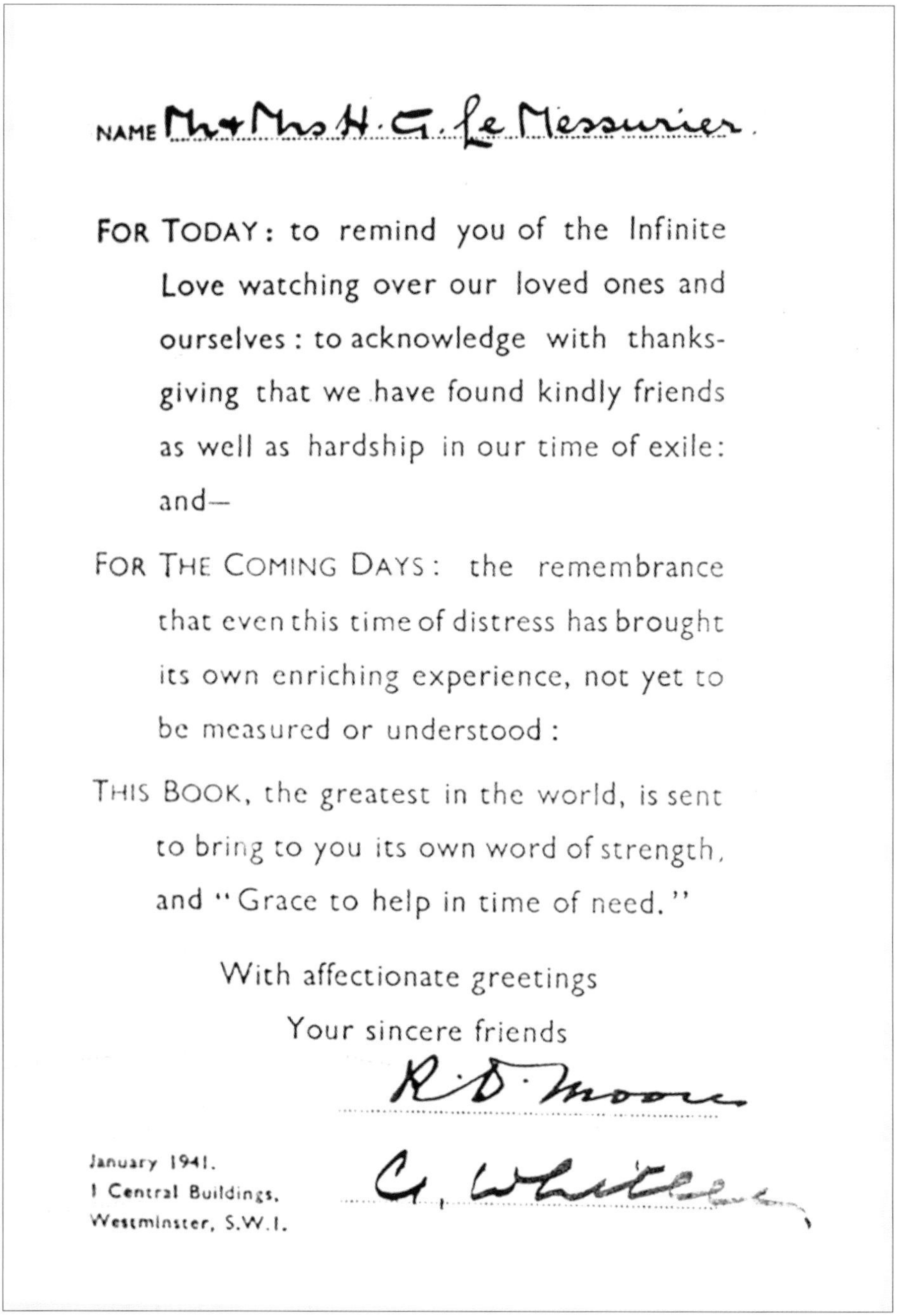

NAME Mr + Mrs H. G. Le Messurier.

FOR TODAY : to remind you of the Infinite
Love watching over our loved ones and
ourselves : to acknowledge with thanksgiving that we have found kindly friends
as well as hardship in our time of exile:
and—

FOR THE COMING DAYS : the remembrance
that even this time of distress has brought
its own enriching experience, not yet to
be measured or understood :

THIS BOOK, the greatest in the world, is sent
to bring to you its own word of strength,
and "Grace to help in time of need."

With affectionate greetings
Your sincere friends

R. D. Moore

January 1941.
1 Central Buildings,
Westminster, S.W.1.

G. White

Figure 10.1: Book plate in bibles presented to Channel Island refugees in Britain by Rev. Douglas Moore (Author's Collection)

the shortage of domestic servants caused by war service.

As self-appointed guardian of refugees' interests, Moore occasionally offered advice in his newspaper column. In August 1940 he pointed out that the Government compensation scheme for war damage did not apply in the case of property that fell into enemy hands. Nevertheless, the rules might change in future so islanders should still register a claim.[14] In February 1941 he reported that Channel Islanders were receiving invoices from local authorities for the billeting of children, despite the fact that they were exempt from payment because of their status as refugees. He promised support to anyone in dispute with their local authority over such a bill.[15] When brief messages from the Channel Islands began arriving in Britain via the International Red Cross he explained how to send replies through Lisbon.[16]

As a result of his network of contacts, Moore became a clearinghouse for information about the Channel Islands gleaned from a variety of sources. Few people outside the ranks of Military Intelligence were as well informed about what was happening in the islands. In September 1940 he passed on reports in an Italian newspaper about life in Jersey: there was a chronic shortage of soap; tea was rationed; coffee and beer were unobtainable; and German currency had been introduced at 7RM to the pound.[17] When Red Cross messages from the Channel Islands began to arrive Moore saw hundreds of them.[18] In September 1942 he conjectured the weekly rations in the islands based on information obtained from Red Cross messages.[19]

The most ambitious aspect of Moore's mission to Channel Island refugees was his provision of practical assistance, chiefly in the form of warm clothing. In August 1940 he reminded *Methodist Recorder* readers that refugees, the majority of them children and the poor, had left their homes in June ill prepared for the coming winter in the north of England. Even those with sufficient financial means were usually no better off since clothing was strictly rationed. Moore appealed for donations of winter clothing for refugees, especially children's clothes, as well as money to buy wool.[20] The response was overwhelming, and soon he was appealing for the loan of a van or car so that he could deliver parcels of clothing around the country.[21]

Having secured the use of a vehicle, in November and December 1940 Moore toured Britain distributing second-hand clothes to Channel Island refugees. The list of places visited in eight weeks illustrates the scope of his activities – Bristol, Glasgow, Dunstable, St Helen's, Bolton, Wigan, Stockport, Oldham, Rochdale, Halifax, Nantwich, Newbury, Devizes, Bowden, and Cheadle Hulme. Refugees living in other areas received parcels by mail. But, despite the large quantity of clothing donated, demand exceeded

supply.[22] The following summer he again appealed for winter clothing.[23] There were further nationwide tours to distribute clothing in 1941 and 1942.[24]

As Moore recognised, there was a certain irony in refugees from the affluent Channel Islands being on the receiving end of charitable handouts. A refugee from Jersey wrote to Moore describing how in the 1930s Sunday school children in the Jersey (Wesley) Circuit had sent clothing parcels to families in Blaina, a town in South Wales suffering the effects of economic recession. As a result, a bond was forged between the two Methodist communities. Now, hearing of the plight of Channel Island refugees, Methodists in Blaina sent £3 to their Jersey contact to purchase wool for making clothes.[25]

Wisely, therefore, Moore's appeals for practical assistance were not all one way. In December 1940 he encouraged refugees to knit clothing for Channel Islanders serving in the armed forces.[26] Moreover, in a move reminiscent of St Paul's collection among the Gentile churches, he urged Channel Islanders living in Britain to make a financial contribution to British Methodism on behalf of the Channel Islands District. Methodists in Jersey and Guernsey were known to be generous contributors to connexional funds but since 1940 the Methodist Church in Great Britain had not received any financial contributions from the Channel Islands because of the German Occupation. Again in February 1944 George Whitley wrote in the *Methodist Recorder* urging islanders resident in Britain to contribute to connexional funds on behalf of Methodists in Guernsey and Jersey. A benefactor was offering to match donations pound for pound towards a target of £957.[27] That the target was eventually exceeded reflects the loyalty that many Channel Island Methodists felt towards the mother church.

Aside from charitable motives, Moore's efforts to provide information, advice and clothing for Channel Island refugees were intended to strengthen links with Methodism. Writing in the *Methodist Recorder*, he suggested various other means to achieving the same end. In July 1940 he published an extract from a letter written by a refugee from Guernsey whose husband was still in the island. She and her children were billeted with a Methodist lady who was 'a great spiritual help'.[28] As he no doubt hoped would happen, a number of Methodists promptly wrote offering homes to Channel Island refugees with Methodist connections.[29] Occasionally, he reminded readers that Channel Island Methodists could make a useful contribution to Methodism in Britain. For instance, refugees attending a church near Weymouth had started a Sunday school for local children.[30] Above all, he urged refugees to form Channel Island Methodist Fellowships consisting of

up to a dozen people of all ages, including children, meeting weekly in homes or in the church vestry in order to share news and to discover how others were faring.[31] This was a variant of the traditional Methodist class meeting.

Paternalistic or not (and it would be anachronistic to judge by present standards), Moore's concern for the spiritual and material welfare of Channel Island refugees compares favourably with the indifferent attitude displayed by certain other parts of British Methodism. In July 1940, following the evacuation of large numbers from the Kent coast as well as from the Channel Islands, the *Methodist Recorder* ran an advertisement on behalf of the Women's Work section of the Methodist Missionary Society urging local church officers:

1. Watch for those who are temporarily changing homes and welcome them into the fellowship of Women's Work;
2. Arrange for the regular opening of the boxes of those that have been evacuated;
3. Distribute 'Women's Work' magazine to those who are subscribers.

It all depends on me and I depend on God.[32]

Clearly, whatever else they may have left behind, Methodist evacuees were expected to have kept hold of their Methodist Missionary Society collecting box. The advertisement makes no mention of any support that evacuees might need from their local church.

Another, more controversial, aspect of Moore's activities on behalf of Channel Island refugees had an overtly political purpose that ultimately proved unsuccessful in its aim to influence constitutional change in the islands. In a number of places refugees set up local societies to further their common interests. One of the largest and most vigorous was the Stockport and District Channel Islands Society, which even began publishing its own journal. Circulation increased until the *Channel Islands Monthly Review* became a national forum for news and debate amongst refugees. At the height of its popularity, the review claimed 8,500 subscribers throughout Britain.

Moore took a keen interest in the development of Channel Island societies, several of which met on Methodist premises.[33] In December 1940 he passed on hundreds of names and addresses to the Bristol Channel Islanders Association, which sought his assistance in contacting refugees.[34] In January 1942 he used his *Methodist Recorder* column to urge refugees to attend meetings of their nearest society and subscribe to the *Monthly Review*.[35] He

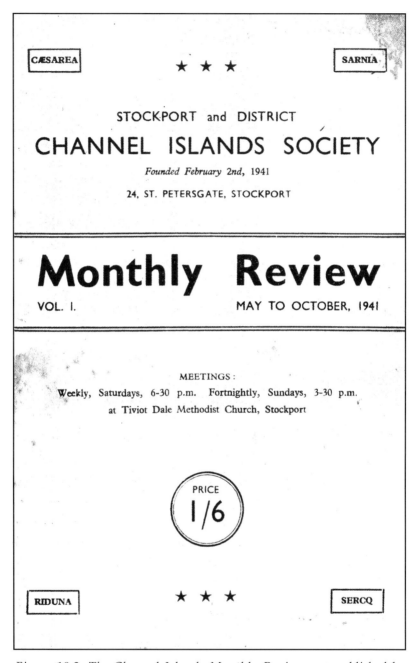

Figure 10.2: The Channel Islands Monthly Review was published by the Stockport and District Channel Islands Society (Courtesy Island Archives, Guernsey)

was a frequent speaker at such meetings where he was greeted as an old friend and praised for his efforts on behalf of refugees.[36]

In a lengthy editorial published in the *Channel Islands Monthly Review* in January 1942 Moore urged refugees to become actively involved in shaping the political future of the islands. After advising islanders not to expect to return home in the immediate future, he gave a pessimistic assessment of the likely economic situation in the islands at the end of the war when, he predicted, the German currency in circulation would be worthless. Refugees must therefore make sacrifices in order to save as much money as they could for their eventual return home. Meanwhile, the present situation created an unprecedented opportunity to campaign for constitutional reform that would lead to greater democracy in the administration of the Channel Islands after the war.

> You may be perfectly sure that there will be great changes also, not only in the business life, but in the social structure, and perhaps in the administration of the Islands. After such an upheaval it could hardly be otherwise. Do you realise the extent to which these changes have already taken place – especially in Guernsey? Does anyone imagine that when the war is over and the exiles return everything will slip back smoothly into its old place again, and go on just as before? I doubt it greatly. But if there are to be changes will they be for the better or the worse? ... I believe, without reserve, in democracy – *and therefore I come, quite deliberately, to the conclusion that it is now more important than it ever was that you should be good citizens; well-informed, intelligent, active and united.* Your influence will count greatly – perhaps decisively, if you are prepared to fulfil the necessary conditions.[37]

The target of Moore's attack was the 'don't want to be bothered attitude of mind' that he observed in many Channel Islanders who were more interested in a '"pubs and pictures" type of life' than being involved in the political process. To counter indifference, he hoped the Channel Island societies would be 'centres of enlightenment' fostering a sense of democratic citizenship rather than just a forum for the exchange of information or, worse still, a social club. Therefore, he welcomed news that 'efforts are now being made to federate all the local Societies'.

Such a federation, representing the interests of many thousands of Channel Island refugees, would have a powerful voice in any organised

campaign for constitutional change in the islands after their liberation. However, Moore made no mention of this in the reasons he advanced in favour of uniting the Channel Island societies: (1) to enable refugees to speak with a united voice; (2) 'remembering the chaos of evacuation' to represent the interests of refugees in dealings with the Government concerning their eventual return; and (3) to represent the legal interests of refugees in questions relating to property, contracts, rents, debts and income tax.

The reaction to Moore's politicking was mixed. A number of correspondents in the *Channel Islands Monthly Review* criticised him for being unduly pessimistic about the economic outlook, forecasting – accurately, as it turned out – that the Government would not see the islands ruined for the lack of a few million pounds' investment when it was spending vast sums on defeating Germany.[38] (At the Liberation, the British Government set a generous exchange rate in the islands so as to avoid economic collapse.) Several correspondents saw no need for a federation to defend their interests and would happily have endured a chaotic repatriation knowing they were returning home. One asked whether Moore was a true islander, since he 'lacks that cheerful optimistic courage which is inborn in the characters of my fellow islanders'. Others echoed Moore's concern about indifference to the political process and welcomed his call for greater democracy.

If Moore hoped his gloomy economic forecast for the Channel Islands would win support for the federation movement, on balance it probably had the opposite effect. To most neutral observers, Moore was so obviously alarmist that he must have a political axe to grind. The debate rumbled on for several more months. In August 1942, when the federation movement was already effectively dead in the water, a correspondent complained that people were 'still harping on Federation'.[39]

By this time, conservative voices or else common sense (depending on one's viewpoint) had mobilised to scupper the federation movement. To Victor Coysh, a prominent Guernseyman, a federation of Channel Island societies sounded innocuous enough, but he feared the real intention was to set up some kind of government-in-exile as several of the conquered European nations had done.[40] Since the island administrations had remained at their post, refugees should support their efforts on behalf of islanders. Coysh spoke for many in the Channel Islands' 'establishment' now resident in Britain for whom the prospect of a government-in-exile attempting to undermine the authority of the island parliaments was abhorrent.

The federation movement was finally vanquished in July 1942 at a tripartite conference involving delegates of the Channel Island societies,

representatives of the government-sponsored Channel Islands Refugee Committee and members of the Jersey Society (the latter consisting of prominent Channel Islanders resident in Britain before the evacuation) under the chairmanship of Jerseyman Sir Herbert du Parcq. Adopting a spoiling proposal from the Bristol society, it was unanimously agreed that the Channel Islands Refugee Committee would 'act as a central office for all such Societies in the United Kingdom'.[41]

Robbed of its *raison d'être*, the federation movement promptly collapsed, though a northern federation of Channel Island societies was later set up which enjoyed a tense relationship with the Refugee Committee. A conference organised by the northern federation in April 1945 attracted 400 delegates but no representatives from the Refugee Committee.[42] By this stage, the Refugee Committee was in an unassailable position as guardian of the interests of Channel Island refugees in Britain. As early as January 1943, members of the committee met with the Home Secretary, Ernest Bevin, and the Minister of Health to discuss issues of present and future concern to islanders.[43] Neither Moore nor anyone else associated with the federation movement was present.

Moore's attempt to influence island politics having failed, his interest in the Channel Island societies appears to have waned. His name fades from the pages of the *Channel Islands Monthly Review*, and his involvement with the societies became marginal, allowing Rev. George Whitley to maintain the link on behalf of Methodism. In January 1943 the BBC broadcast a service from St Martin-in-the-Fields, Trafalgar Square, in which Channel Islanders were specially remembered. The service was led by the Archbishop of York (a former bishop of Winchester in whose diocese the Channel Islands lie). Rev. George Whitley read one of the lessons.[44] In the summer of 1945 Whitley, rather than Moore, addressed a thanksgiving service for the Channel Island societies held at Westminster Central Hall.[45]

It would appear that Methodist leaders in Britain also grew weary of Moore's dabbling in Channel Island politics, though he was not without his supporters. In 1941 the Hull District Synod petitioned the Conference: 'In view of the special needs of Methodist Channel Island Refugees now resident in Great Britain, the Synod suggests that the Rev. R. Douglas Moore be set apart to have pastoral oversight of this large section of our Church now scattered throughout the Connexion.'[46] Not surprisingly, however, Methodist leaders were unwilling to take away pastoral oversight of Methodists from local ministers. Nor did they want to be seen encouraging constitutional reform in the Channel Islands. The Conference declined the Hull District's

suggestion.

Unable to sustain his mission to Channel Island refugees without the necessary support of the Conference, in September 1941 Moore was appointed superintendent of the Kent Mission with responsibility for 29 chapels – a post presumably intended to preclude extra-curricular activities. Whilst Moore had no intention of giving up his refugee work entirely, circuit responsibilities meant it had to be scaled back. The demise of his regular column in the *Methodist Recorder* tells its own story.

Moore's first article in the *Methodist Recorder* in six months was published in January 1942; the next did not appear until the following September, and this proved to be the last. Nevertheless, despite some loss of momentum, Moore continued with his welfare activities on behalf of refugees. The largest room in the manse was used to store clothing that was still arriving in response to earlier appeals and which he continued to distribute. There were also visits to Channel Island societies and Methodist churches around the country. For instance, in January 1943 he addressed Methodists in Wisbeach on the subject of Channel Island refugees before receiving a generous donation for his work.[47]

In fact, by the end of 1942 the need for practical assistance for Channel Island refugees had greatly diminished, thanks largely to the efforts of the Channel Islands Refugee Committee, which could provide far greater assistance than Moore with his limited resources and contacts could ever have done. Even so, in the months immediately following the evacuation Moore demonstrated how a small voluntary organisation could make a difference to the lives of refugees. To what extent he succeeded in fulfilling his main objective of strengthening Methodist identity amongst the refugees is difficult to say since there are no statistics to evaluate. Inevitably, many Channel Islanders were lost to Methodism as a result of being in unfamiliar surroundings without the subtle pressures to conform to ingrained church-going habits. Still, there were those who found spiritual fellowship in Methodist congregations in Britain which sustained them until they were eventually able to return to their home churches.

Deportation

The deportation in September 1942 of nearly 2,000 British-born civilians to internment camps in Germany in reprisal for Britain's internment of a similar number of Germans in Iran caused great alarm. In Guernsey and in Jersey the civilian administration protested against this violation of the German undertaking that, in the event of their peaceful surrender, the lives of the

inhabitants were guaranteed. However, since the orders came from Berlin, there was little room for manoeuvre.

The prospect of the majority of active clergy being deported to Germany created a crisis for the churches. In Guernsey, after urgent negotiations with the German authorities, the President of the Controlling Committee, John Leale, announced to an anxious gathering of clergy that a total of thirteen ministers across all denominations would be allowed to stay. The ten Church of England parishes were left in the care of five retired Anglican priests over seventy years of age plus two Guernsey-born and one French priest.[48] With Flint, Ord and Romeril all scheduled for deportation, Methodism in Guernsey would have to rely on Beaugié and Foss. In Jersey Fell, South, Skyrme, Scott and Mylne were eligible for deportation.

In Guernsey Beaugié wrote to the German authorities asking that his colleagues 'be permitted to continue their work amongst us [....] in the highest interests of our Island'.[49] Whether or not this had any effect, some were reprieved. As the leader of Methodism in the Channel Islands, Flint learned that he was exempt from deportation. However, he immediately volunteered to go to Germany so that he could minister to those deported. Romeril successfully appealed against deportation, presumably because the Germans valued his work at the labour office. When Rev. John Scott in Jersey received his deportation order he called together his congregation for a prayer service 'characterized by confidence, hope and joy'.[50] The order was later rescinded. For reasons that are not entirely clear, none of the other Methodist ministers in Jersey were deported.

Douglas Ord was stunned to receive his deportation order ('a dreadful blow') but resigned himself to the inevitable.[51] However, a few days later Beaugié phoned to say that Ord and his wife would not, after all, be deported. Rev. Donald Stuart from Jersey was to be deported in his place. On arriving in St Peter Port from Jersey that morning, Stuart was informed that he must register for deportation because he was born in Britain.[52] Beaugié managed to persuade the German authorities that if Stuart was to be deported in any event then it should be as a clergyman. Beaugié watched as Ord's name was deleted from the list and that of Stuart added.[53]

Marie Ozanne, the Salvation Army officer who defiantly preached in uniform after the organisation was suppressed, also tried to volunteer for deportation.[54] Her offer was rejected – the German authorities rightly suspecting that she would prove even more troublesome in an internment camp.

Even if few went so far as to volunteer, clergy generally resigned

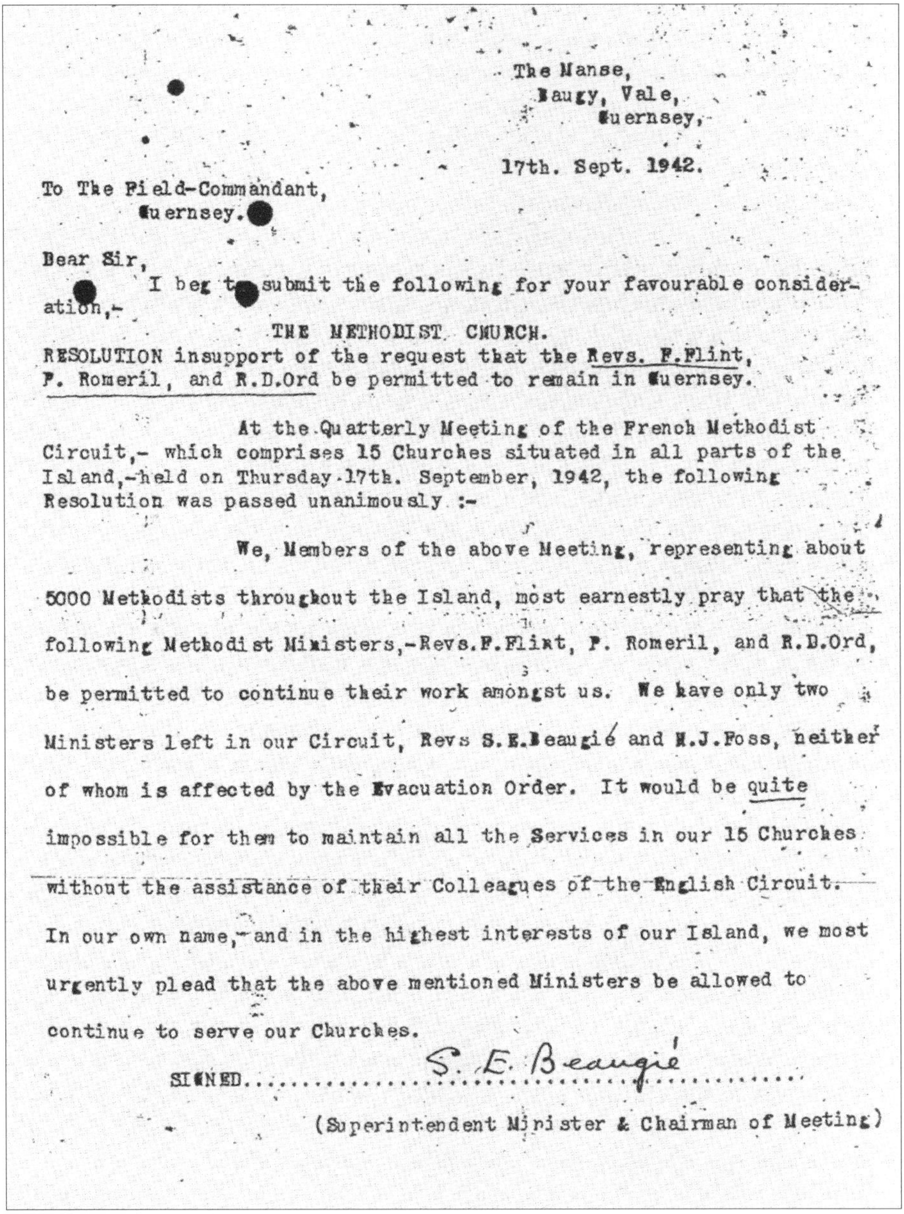

The Manse,
Baugy, Vale,
Guernsey,

17th. Sept. 1942.

To The Field-Commandant,
Guernsey.

Dear Sir,

I beg to submit the following for your favourable consideration,-

THE METHODIST CHURCH.

RESOLUTION in support of the request that the Revs. F.Flint, F. Romeril, and R.D.Ord be permitted to remain in Guernsey.

At the Quarterly Meeting of the French Methodist Circuit,- which comprises 15 Churches situated in all parts of the Island,-held on Thursday 17th. September, 1942, the following Resolution was passed unanimously :-

We, Members of the above Meeting, representing about 5000 Methodists throughout the Island, most earnestly pray that the following Methodist Ministers,-Revs.F.Flint, F. Romeril, and R.D.Ord, be permitted to continue their work amongst us. We have only two Ministers left in our Circuit, Revs S.E.Beaugié and H.J.Foss, neither of whom is affected by the Evacuation Order. It would be quite impossible for them to maintain all the Services in our 15 Churches without the assistance of their Colleagues of the English Circuit. In our own name,- and in the highest interests of our Island, we most urgently plead that the above mentioned Ministers be allowed to continue to serve our Churches.

SIGNED.............. *S. E. Beaugié* ....

(Superintendent Minister & Chairman of Meeting)

Figure 10.3: Letter of Rev. Sidney Beaugié to German Commandant appealing against the deportation of Methodist ministers in Guernsey (Courtesy of Island Archives, Guernsey)

184

themselves to the fact that deportation presented an opportunity to minister to those in the same position. Exceptionally, Rev. Edwin Foley of Spurgeon Memorial Baptist Church in St Peter Port wrote to the Commandant asking that he and his wife might be spared deportation on grounds of age and because he was the only English-speaking Baptist minister in the island. He added a confidential postscript that was ingratiating and unpatriotic:

> Though I am English born, I am very, very sorry for all the wrong which I believe England has done to Germany. I was not in favour of England declaring war on Germany in 1914, and got into some trouble for saying so.
>
> I believe the Treaty of Versailles was iniquitous (*löse*) and did much wrong to Germany.
>
> I often said, too, that I thought the Allied blockade of Germany during the long months of the so-called Peace Conference in 1918-19 was very wicked, and I was not in favour of England declaring war on Germany in 1939.
>
> For nearly forty years I have tried hard to foster friendly relations with Germany and a saner policy. I know that some English-speaking people in Guernsey and many in England think and feel as I do, but unfortunately we have been and at present are in a minority – the propaganda forces have been too strong for us.[55]

Foley and his wife were allowed to stay, but for the majority there was no reprieve, though several wrote poignant letters seeking exemption, and a handful committed suicide rather than face internment.[56] At Les Camps in the Guernsey and Sark (French) Circuit, Ken Lewis observed a group of Methodists after the morning service leaving for the harbour to be deported: 'it was a heartbreaking scene though everyone present was very brave to the last.'[57] At the Rohais church, harvest goods of fruit and vegetables were handed over to the civilian authorities for the benefit of the deportees.[58]

In the event, the situation of those interned in Germany was not as bad as was at first feared, and in the final months of the war may actually have been better in some respects than in Jersey and Guernsey. Channel Islanders were grouped together in one of three internment camps in Bavaria where they enjoyed limited freedom and were safe from the danger of Allied bombing. The camps were run by benign local officials, who often did their best to make conditions as tolerable as possible. Unaccompanied men were

housed in the castle at Laufen; married couples, families and single women were accommodated in the castle at Würzach or in a former prisoner of war camp at Biberach. Conditions were tolerable, and the International Red Cross and YMCA made regular visits. It was even possible to communicate with families at home.

With the permission of the camp authorities, clergy lost no time in arranging Sunday services. On the first Sunday following the deportation, some 350 people attended a service in Würzach led by Rev. Cecil Atyeo, rector of St Luke's, Jersey. According to Joan Coles, who was to become a regular attendee at camp services, 'Many tears were shed when prayers were read for "absent friends".'[59]

Services of Holy Communion were held in the makeshift chapel using vessels obtained from the nearby village church. The main Christian festivals were also observed. At Christmas, thanks to the generosity of the local Roman Catholic priest, the chapel was decorated with a crib and Holy Child; the simple wooden altar 'was complete with hand-embroidered altar linen and exquisite vessels'.[60] Between 50 and 60 people received holy communion at Christmas – rather fewer than the number attending the carol service. The Easter schedule gives the impression of a typical Anglican parish church. On Good Friday a service was held at which a small choir sang. On Easter Day Anglican communion services were held at 7.00am and 10.30am with Evensong at 6.30pm.[61]

Clergy occasionally conducted baptisms and funerals. Over a period of 30 months at Würzach there was one infant baptism and seven funerals, including a service for a child that died of meningitis.[62] Burials were permitted in the local churchyard. Whether perhaps they sensed the end of the war was approaching and wished to appear benevolent, in 1944 the camp authorities allowed an Armistice Day service to be held.

Donald Stuart, his wife and daughter were interned at Biberach. In February 1943 he wrote to friends in England informing them that he had 'volunteered to accompany a party of deportees to Germany'.[63] Soon after, his brother learned that Stuart was the only Free Church minister in the camp and that he was conducting services twice on Sundays. He had even started a Sunday school and was running a midweek women's meeting. During the week, he taught several subjects at the day school organised by internees.[64] Three Anglican priests were also interned in Biberach. One or other of them took turns to conduct Sunday services, and a Roman Catholic priest from the village visited fortnightly to say Mass.[65] At Easter internees were permitted to attend Mass at the adjacent convent.[66]

As an unaccompanied man (his wife evacuated to England in June 1940), Flint was interned in Laufen along with four Anglican clergy. Hartley Jackson and another priest were soon transferred to prisoner of war camps to become chaplains, leaving Flint and two Anglican priests to share the duties of leading Sunday worship. Unfortunately, few details of these have survived, though presumably arrangements were similar to those in other camps. According to Ambrose Sherwill, camp senior, evening services were 'attractive and well attended'; at harvest the chapel was decorated with flowers and 'fruits of the earth', which were later donated to the local hospital in gratitude for the care given to patients from the camp.[67]

A dynamic character and natural leader, Flint was placed in charge of a dormitory of 60 men. In July 1943 he was elected by internees to the camp senior's advisory council – an unofficial court handling disciplinary cases amongst the men.[68] Many years later, Sherwill acknowledged with gratitude the ministry of 'Padres Gerhold, Flint and Leedham' during the long internment at Laufen.[69]

In February 1943 a further round of deportations from the Channel Islands was ordered to make up for a shortfall in the original quota. Among those deported were several native islanders described by the Germans as 'undesirables', including Rev. Henry Foss.[70] Why Foss was deported as an undesirable has never been established, though it was probably due to his outspokenness in the pulpit. He was widely known to have criticised the personal morality of several high-ranking German officers. Beaugié and Ord both appealed against his deportation but without success.[71]

Despite his poor health, Foss was deported along with his frail elderly wife and daughter. They were interned at Compiègne near Paris for four months before being sent

Figure 10.4: Rev. Henry Foss, photographed in 1941 for identity card
(Courtesy of Island Archives, Guernsey)

Ministers now residing outside the
Circuit.

Rev. GEORGE WHITLEY,
ENGLAND.

Rev. FREDERICK FLINT,
GERMANY.

Rev. DONALD STUART,
GERMANY.

Supernumeraries.

Rev. F. J. PAINE,
"Calumet," Les Blanche Pierres, St. Martin's.

Rev. A. BERNARD BROCKWAY, B.A., B.D.,
Hendford, St. Martin's.

Rev. JOHN LEALE, M.A., Ormond, St. Sampson's.

*Figure 10.5: Notice printed in the Guernsey (English) Circuit
plan after the deportation of ministers* (Author's Collection)

to Biberach in June 1943. Although suffering from high blood pressure, Foss assisted Stuart in ministering to the camp's Nonconformists, regularly conducting worship and leading evening prayers.[72] Fellow internees in both camps later remembered with gratitude his 'faithful ministry'.[73]

Like everyone else, clergy were subject to the stress created by the close confinement of several hundred people in conditions where enforced inactivity generated boredom, petty quarrels and depression. Flint, Stuart and Foss all suffered under the strain of performing ministerial duties and mediating in disputes between internees which in the circumstances assumed disproportionate importance and threatened to undermine the equilibrium of the camp. Stuart's health deteriorated to such an extent that he and his wife were included in a batch of 212 Channel Island internees repatriated to England in March 1945.[74] Others were less fortunate. In Würzach Cecil Atyeo, exhausted by the strains of ministry, succumbed to illness and died in February 1945. A large congregation attended his funeral in the camp chapel. His body was buried in the village cemetery.[75]

Besides religious activities, efforts to maintain morale by staving off boredom included self-improving education. Emblazoned across the 'Education Syllabus for Winter 1943/44' at Laufen was the imperative: 'Time drags! Spend it wisely! Invest in Yourself! Join a class!' There was no shortage of classes either, in subjects as diverse as art appreciation, commercial arithmetic and comparative religion, as well as five foreign languages. The education officer hoped to be able to commence classes in anatomy, physiology, ancient Greek history, architecture, structural engineering, elocution and Latin. Certificates would be issued for proficiency in the subject and regular attendance at classes. The brochure promised that letters would be dispatched to various institutions, including London University, the Royal Society of Arts and the London Chamber of Commerce, for permission to hold examinations in the camp.[76] The YMCA in Geneva provided a library of 1,500 books so that internees could study.[77]

Superficially, the weekly programme of education, entertainment and Sunday worship might convey the impression that Channel Islanders' experience of internment in Germany was little worse than attending a particularly austere boarding school. However, despite efforts to maintain morale, life in the camps was unremittingly dreary, debilitating in body, mind and spirit, and tinged with tragedy. When the Allies finally overran the internment camps towards the end of April 1945 the internees' undoubted joy was tempered by concern for the situation in the Channel Islands where the Germans were still firmly in control.

Chapter 11

Liberation

Following the reinforcement of the German garrison in the Channel Islands in 1941 and the construction of major defences, the British Government concluded that retaking the islands by force was not a viable option since the loss of civilian life resulting from a full-scale assault would be unacceptably high. The Channel Islands would be liberated only after Germany had surrendered – a distant prospect until the fortunes of war eventually began to turn in the middle of 1943. Ironically, because of their strategic irrelevance and the high density of civilians in close proximity to military establishments, the Channel Islands became one of the safest places in Europe, virtually immune from serious Allied attack. Along with millions of others in the German-occupied territories, islanders pinned their hopes for liberation on the promised Second Front.

The Allied invasion of northwest Europe on 6 June 1944 encouraged Channel Islanders for the first time to believe that their liberation might be at hand. In Guernsey Douglas Ord heard the drone of Allied aircraft on a massive scale on the night of 5/6 June and realised straightaway that the invasion was underway.[1] Next morning, German soldiers wearing full battle order were much in evidence, frenziedly preparing to repel an attack expected imminently. When islanders learned that the Allies were as close as Normandy most imagined it would not be long before the German garrison was forced to withdraw from the Channel Islands or face being marooned as British and American forces advanced deep into France. The following Sunday Ord took as the biblical text for his sermon John 12.23: 'The hour has come.'[2]

Reflecting the general mood of optimism, Methodists began to plan for the cessation of hostilities. In September 1944 the Guernsey and Sark (French) Circuit set up a committee to make arrangements for a service of thanksgiving to mark the island's liberation.[3] The local preachers had already proposed a service be held on the day after the island was freed.[4]

190

Posters advertising the thanksgiving service would be displayed outside every church in the circuit as soon as news of liberation was received; if time permitted, a notice would be placed in the newspaper. Not to be outdone by Guernsey, Methodists on Sark made their own arrangements for a thanksgiving service on the day of liberation. The lay pastor and a church steward were deputed to prepare an order of service, which was to include a collection for the Red Cross.[5] Discreetly, churches in the Guernsey (English) Circuit also began to prepare for the island's liberation.[6] At Brock Road, the organist had been actively planning for the end of hostilities since February 1943.[7]

In Jersey, planning for the liberation of the island began shortly before the Normandy landings. In May 1944, with uncanny prescience, the Free Church ministers' meeting considered how best to mark the end of hostilities in Europe. This was the first time the subject had arisen in that forum since the beginning of the Occupation, and why it was aired on this occasion is not clear since the war news provided no special grounds for optimism. For whatever reason, the Baptist minister, S.J. Smurthwaite, proposed that the Free Churches of Jersey arrange a united service of thanksgiving to commemorate the island's liberation. However, the Methodist ministers present received the proposal with little enthusiasm, believing that most churches would want to make their own arrangements. Besides, no single venue was large enough to accommodate the congregation that could be expected to attend on such a momentous occasion.[8] Instead it was decided that there would be a number of simultaneous united services for Nonconformists at various locations throughout the island. An order of service was commissioned.

Two days after the Allied invasion of Normandy, a timely quarterly meeting of the Jersey (Grove Place) Circuit 'resolved that a committee be appointed to arrange special thanksgiving services on termination of hostilities'.[9] A few days later, the Jersey (Great Union Road) Circuit also established a committee to plan a thanksgiving service for the evening of the island's liberation or the following day.[10] Later these arrangements were incorporated into the island-wide programme of thanksgiving services for Nonconformists.

However, it soon became apparent that plans to mark the liberation were premature since German forces were preparing for a long siege. From September 1944 onwards the Channel Islands were cut off from the outside world as the Allies advanced southwards and eastwards through France towards Germany. Apart from radio, the only means of communication with

Germany was by hazardous night flights at low level over Allied-occupied territory. Yet the garrison stubbornly held on, despite near starvation conditions.

As the British Government had always intended, besieged islanders would be obliged to wait until the very end of the war in Europe before they were liberated. Only on 8 May 1945, Victory in Europe (VE) Day, were British forces finally able to commence surrender negotiations with representatives of the German Commandant of the Channel Islands, Vice-Admiral Huffmeier, a fanatical Nazi. Under pressure from Dönitz, Huffmeier surrendered the islands unconditionally in the early hours of the following morning. Amidst jubilant scenes, British forces began disembarking in Guernsey and in Jersey on 9 May 1945, Liberation Day.

In an emotional speech to islanders on VE Day, the Bailiff of Jersey declared his 'earnest wish that services should be held in all places of worship in the same manner as services are being held in the United Kingdom and in other parts of the Empire'.[11] Churches hardly needed any encouragement: longstanding plans were immediately put into effect or else arrangements were hastily improvised.

With impeccable timing, First Tower Methodist Church placed a newspaper advertisement on 5 May (carefully worded to get round the German censor) announcing that the choir would perform a special programme of 'Topical and Popular Hymns reflecting the Present Situation – National, Social and World Peace Hymns' on the evening of Wednesday 9 May.

For Anglicans and Roman Catholics, the church calendar provided a ready-made occasion to mark the Liberation. The day after British forces landed was the Feast of the Ascension, and Anglican and Roman Catholic parish churches were due to hold services. These were quickly adapted to take account of the Liberation. Services on the first Sunday after the Liberation became occasions for special thanksgiving, and many churches held collections for the Red Cross.

The Jersey Free Church Council's united services of thanksgiving for the Liberation were held simultaneously in nine different Methodist churches throughout the island on the evening of Friday 11 May – a feat of organisation that would not have been possible without many weeks of planning.[12] In St Helier a service was held at Grove Place church led by Rev. William Ward.[13]

In both islands feelings were running high as pent up emotions were released. Civic leaders feared an outpouring of hostility towards the defeated enemy and those islanders whose behaviour was judged, rightly or wrongly,

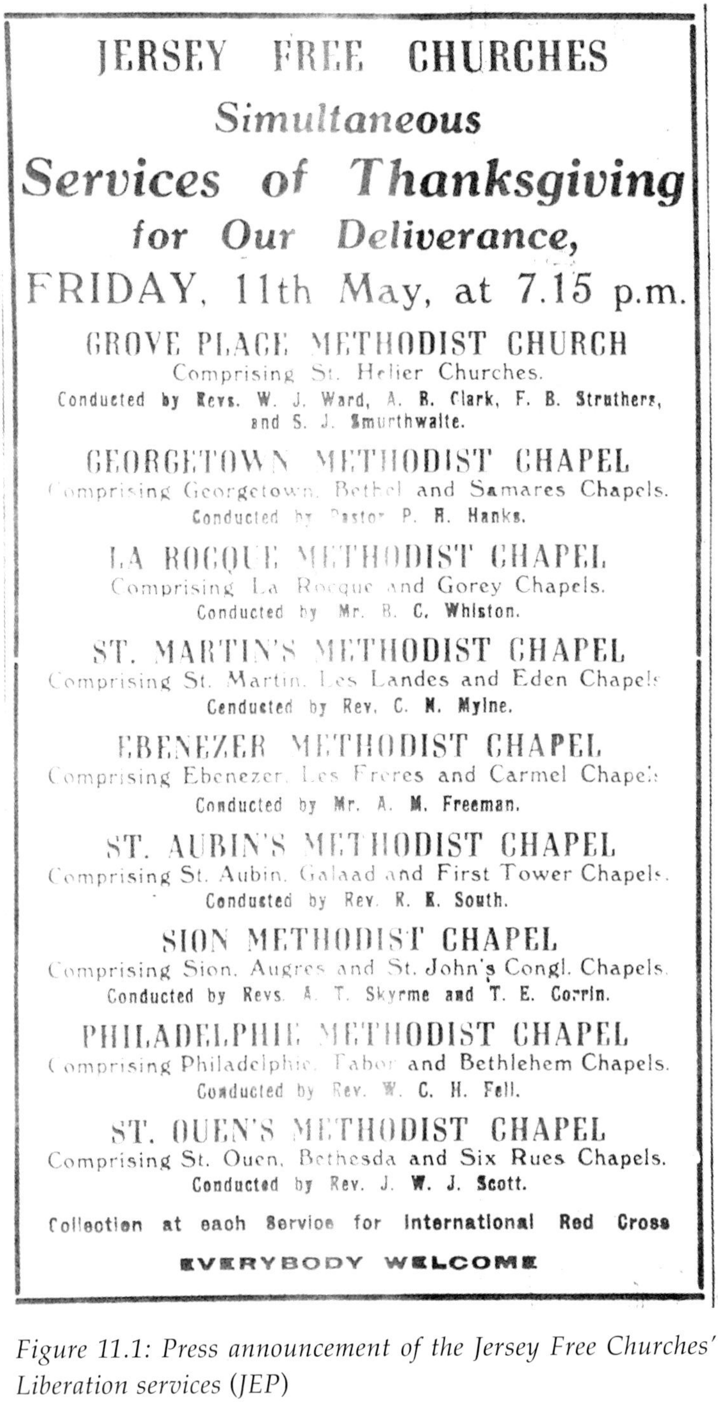

JERSEY FREE CHURCHES

Simultaneous

Services of Thanksgiving
for Our Deliverance,
FRIDAY, 11th May, at 7.15 p.m.

GROVE PLACE METHODIST CHURCH
Comprising St. Helier Churches.
Conducted by Revs. W. J. Ward, A. R. Clark, F. B. Struthers,
and S. J. Smurthwalte.

GEORGETOWN METHODIST CHAPEL
Comprising Georgetown, Bethel and Samares Chapels.
Conducted by Pastor P. H. Hanks.

LA ROCQUE METHODIST CHAPEL
Comprising La Rocque and Gorey Chapels.
Conducted by Mr. R. C. Whiston.

ST. MARTIN'S METHODIST CHAPEL
Comprising St. Martin, Les Landes and Eden Chapels
Conducted by Rev. C. N. Mylne.

EBENEZER METHODIST CHAPEL
Comprising Ebenezer, Les Freres and Carmel Chapels
Conducted by Mr. A. M. Freeman.

ST. AUBIN'S METHODIST CHAPEL
Comprising St. Aubin, Galaad and First Tower Chapels.
Conducted by Rev. R. K. South.

SION METHODIST CHAPEL
Comprising Sion, Augres and St. John's Congl. Chapels.
Conducted by Revs. A. T. Skyrme and T. E. Corrin.

PHILADELPHIE METHODIST CHAPEL
Comprising Philadelphie, Tabor and Bethlehem Chapels.
Conducted by Rev. W. C. H. Fell.

ST. OUEN'S METHODIST CHAPEL
Comprising St. Ouen, Bethesda and Six Rues Chapels.
Conducted by Rev. J. W. J. Scott.

Collection at each Service for International Red Cross

EVERYBODY WELCOME

*Figure 11.1: Press announcement of the Jersey Free Churches'
Liberation services (JEP)*

to have been unpatriotic. In Guernsey, even before the Liberation, a group styling itself the Guernsey Underground Barbers was threatening to shave the heads of 'jerrybags' as soon as the opportunity arose. Against this backdrop, thanksgiving services afforded an opportunity for more sober reflection on the Occupation.

The printed order of service for the Jersey Free Churches' service of thanksgiving is both dignified and restrained. The opening statement sets the tone for what follows:

We are gathered here today to give thanks for our Liberation from foreign occupation on 9 May 1945. We thank God for the Peace which came to Europe then and pray that it may grow from more to more. We shall hold in our memory those who laid down their lives or made great sacrifices to win our freedom and we shall pray that we may use worthily the great opportunities which are now ours. From this Thanksgiving let there be born a new consecration to the cause of brotherhood, righteousness and faith.[14]

The prayers of thanksgiving address obvious themes: for those who opened their homes to evacuees; for 'the friendliness and willing service of the liberating forces'; for the International Red Cross and the aid it provided. Members of the congregation were then invited to look to the future.

For this new era of Liberty, with its larger opportunities of service to one another and to all men:
Pray that peace and righteousness may grow from more to more, that men may practice goodwill to one another, that, by the power of Thy Gospel we may cast out want, unjustice [sic] and bitterness, pride and cruelty, and that Christ the Prince of Peace may reign in our midst.
[Pray that] our hearts may be cleansed from selfishness and that we may have a greater part in the coming of Thy Kingdom. Lead us to the Cross of Christ that we may listen to his words and repent of our sin and receive Thy Holy Spirit.
Grant unto our leaders and to those who train young people special grace and wisdom. Enable us all in our Island life to overcome evil with good. Endue us with strength from on high to build a community wherein dwelleth righteousness, where Thy will shall be done with gladness and Thy name be our Everlasting Refuge.

The liturgy is devoid of triumphalism or recrimination. While the former occupying forces are not specifically mentioned, neither are they demonised. Instead, the focus of attention is on islanders and the future. Members of the congregation are invited to repent of their sins prior to 'consecrating' themselves in the pursuit of 'brotherhood'. The inclusion of prayers for young people probably reflects a perennial concern for the spiritual welfare of a rising generation, coupled in this case with awareness that life in the post-war world would be more complicated than ever before.

In Guernsey Douglas Ord and his wife chose to celebrate the Liberation quietly at home with friends by opening a tin of nectarines, carefully preserved during five long years for this very day.[15] Ord had more reason than most to feel bitter towards the German people, who had twice robbed him of his liberty. Yet he considered it essential for British people to develop a good relationship with the former enemy as the basis for enduring peace. Likewise, he could not bring himself to condemn islanders whose behaviour during the Occupation was judged to have been unpatriotic. Unlike the hotheads out for revenge, he harboured no resentment against women who had formed relationships with German soldiers. As Ord saw it, 'girls with German babies will have their own burdens to bear long after public feeling has cooled.'[16]

Thus it was in reflective mood that Ord sat down to write the final entry in his Occupation diary, dated 12 May 1945. Characteristically, the journal ends with a heartfelt prayer that displays remarkable generosity of spirit:

O God, whose mercies are numberless and beyond our deserts, cleanse our hearts of a facile hatred, that, at this time we may do justly, love mercy, and walk humbly with Thee. Forgive us, if, in our sorrows, we have given way to bitterness and forgotten Thy love. May those now leaving our Island have cause to remember not our frailty nor our unworthiness, but such character and goodness as we would that men should perceive in us, that in the days to come there may be healing and not strife. And this we ask in the Name of Jesus Christ our common Lord and Saviour. Amen.

An appendix to Ord's diary contains a copy of an entry made by a German army chaplain in the visitors' book at St Sampson's parish church at the close of a service held by members of the occupying forces on the eve of the Liberation:

May 8. End of War:
I express my thanks for all the love of Christ which has come down to us in this House of God during our stay in Guernsey. I pray that the Lord may lead the world towards the Eternal Goal of His Heavenly Kingdom and establish peace higher than all human understanding. Jesus Christ is the same, yesterday, today and forever.

Significantly, the padre took as the biblical text for his sermon Hosea 6.1: 'Let us return unto the Lord, for He has torn us; He will heal us; He has wounded; He will bind us up.' Belatedly, many Germans were beginning to realise the true nature of National Socialism.

On 16 May, exactly one week after the Liberation, Ord gave the address at a 'Service of Remembrance and Thanksgiving' held at Brock Road church. More of a lecture than a sermon, the address was later published in pamphlet form.[17]

Ord's address begins with a survey of German militarism and the rise of National Socialism before referring briefly to the Occupation. Aware of the criticisms that some islanders were openly voicing against their own leaders, he reminded the congregation of 'the burden which has lain upon those whose public utterances might so easily be distorted by Quislings, of whom we have had a number to our shame'. Could perhaps the clergy have spoken out more against injustices during the Occupation? Disarmingly, he admits that 'It has not been at all easy during these five years to speak the truth of God in public when even the walls had ears.'

Rather than dwell on past events, however, Ord turns his attention to the future. At a time when many in Guernsey were saying that 'the only good German is one that is either disarmed or dead', Ord was anxious to avoid recriminations against the German people as a whole. As a sign of hope, he refers to 'a great rally of Youth of the Allied Nations' broadcast by the BBC a few days earlier in which a young German speaker was introduced 'as representing *the other Germany*'. For Ord, this was a timely reminder that not all Germans were Nazis. The downfall of the Hitler regime had also liberated many anti-Nazis within the German population. The German opposition included men like Martin Niemöller 'whose resistance to the Nazis has struck the world's imagination'. From his own contacts with the German opposition Ord had acquired respect for the Confessing Church in Germany. 'Not in vain have the martyrs of the Church of Christ in Germany these dozen years past shed their blood or ended their days in bestial camps. They were faithful unto death and the seed they have sown will bear fruit in due season.'

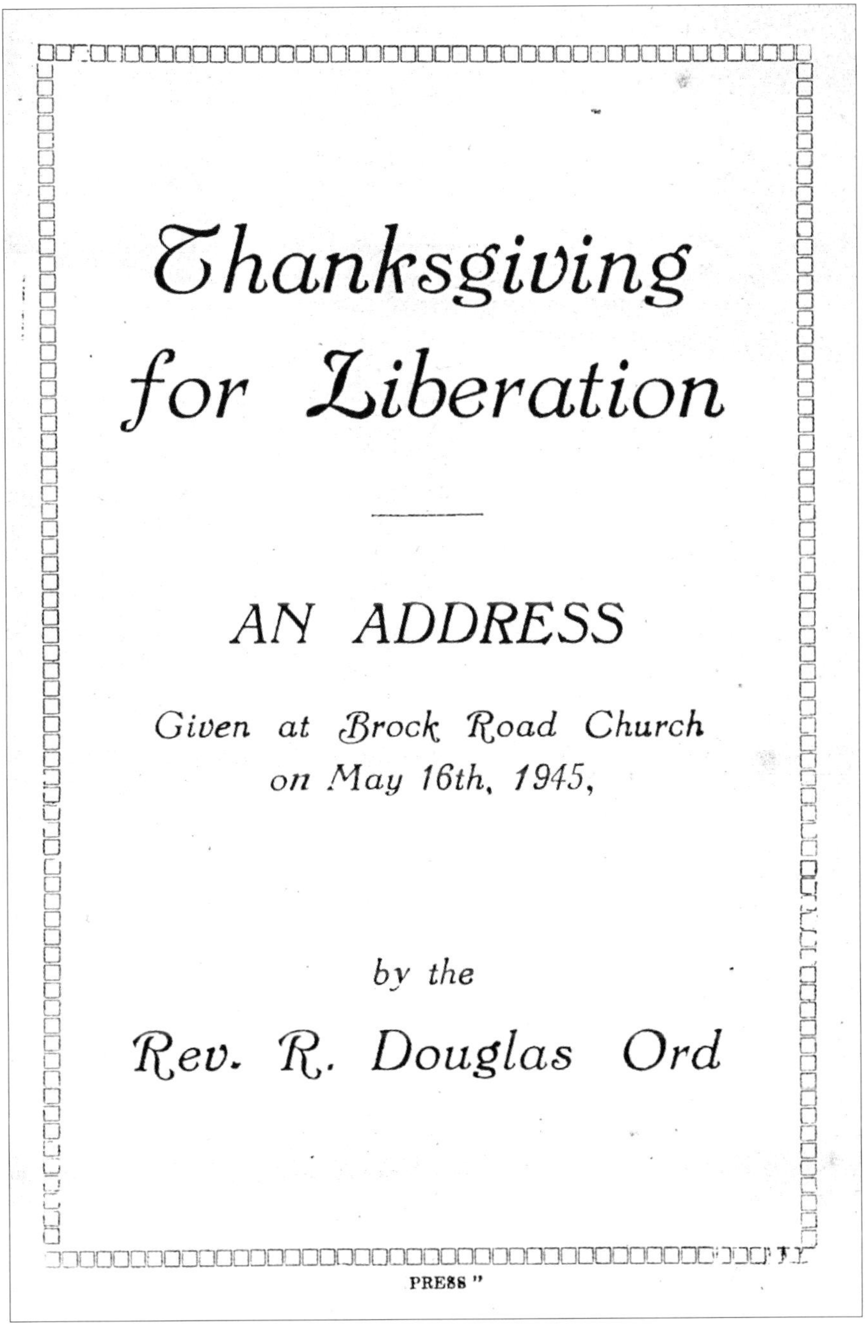

Thanksgiving
for Liberation

AN ADDRESS

Given at Brock Road Church
on May 16th, 1945,

by the

Rev. R. Douglas Ord

PRESS "

Figure 11.2: Ord's address at the Liberation service for Guernsey's Nonconformists was later published (Author's Collection)

Service of Remembrance & Thanksgiving

Peace celebrations in Guernsey, so far as nonconformist interests were concerned, culminated in a special service of Remembrance and Thanksgiving held at Brock Road Church on Wednesday, May 16th at 7.30pm. The programme was carried out under the presidency of Revd R.D. Ord who gave a stirring address. He was supported by Augmented Choirs who rendered the programme enclosed. A special extra item was the Unison Song given by the School Choir, a capable group under the control of Misses Mary Le Lacheur & Molly Winterflood. One innovation was the poem "For the Fallen" (Laurence Binyon) effectively and dramatically recited by Miss Mary Le Lacheur. The offertory was given over to Red Cross Funds, the amount being £24.10.8. Programmes for choir use were kindly provided by Mr. C.H. Butt. Floral decoration was carried into effect by Misses Rougier, Nightingale and Mr. W. Mauger.

Figure 11.3: Handwritten souvenir of the Liberation service at Brock Road church, 16 May 1945 (Herbert White Collection)

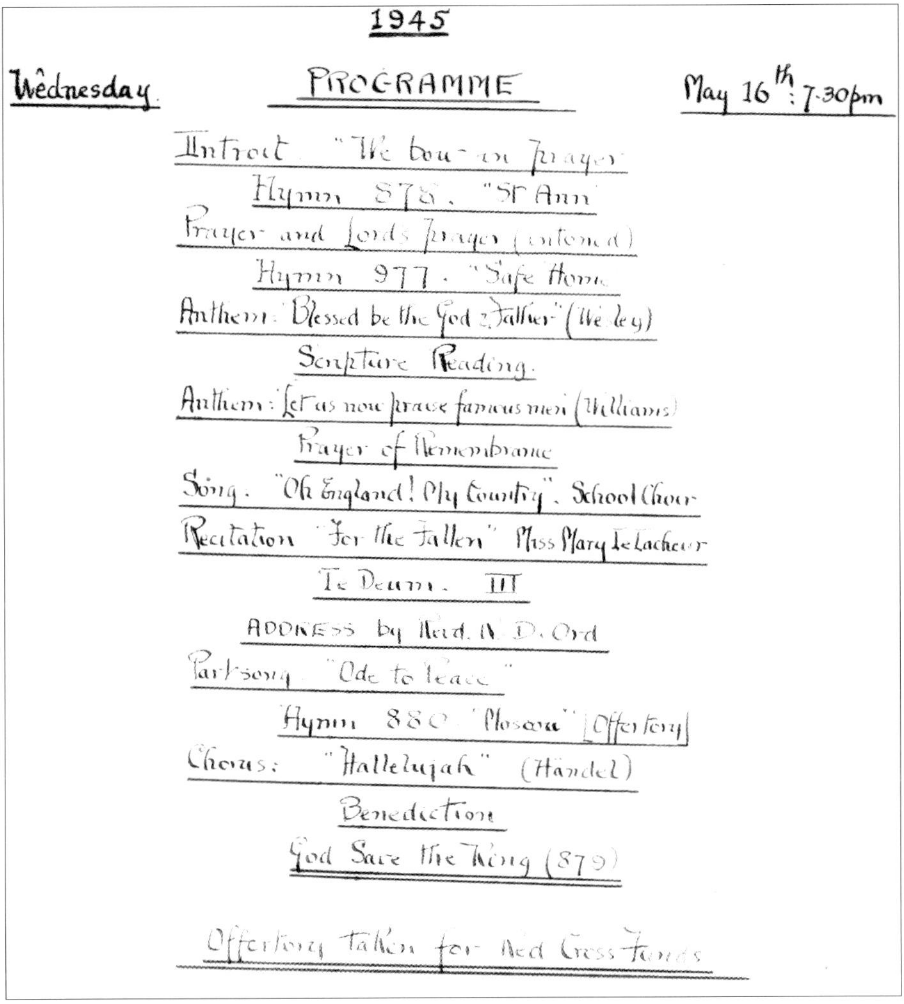

<u>**1945**</u>

Wednesday   <u>PROGRAMME</u   May 16th 7.30pm

Introit   "We bow in prayer"
Hymn   878. "St Ann"
Prayer and Lords prayer (intoned)
Hymn   977. "Safe Home"
Anthem: Blessed be the God & Father" (We beg)
Scripture Reading.
Anthem: Let us now praise famous men (Williams)
Prayer of Remembrance
Song. "Oh England! My Country". School Choir
Recitation "For the Fallen" Miss Mary Le Lacheur
Te Deum.   III
ADDRESS by Revd. N. D. Ord
Part-song "Ode to Peace"
Hymn   880 "Blossom" Offertory
Chorus: "Hallelujah" (Handel)
Benediction
God Save the King (879)

Offertory taken for Red Cross Funds

Figure 11.4: Programme for the Liberation service held at Brock Road church, 16 May 1945 (Herbert White Collection)

Mindful that the rise of Hitler had its origins in a punitive peace treaty imposed on Germany after the First World War, Ord reflected on the challenge of establishing lasting peace in Europe.

Before us now lie the problems of the peace, more intricate and subtle, difficult of solution, perhaps, and fragile. In what spirit do we approach this final testing of our national character? It is easy now to be patriotic and shout with the crowd. It is hard to be just and

199

honourable, even to the foe now rapidly being conducted from our shores. We have need of strong guidance. Where shall we find it? Let Mr Churchill speak again: 'We shall not in the hour of victory lose our poise and balance, nor strain our victorious arms with deeds of shame.' May our people be given grace to fulfil that noble pledge.

What is striking about Ord's address is its stand against anti-German sentiment in Guernsey. Ord goes out of his way to exonerate the German population of blame for the crimes of National Socialism. Yet he was hardly justified in absolving German people of all responsibility for National Socialism. His romantic description of the Confessing Church ignores the fact that the vast majority of Christians in Germany, including Martin Niemöller, considered it their duty to support the state when war broke out in 1939.[18] Equally, his account of German militarism glosses over civilian acquiescence in the dismantling of the law in Nazi Germany in the years before the Second World War. Judge Gunkel and others like him may have bemoaned the demise of justice in Nazi Germany but they saw themselves primarily as victims and did little to protest against the attack on civilised human values.

Given the strength of anti-German sentiment in the Channel Islands following the Liberation, it is understandable that Ord should try to defuse tensions by portraying the German population in a sympathetic light. By drawing attention to 'the problems of the peace', he encouraged islanders to look to the future instead of the past. He also contrived to give Churchill's words Christian content and an individual slant by appealing to the grace of God. The fact his address was subsequently published suggests it was valued within the Nonconformist community. Leaving aside his credulous description of the Confessing Church in Germany, Ord deserves credit for his lack of triumphalism in the moment of victory.

Of course, Ord was not alone in believing that lasting peace in Europe required a commitment to reconciliation and a willingness to forego retribution. Ordinary voices were saying the same, though these were seldom recorded for posterity. At Les Camps Sunday school on the first Sunday of 1945 the superintendent told the children to be 'on the lookout for peace'. It was the duty of everyone to consider their words and actions carefully so that when peace came they would do their best to make the world a better place.[19] On the Sunday following the Liberation, he reminded the children of his words to them at the beginning of the year.[20]

Detached from its context such advice may sound platitudinous.

However, the hardship endured by islanders during the Occupation meant that a rejection of hatred for the enemy was far from being an easy option.

If the future was what counted now the islands were free, the past could not simply be swept under the carpet. During the previous five years, anyone possessed of even modest foresight could see that the liberation of the Channel Islands from German Occupation would bring in its wake a day of reckoning in which individuals and institutions would have to account for their actions. Decisions taken in complicated circumstances with the best of intentions might subsequently have to be defended when subjected to scrutiny by others who had not shared the same experience. The civil authorities in particular would have to justify their conduct.

Whilst churches would not be exposed to the same degree of scrutiny as the civil authorities, they too would have to account for themselves to denominational authorities. As early as 2 June 1944 the advisory committee of the Jersey (Wesley) Circuit recommended that the quarterly meeting appoint a small group to prepare a report about the circuit during the Occupation for the benefit of the Secretary of the Methodist Conference who, it was assumed, would visit the islands as soon as possible after the Liberation.[21]

The Allied invasion of France four days later gave the proposal greater urgency, and the quarterly meeting accepted its advisory committee's recommendation. Six people were appointed to draft a report: South, as acting superintendent; the secretary of the quarterly meeting; the two circuit stewards; and the two former circuit stewards who had resigned when Donald Stuart was re-invited in 1941.[22] The finished report was approved by the quarterly meeting in September.[23] However, it would be many more months before the 'Official Report of the English Circuit for the period of the German Occupation of Jersey' could be sent to the Secretary of the Conference in London.

The report summarises circuit life under four headings – finance, administration, worship and the current state of churches.[24] The financial arrangements made in the summer of 1940 regarding the payment of ministerial stipends are set out along with subsequent revisions. Events leading up to the termination of Stuart's appointment are outlined. The report requests permission from the Methodist Conference to retain money held by the circuit for Home Missions in order to help the circuit maintain 'financial stability during the difficult transitional period following the end of the war'. However, money collected for other connexional funds would

be paid over at the earliest opportunity. In particular, 'A considerable sum of money is available for the use of Overseas Missions[…] This vital part of Church life has not been neglected despite adverse conditions.' With justifiable satisfaction, the report concludes:

> Despite the conditions and limitations imposed by enemy occupation, affecting transport, lighting and heating, and a depleted preaching staff, services twice a Sunday have been held in all our Churches. Week day activities, while not on the same elaborate scale as pre-war days, have been vigorous. Our Sunday Schools have also maintained a high standard.

None of the other circuits in the Channel Islands felt the need to prepare an official report for the period of the Occupation, presumably because they had experienced nothing like the turbulence in the Jersey (Wesley) Circuit. Indeed, it is a curious fact that circuit and church records make little mention of the Liberation. Pulpit announcements in May 1945 stuck doggedly to the usual formula – reporting the previous week's collection and the preachers appointed for the following Sunday. Local preachers in the Guernsey and Sark (French) Circuit met at the end of May 1945 to conduct regular business. The only clue in the minutes that the Occupation was over is a reference to the presence of 'a visitor from His Majesty's Forces'.[25] Just as the arrival of German forces in the Channel Islands was barely acknowledged in church records, so too their departure was greeted mostly with silence. To a certain extent, this may be explained by the formal style of minute-taking characteristic of the period. But this is not wholly convincing, and a more satisfactory explanation is required.

The most likely explanation is that there was a tacit understanding that the enemy would not be permitted to violate the spiritual, if not the physical, space which Methodism occupied in the lives of islanders. If so, it was hardly the case that religion provided a parallel world for the faithful – the effects of living in close proximity to the enemy were too invasive to permit that kind of flight from reality. Instead, by unconsciously distinguishing between ecclesial and secular spheres of life, Methodists were able to function under oppressive conditions without experiencing the complete surrender of their identity. Hence, as far as possible, neither the arrival nor the departure of the invader was allowed to impinge upon the spiritual realm recorded in the minutes of church meetings.

Exceptionally, Methodists in the Jersey (Grove Place) Circuit recorded

their feelings at the end of the Occupation:

> On the occasion of holding our first Quarterly Meeting after the liberation of our beloved Island from enemy occupation we desire to place on record our gratitude to Almighty God for His preserving mercies and protecting care. With almost unimpaired religious liberty, our people for the greater part have remained loyal to the Church, its claims and challenge, and this despite hardships at home and deprivation of light and heat in the winter months. Our steady membership and wonderfully increased finances bear witness to God's blessing resting upon us. With profound gratitude we exclaim 'To God be all the praise'.[26]

It was a fair assessment of the situation at the Liberation and one that, to a greater or lesser extent, could be echoed by other churches and denominations.

In Britain, the first news of the liberation of the Channel Islands came in Winston Churchill's radio broadcast at 3pm on VE Day. After referring to the end of hostilities in Europe, he announced 'And our dear Channel Islands are also to be freed today.' Islanders, listening on their radios or via loudspeakers in public places, knew the announcement to be premature, but it was reassuring to learn that the British Government had not forgotten them. For Channel Island refugees in Britain, fearful of a bloodbath in the islands, Churchill's matter-of-fact announcement came as a huge relief. Before long, they were avidly pouring over reports in British newspapers about life in the islands during the German Occupation.

Naturally, evacuees were anxious to return home as soon as possible, though the need for the situation in the islands to stabilise meant a frustrating delay before travel permits were issued.[27] A small minority of refugees chose to remain in England for personal reasons. Some had discovered new horizons in Britain and were unwilling to return to their former way of life. The vast majority, however, looked forward to being reunited with families and friends just as soon as arrangements could be made.

By the summer of 1945 Lois Brehaut, whose evacuation we noted in Chapter 10, was Head Girl at the States of Guernsey Intermediate School temporarily located in Rochdale. She returned to Guernsey with her compatriots on 15 August to be greeted at the quayside by her overjoyed parents. Yet the long years of separation often made such homecomings

awkward occasions. Years later, she wrote: 'I felt enormously distanced. Here were two people claiming me as if I were theirs already and they didn't even know me.'[28] Sensitivity would be required on all sides if former relationships were to be restored.

It was not only evacuees who were anxious to reach the Channel Islands. Denominational leaders naturally wanted to re-establish contact with churches in the islands as soon as possible. The (Roman Catholic) bishop of Portsmouth, the (Anglican) bishop of Winchester and the national Moderator of the Free Church Federal Council sent messages of greeting to their respective constituencies in the islands, hailing their liberation and assuring islanders they had not been forgotten during the Occupation.[29] As soon as travel permits could be arranged, the bishops visited the islands to deal with a backlog of candidates for confirmation. In Jersey alone the bishop of Portsmouth confirmed 867 candidates.[30] In Guernsey the bishop of Winchester confirmed 'hundreds' of candidates and licensed several lay readers.[31] For Salvation Army leaders in Britain, the most urgent task in the islands was to re-start activities as soon as possible.[32]

The President of the Methodist Conference, Rev. Wilbert Howard, made a morale-boosting visit to the Channel Islands in July accompanied by Rev. Colin Roberts of the Home Missions Department. In Guernsey he preached in the afternoon at the Vale church and then at an evening rally at Ebenezer 'chaired' by John Leale. The singing was led by a massed choir drawn from the 23 Methodist congregations represented at the rally.[33] Similarly, in Jersey there was a capacity congregation at Grove Place church for a service of celebration 'chaired' by the island's Solicitor General and prominent Methodist layman, Cecil Harrison. Here the combined choirs mustered 170 voices.[34] It was the first time that a serving President of the Conference had visited the islands since Methodist Union.

Besides encouraging Methodists in the Channel Islands, Howard's visit was also a fact-finding mission that Douglas Moore in Britain was anxious should result in substantial financial aid from British Methodism. Moore's personal interest can be explained by the fact that he was due to become superintendent of the Guernsey and Sark (French) Circuit in place of Beaugié. Initial reports emanating from the islands after the Liberation suggested that Methodism was in a stronger financial position than expected. Beaugié himself proudly reported to Moore that the circuit was entirely free of debt. Ever the politician, Moore realised the negative effect such reports would have on those responsible for allocating central Methodist funds to alleviate war damage.

Shortly before the president's visit, Moore wrote confidentially to Beaugié informing him that the Conference had already set aside £2,000 to help Methodism in the Channel Islands after the end of the war.[35] More funds were readily available since 'the war emergency fund is simply rolling in money'. For Beaugié to present the financial situation at the end of the Occupation in a favourable light would be 'sadly misleading'. Instead he should emphasise the shortages and difficulties facing Methodism in the Channel Islands in the immediate post-war period so that the president made a sympathetic report to the advisory committee responsible for allocating funds. Above all, Beaugié was not to minimise the current situation: 'C[olin] R[oberts] will do that for you.' Underlining the point for emphasis, Moore insisted 'Don't hesitate a bit about presenting a formidable schedule of needs and press them strongly.'[36]

Whether as a result of Moore's interventions, in the end the Conference wrote off the levy to central funds which went uncollected in the Channel Islands during the Occupation.[37] In addition, sufficient money from central funds was made available to allow building repairs to proceed without the need for substantial local fundraising. In the post-war world Methodism in the Channel Islands would not have to face undue financial problems created by the Occupation.[38]

In addition to distinguished visitors and a trail of civil servants and technical advisors, the presence in the islands of a significant number of British service personnel from all three branches of the armed forces presented a different kind of challenge to islanders more used to maintaining correct relations with German personnel. In view of the lack of suitable leisure facilities other than pubs, a number of congregations opened their premises to members of the armed forces.

At Grove Place church in St Helier one room was set aside for quiet reading, another for writing. The large schoolroom provided facilities for table tennis and snooker. After conferring, the trustees agreed that smoking would be permitted on the premises on games' night. The ladies of the church undertook to provide tea and biscuits, and several men mounted patrols 'to see that nothing was done on our premises which did not comply with the rules of our church'.[39] Liberators or not, British soldiers could not be permitted to drink alcohol or dance on church premises. But even Methodist trustees could not stifle romance. On 23 June Douglas Ord in Guernsey conducted the marriage of a Royal Navy stores assistant and a local girl by special licence.[40]

When the euphoria of liberation eventually subsided and a succession of visiting dignitaries (including the King and Queen) had returned to the mainland, the churches were left with the task of integrating returning evacuees into church life alongside those who had remained in the islands during the Occupation. The vastly different experience of these two groups generated tensions that unsettled families, churches and the wider community. Those who experienced the Occupation resented the fact that evacuees had not endured the same hardships or had to make difficult decisions about how to live alongside the enemy. Conversely, evacuees were inclined to believe that, whilst they were contributing to the war effort, those left in the islands had been passively waiting to be freed.

The role of the churches in helping reconcile these two groups within island life is difficult to quantify. By its nature, such work is pastoral and thus not recorded in official records, which deal mostly with administration and finance. Nevertheless, the problems posed by reintegration were not unforeseen. Even before the end of the Occupation, Methodists were aware that the different experience of evacuees would cause tensions when they eventually returned home. One reason for maintaining the names of evacuees on church membership lists was to avoid giving the impression they had been forgotten.

During the summer of 1945, congregations made real efforts to integrate returning evacuees into church life, especially in Guernsey where nearly half the population had left in June 1940. For strategic reasons, attempts at reintegration centred on children. In the Guernsey and Sark (French) Circuit Sidney Beaugié arranged for printed invitations to be sent to former Sunday school scholars as soon as they arrived back in the island. Although the recipients had 'changed very much in many ways', Beaugié nevertheless hoped they still loved their 'old Church and School'. A warm welcome and a place in the Sunday school awaited all returning children. Those now too old for Sunday school classes could make themselves useful as teachers or else join the choir. Then an anxious request that reflected the concerns uppermost in many people's minds:

> Many of you will return with new ideas and new ways and perhaps find some of us a little behind the times – but you will not be too hard on us, will you? – and you will be very careful how you press these new ideas on the people at home, won't you? We shall try to welcome every new idea, and adopt every new way, in so far as they appear good to us.'[41]

B.

The Methodist Church

GUERNSEY & SARK (FRENCH) CIRCUIT.

Carmel Methodist Church. June, 1945.

Dear *Thomas*

Guernsey calling ! Your old Church and Sunday School greet you !

We are looking forward eagerly to seeing you back again and want you to feel that a *very* warm welcome awaits you, not only from your relatives and friends, but from your Church as well.

You will have changed very much in many ways—one thing sure, you are five years older than when we saw you last ! but we do hope that in one thing you have *not* changed, in your love for your old Church and School. We are hoping to see you all back in your old place and to see those of you who are now quite grown-up making yourselves useful in the Church, as for instsance, in the School as Teachers, in the Choir (*if* you can sing !) and so on. Please understand that we need you all badly, *every* one.

Many of you will return with new ideas and new ways and perhaps find some of us a little behind the times—but you will not be too hard on us, will you ?—and you will be very careful how you press these new ideas on the people at home, won't you ? We shall try to welcome every new idea, and adopt every new way, in so far as they appear good to us.

We are so pleased to hear that some of you have made the Great Choice and now belong to Christ, the very best Friend of all. We should like to think that you all have taken your stand on His side. For remember! Your friends, your Church and your Island need you at your best.

So come back soon and join us. There's a place waiting for you.

All the very best to you,

Your sincere friends,

S. E. BEAUGIÉ, *Superintendent*.

John Le Ray Secretary for

Carmel Church.

In case you should wish to reply (and we'd very much like a short note from you,) the Secretary's address is :—

J. Le Ray
Le Pron
St. Saviour's.

Figure 11.5: Letter sent to returning Sunday school children in the Guernsey and Sark (French) Circuit (Herbert White Collection)

Besides printed invitations, practical steps were taken to welcome returning evacuees. At Les Capelles in the Guernsey and Sark (French) Circuit the Sunday school council arranged for the annual outing in August to take the form of a bus ride followed by tea. However, the date was not fixed until it was known when the evacuees would return so that they could be included. By the end of September, the Sunday school council was reporting a 'steady flow of returning evacuees', though the average weekly attendance at classes was still considered low.[42] Les Camps arranged a children's sports day, followed by tea in the schoolroom and a social evening 'to welcome scholars who had evacuated to the mainland in 1940 together with the present scholars'. Altogether, 68 children sat down to tea. Diplomatically, the evening closed with the singing of *Sarnia chérie* and *Auld Lang Syne*.[43]

By the late summer of 1945 conditions on all fronts were steadily improving, though property repairs would take several more years to complete. Surveying the recent past, islanders began to reflect that their experience in the previous five years could have been a great deal worse. Many would have echoed the words of the Sunday school superintendent at Torteval in the Guernsey and Sark (French) Circuit in a speech given at the first Sunday school anniversary service following the Liberation. Reading from a longhand script that reveals a lack of finesse in English grammar, he managed nevertheless to place the previous five years into a broader context:

> When we think of all the other countries who have been ravaged and destroyed by the effects of the war and yet we have been allowed to remain almost in peace. Are we really thankful to God for all he has done for us? Yet many a time we have grumbled at our position had we cause to do so. Today we realise that we could have been much worse than we have been but we can say God moves in a mysterious way his wonders to perform. Our liberation has come we are free to speak and act, but we are thankful that during the Occupation we have been able to carry on our Sunday school work just the same.[44]

Whilst some psychological wounds would take a long time to heal, other aspects of the Occupation were rapidly fading from the collective consciousness, including things that had once seemed important to remember when peace came. At the annual general meeting of the Sisterhood at St Sampson's in the Guernsey (English) Circuit in September 1945 the president reflected on the previous five years. During the Occupation,

women often remarked how they would never again take for granted those things they had to live without. Now that the island was free again, however, she wondered whether women were in danger of forgetting what they had said time and again during the Occupation.[45] Evidently, life was beginning to return to normal.

FIRST TOWER METHODIST CHURCH

THE CHOIR SUPPORTED BY ORGAN, PIANO AND STRINGS

PRESENTS
SPECIAL
PROGRAMME

Topical and popular Hymns reflecting the
PRESENT SITUATION.
National, Social and World Peace Hymns

WEDNESDAY, MAY 9th, at 7.30 p.m.

ENTIRE PROCEEDS OF PAPER COLLECTION FOR **RED CROSS FUNDS**

Figure 11.6: Some churches arranged events to mark the end of hostilities in Europe

Chapter 12

Aftermath

The liberation of the Channel Islands in May 1945 brought in its wake a period of constitutional reform as the population adjusted to new realities following the massive social dislocation caused by the evacuation of civilians in 1940 and the subsequent German Occupation. Inevitably, the return of thousands of refugees and servicemen, bringing with them experience of horizons beyond the Channel Islands, meant that things would never be quite the same again. Even without the efforts of Douglas Moore to stimulate interest in the political process, it was widely recognised that change was required in order to fulfil the aspirations of islanders in the post-war world.[1]

So far as Methodism was concerned, a radical institutional overhaul was desperately needed in response to a contemporary situation very different to the environment in which the movement flourished in the nineteenth century. During the war years, some whose lives once centred on Methodism had discovered alternative interests with the result that the former pattern of Sunday observance was difficult to re-establish. Strategic decisions long overdue could no longer be postponed despite efforts by diehards to restore things to the way they were before the Occupation. As longstanding rivalries resurfaced following the Liberation, Methodism in the Channel Islands was in danger of becoming hostage to competing interests until the whole system collapsed under the weight of maintaining an infrastructure that reflected the optimism of an earlier, expansionist age. But it was impossible to impose changes on circuits and churches in the absence of local agreement. Despite Methodism's reputation for discipline, there has never been an effective means of exercising central control over the local managing trustees of church buildings.

The impetus for reform was provided by the decision of the Methodist Conference in June 1945 to establish a commission on Methodism in the Channel Islands. Headed by Wilbert Howard, by now the former President

of the Conference, its brief was 'to visit the Channel Islands to consult with Circuits and Churches concerning Post-War Developments and the best use of manpower'.[2] There were ten members, all of them Conference heavyweights, including the Vice-President and the Secretary of the Conference.[3] Their agenda was obvious from the terms of reference: 'the best use of manpower' could mean only one thing – a reduction in the number of ministers leading to a rationalisation of buildings. Crucially, however, the commission had no power to implement its proposals. Instead it would be up to circuit quarterly meetings and the trustees of churches to decide what to do in the light of any recommendations. In practice, this gave congregations a veto over proposals that threatened their interests, irrespective of how narrow or short-sighted these might appear to others.

Pending further developments, there were a number of immediate changes in ministerial staff in the summer of 1945.[4] Frederick Flint returned from internment in Germany to serve a valedictory year as Chairman of the District and superintendent of the Guernsey (English) Circuit before retiring in 1946. Mark Lund (minister of a church in Stockport with a strong contingent of Channel Island refugees) arrived in the circuit as the fourth member of staff in place of David Ball, who evacuated in 1940. In the Guernsey and Sark (French) Circuit Henry Foss returned from internment for a final year before he too retired. Sidney Beaugié moved to Deal in Kent, while Douglas Moore returned from England as superintendent. The addition of Eric Sarchet and Donald Collings restored the ministerial strength to its pre-war level. The Alderney Circuit was left vacant since it would be several months before islanders would be able to return to their ravaged homes.

In Jersey W. Vere Coxon arrived as superintendent of the Jersey (Wesley) Circuit in place of Donald Stuart, who took up a circuit appointment in Bradford following his return from internment in Germany. His health shattered, he retired to Guernsey the following year where he died in December 1948.[5] From the Jersey (Grove Place) Circuit William Ward moved to Rothwell, Anthony Skyrme to Yarm-on-Tees, and Alan Freeman to the Forest of Dean. They were replaced by Peter Hanks (lay pastor during the Occupation and now a probationer minister), Eric Walker, and Robert Rider as superintendent and Flint's designated successor as Chairman of the District.

It came as no surprise that the Conference commission recommended a single circuit covering the whole of Jersey. However, there was strong opposition to change in Jersey stemming from historic rivalries between

the Wesleyan, Primitive Methodist and Bible Christian traditions. As a compromise, the circuit stewards proposed the amalgamation of the Jersey (Wesley) and Jersey (Grove Place) Circuits since both were formerly Wesleyan Methodist and considerations of language no longer applied.[6] The case for combining the two circuits was overwhelming and resistance was short lived. In 1947 these came together to form the Jersey (Wesley Grove) Circuit. A single circuit for Jersey eventually came about in 1960, by which time declining congregations and fading memories had eroded much of the opposition.

In Guernsey, the non-Wesleyan churches, numerically weak, had been absorbed relatively painlessly into the Guernsey (English) Circuit before the war. By 1945 the majority of services in the Guernsey and Sark (French) Circuit were in English, strengthening the case for uniting the two circuits. Yet institutional change was painfully slow in the face of determined opposition. In 1946 the Guernsey (English) Circuit and the Alderney Circuit amalgamated to become the Guernsey and Alderney (English) Circuit, a development long overdue and relatively easy to achieve. In 1948 the Guernsey and Sark (French) Circuit finally dropped the language reference from its title. The following year it changed its name to the Guernsey (Victoria) and Sark Circuit, after its flagship church in Victoria Road, St Peter Port. Since there was no longer a French circuit as such, the other was renamed the Guernsey and Alderney Circuit. After this superficial tinkering with the system, reorganisation ground to a standstill. It was not until 1976 that the two circuits finally amalgamated to form a single Bailiwick of Guernsey Circuit.

If simply reducing the number of circuits in the Channel Islands proved controversial and difficult to achieve, rationalising the number of churches was even more contentious, consuming a great deal of energy that would have been better devoted to consolidating viable causes. Ministers in particular bore the brunt of islanders' wrath and were often accused of having been sent by the Conference to close a particular church. Whilst similar concerns were expressed elsewhere in British Methodism, in the Channel Islands these were exacerbated by a deep suspicion of outsiders and geographical remoteness from the Conference.

Some of the difficulties encountered in reducing the number of Methodist churches in the Channel Islands are evident in the saga of Salem chapel in St Peter Port which closed temporarily in July 1940 as a result of staffing difficulties following the evacuation of two ministers from the Guernsey

(English) Circuit. Its congregation dispersed between Brock Road and Ebenezer, Salem found a new role during the Occupation providing storage facilities for the States' Education Council. But, even with reinforcements from Salem, Ord found that the loss of young people in 1940 made it difficult to carry on midweek activities at Brock Road.[7] Looking to the future, it was by no means certain that evacuees would return to their former churches. To Ord's way of thinking, there were too many Methodist churches in St Peter Port: therefore, it made little sense to reopen Salem after the war.

In June 1945 the Guernsey (English) Circuit quarterly meeting discussed the future of Salem. Ord drew attention to the strain on resources which would be created by re-opening a building that was surplus to requirements given the close proximity of other Methodist churches in the town. However, not only was his view in a small minority, he was vehemently denounced for expressing it. The discussion became acrimonious, obliging Ord to say that of course he would welcome the re-opening of Salem.[8] After considerable effort on the part of the congregation to repair the building, Salem reopened for worship on the first Sunday in September. Inevitably, the *Guernsey Evening Press* reported the reopening as a success story but the underlying reality was altogether different.[9]

A series of events concerning Ebenezer in the same circuit confirms that the furore over Salem was not an isolated example. In June 1944 a bomb exploding in St Peter Port harbour during a rare Allied air raid blew out the windows of Ebenezer rendering it uninhabitable. A hurriedly convened meeting between officials of Ebenezer and Brock Road agreed that the two congregations would worship together at the latter premises 'probably for the duration'. However, there was still one delicate issue to be resolved.

The minister now in pastoral charge at Salem, Philip Romeril, requested that Ord cease using the liturgical Order of Morning Prayer at Brock Road. Ord refused, to his surprise finding support from several lay officials who, until recently, had been members at Salem. Having previously not been used to the liturgy, they now expressed their appreciation of it. Nevertheless, as a gesture of goodwill, Ord agreed that the Order of Morning Prayer would alternate on Sundays with a preaching service. Romeril would occupy the pulpit only on those occasions when the liturgy was not used.[10]

Within a few days of the settlement, Ord expressed delight at the outcome. Sunday worship was a great success. The two congregations blended easily, as did their respective choirs: 'Not a discordant note was raised by anyone.' Brock Road was filled for Sunday worship, and the singing was uplifting. For Ord, this was all the more remarkable because of longstanding antipathy

The METHODIST CHURCH

EMERGENCY NOTICE

The congregation of Ebenezer and Brock Road Methodist Churches **WILL WORSHIP, UNTIL FURTHER NOTICE** AT BROCK ROAD

All seats free.   Sunday next at

11.00 a.m. Rev. F. J. Paine. (non liturgical).

6.30 p.m., Rev. R. D. Ord.

A Special Invitation is extended to Ebenezer Choir whose members are asked to essemble in the Choir room.

ST. SAMPSON'S
METHODIST CHURCH.

SUNDAY JUNE 25th.

11.00 a.m., Rev S. E. Beaugié, M.A.

7.00 p.m., Mr. C. Le Page.

Figure 12.1: Press announcement that the Ebenezer congregation would worship at Brock Road church (Guernsey Evening Press)

towards Brock Road on the part of the Ebenezer congregation dating from the nineteenth century. At that time, members of Ebenezer resented a new Methodist building in the vicinity, especially one as attractive as the Brock Road church with its pleasing spire. Elated at this unexpected turn of events, Ord vowed to do everything he could to weld the two congregations and their leaders into a single unit. Why, he wondered, had they not done this in 1940?[11]

But, as Ord well knew, the amalgamation of the two congregations had been achieved only by external means – in this case by an American bomb. In other circumstances negotiations for uniting the two congregations might have dragged on for several years, always assuming there was a desire to commence talks in the first place. By the following Sunday, the newfound unity was shattered:

> This has been a day of great disappointment to the joint congregations worshipping in my church at Brock Road. Notwithstanding the universal delight, the approval of the *Press* and the rich promise for the future, I am sorry to have to record that it pleased Romeril to pretend that he must 'keep Ebenezer going as a trust' on behalf of its minister, the Reverend F. Flint, now in Laufen. How exactly he managed to persuade some of his officials that they should go back on their agreement, I cannot say. The windows of Ebenezer are being patched up and the separate working of the two congregations will be resumed, to the dismay, bewilderment and surprise of almost everyone. Regret is widespread. Time will pass judgement on this arrogant and unbrotherly action.[12]

Livid, the following Sunday Ord took his revenge by preaching at Ebenezer on the merits of the Order of Morning Prayer. Presumably unaware of the negotiations that had previously taken place, Ambrose Robin innocently recorded in his diary an 'interesting talk on the liturgical service', though he was 'not impressed with it as a sermon in these times'.[13] In August Ord addressed the Brock Road congregation on the same theme. On this occasion Robin's pithy observation probably captures the preacher's intention as well as his style: 'Ord gave us another lecture on the liturgical service.'[14] Perhaps not surprisingly, Ord's own diary makes no reference to either occasion.

It is difficult more than sixty years later to apportion blame in what was a classic example of the internecine strife all too common in small churches.

That relations between Ord and Romeril were already strained is evident from several entries in Ord's diary.[15] But more was at stake here than a clash of ministerial personalities. This was a power struggle between factions of the Ebenezer congregation over the future. Given the historic rivalries between the congregations involved, Ord was wildly optimistic to believe that Brock Road could benefit painlessly from the closure of two other town churches. Again, there was nothing unique about all this. Power struggles over property were a common occurrence in British Methodism in the years following Union in 1932 as vested interests thwarted plans for rationalisation. Feuds over property were usually the continuation of earlier turf wars between competing groups of Methodists. As in this case, the dispute was often exacerbated by antipathy to a particular style of worship.

Yet there were also successful attempts to dispose of surplus property in imaginative ways. In July 1940 Morley chapel in the Guernsey (English) Circuit closed to ease staffing difficulties, and its small congregation transferred to Les Camps in the same parish. The trustees, who continued to meet annually throughout the Occupation, arranged for a caretaker to look after the building. In 1943 the Germans took over the premises for use as a flour store but released them in April 1944, whereupon the States of Guernsey used the schoolroom as a furniture depository. At the end of the Occupation the premises were found to be in good condition, but the trustees accepted that St Martin's parish no longer needed their chapel in addition to Les Camps and St Martin's Mission. Alternative uses of the premises were explored, and the building was later turned into a successful youth hostel.[16]

In Jersey the healthy financial position of Methodism at the end of the Occupation obscured the need for rationalisation. Even the Jersey (Wesley) Circuit, hardest hit by the evacuation and internal disputes, looked to the future with renewed confidence. In March 1944 it was reported that all the churches in the circuit were investing financially in the future. St Aubin's intended to buy four properties situated at the rear of the premises in order to expand the schoolroom. Gorey was planning a new system of lighting and heating. Wesley chapel had agreed to spend a thousand pounds on extensive alterations and improvements. First Tower wanted to buy a new organ, and Samarès was contemplating building an entirely new church or schoolroom.[17]

The main challenge facing the Jersey (Wesley) Circuit at the end of the Occupation was what to do with Seaton Place church, which closed in July 1940 'for the duration'. A proposal to sell the premises was presented at the

quarterly meeting in June 1945. According to the circuit stewards, the cost of getting the building into a state where it could once again function as a centre for mission was prohibitive. Other circuits were said to be making plans for 'consolidation', and the disposal of this particular building made sense. The circuit stewards 'appealed to those who would oppose the motion to have a wider vision as to the needs of the circuit'. After a lengthy discussion, the vote was carried by a resounding majority.[18] For the most part, however, further post-war rationalisation in Jersey proceeded slowly and without the benefit of strategic planning.

It was not until December 1945 that the first group of Alderney residents was able to return to the island such was the devastation caused by German forces. Like the vast majority of buildings, the Methodist church was found to be in a poor state of repair and in urgent need of attention.

The task of reviving Methodism in Alderney after the Occupation did not merit the stationing of a resident minister in the straitened financial circumstances of the immediate post-war period. Instead, a resident lay pastor was appointed in 1947, and the District Synod subsequently received an encouraging report about the revival of Methodism in Alderney.[19] Even so, establishing a viable congregation was arduous work, confirming Douglas Moore's belief that Alderney was barren soil for Methodism. A resident minister was eventually appointed, but Methodism in Alderney continued long afterwards to struggle for survival even with financial support from the Home Missions department of British Methodism.

Nowadays Methodism remains influential in the Channel Islands, though not on the same scale as before the Second World War. Despite further closures, in 2008 there were still twelve Methodist churches in Guernsey served by five ministers, and fourteen in Jersey served by six ministers – a large number given the small size of the islands. Brock Road church in St Peter Port, where Douglas Ord hid his diary under the floorboards, closed for worship in 1993 and presently stands empty awaiting disposal, a casualty of prohibitive repair costs. Responsibility for Methodism in Alderney is shared jointly by the Guernsey and Jersey circuits, a sign that it continues to struggle. A lay pastor ministers to the small congregation. On Sark the small Methodist congregation, also in the care of a lay pastor, continues to welcome numerous holidaymakers during the summer months. The inscription carved on the communion table, *Je suis le pain de vie*, reminds visitors of the French influence on Methodism in the Channel Islands.

At the end of the first decade of the twenty-first century, there are an ever dwindling number of people with firsthand experience of life in the Channel Islands during the German Occupation. Consequently, the oral history of church life during the Occupation is in danger of being permanently lost. This is a great pity. For, as we have seen in the case of Methodism, the churches played a significant role during the Occupation, not least as one of the few public spaces in which islanders were able to express their loyalty to an authority beyond that of the occupying forces.

The remnants of Hitler's Atlantic Wall in the Channel Islands bear silent witness to the *hubris* of National Socialism and a thousand-year Reich that lasted for just twelve. In the centuries-long history of Christianity in the islands the five years spent under the German swastika are a fleeting moment. Nevertheless, this short period constitutes a unique chapter in European Church history when British churches found themselves subject to the world's most powerful regime since the Romans. That the churches survived remarkably well was due to a combination of factors, not least of which was the determination of clergy and congregations to maintain public worship despite the difficult circumstances.

The freedom of worship granted by the occupying forces was always a fragile state of affairs that could so easily have been withdrawn at any time should this have served German interests. Had clergy upset the equilibrium by denouncing the actions of the occupier, the churches' experience under enemy occupation could have been significantly different. As it was, by sustaining their normal pattern of public worship and midweek activities during five years of German Occupation, the various churches in the Channel Islands, including Methodism, played a more effective role in subverting the Third Reich and witnessing to a future in which island life would one day return to normal.

APPENDIX

Channel Islands District of the Methodist Church
Ministers and Churches, 1940-45

Chairman of the District   Frederick Flint
Synod Secretary   Walter C.H. Fell
    (Acting Chairman from September 1942)

Guernsey (English) Circuit
Frederick Flint (Superintendent, deported to Germany in October 1942)
Philip Romeril (Acting Superintendent from October 1942)
R. Douglas Ord
David Ball (evacuated in June 1940)
A. Bernard Brockway (retired)
Frederick J. Paine (retired)
George Whitley (retired, evacuated in June 1940)
John Leale (President Controlling Committee of the States of Guernsey
   October 1940 – June 1945)

Churches
Ebenezer (Saumarez Street, St Peter Port)
Brock Road (St Peter Port)
St Sampson's (New Road)
Salem (Vauvert) Closed July 1940
Rohais (Rohais de Bas)
St Martin's Mission (Rue des Caches)
Bailiff's Cross Mission (St Andrew's) Closed July 1940
L'Islet (Route Carré)
Bordeaux Mission (Vale)
Cornet Street Mission (*Rented*)
Morley (Fort Road) Closed July 1940

Guernsey and Sark (French) Circuit
Sidney E. Beaugié (Superintendent)
Henry J. Foss (deported to Germany February 1943)

R. Douglas Moore (evacuated June 1940)
Frederick E. Lines (evacuated June 1940)
William H. Bunting (retired, resident minister on Sark, died May 1940)
Alf Tardiff (lay pastor on Sark, September 1940 to December 1945)

Churches
Victoria (Victoria Road, St Peter Port) Closed July 1940
Wesley (Grand Bouet)
Les Camps (St Martin's)
Forest (Le Bourg) Closed July 1940
Sion (St Pierre du Bois)
Torteval (La Bellée)
Les Adams (L'Erée)
Rocquaine (Le Coudré)
Carmel (Les Bordages, St Saviour's)
St Andrew's (Le Four Cabot)
Delisle (Castel)
Galaad (Grandes Rocques)
Les Capelles (St Sampson's)
Vale (Belval Road)
La Moye (L'Ancresse, Vale)
Sark

Alderney
Edgar Calvert (Superintendent, evacuated with civilian population June 1940)

Churches
The Butes (closed June 1940)

Jersey (Wesley)
Donald Stuart (Superintendent, deported to Germany October 1942)
Ronald E. South (Acting Superintendent from 1941)

Churches
Wesley (St Helier)
St Aubin's
Gorey
First Tower
Seaton Place Closed July 1940

Samarès

Jersey (Aquila Road)
Walter C.H. Fell (Superintendent)
J. Watson Grayson (retired)

Churches
Aquila Road

Jersey (Great Union Road)
Clement N. Mylne (Superintendent)
John C. Pye (retired)

Churches
Great Union Road
Royal Crescent (Don Road)
Les Landes (St Martin's)

Jersey (Grove Place)
William J. Ward (Superintendent)
Anthony T. Skyrme
John W.J. Scott
Alan M. Freeman
Peter Hanks (lay pastor)

Churches
Sion
Les Augrés (Trinity)
Les Fréres
Six Roads
Galaad
St Martin's
Ebenezer (Trinity)
Eden (St Saviour)
La Rocque
Carmel (Rozel)
Tabor (St Brelade)
Philadelphie (St Peter's)
Bethlehem (St Mary's)

St Ouen's
Bethesda (Val-de-la-Mare)
Bethel (La Hocq Lane, Samarès)
Georgetown
Grove Place

NOTES AND REFERENCES

Chapter 1

1 Mark Patton, *Jersey in Prehistory* (La Haule: La Haule Books, 1987).

2 For a general history of the Channel Islands see G. R. Balleine, *A history of the Island of Jersey from the cave men to the German occupation and after* (London: Staples, 1950; revd edn 1998); Raoul Lemprière, *A History of the Channel Islands* (London: Hale, 1980).

3 The standard study of this period in Channel Island ecclesiastical history is A.J. Eagleston, *The Channel Islands under Tudor Government 1485-1642* (Cambridge: Cambridge University Press, 1949). For a detailed study of the Reformation in Guernsey see Darryl Ogier, *Reformation and Society in Guernsey* (Woodbridge: Boydell, 1996). There is no equivalent study for Jersey.

4 See C.S.L. Davies, 'International Politics and the Establishment of Presbyterianism in the Channel Islands: The Coutances Connection', *Journal of Ecclesiastical History* 50/3 (1999), pp. 498-522. I am indebted to Sue Laker, Deputy Librarian at the Priaulx Library in Guernsey, for this reference.

5 David Hempton, *Methodism: Empire of the Spirit* (Yale: Yale University Press, 2005).

6 Coughlan was an Irish Roman Catholic who became a Methodist preacher. On the recommendation of John Wesley, he was ordained by the bishop of London and sent by the SPCK to Newfoundland where he gathered converts into classes. Entry in John Vickers (ed.), *A Dictionary of Methodism in Britain and Ireland* (Peterborough: Epworth, 2000), p. 80. The earliest written account of the arrival of Methodism in the Channel Islands is William Toase, 'The Grace of God manifested: A memoir of the late Mrs Elizabeth Arrivé of Guernsey', *The Methodist Magazine* (1820), pp. 144-51, 186-95.

7 'Memoir of Peter Le Sueur', *Methodist Magazine* (1820), pp. 401-8.

8 John Wesley to Robert Carr Brackenbury, 4 January 1784. John Telford (ed.), *The Letters of the Rev. John Wesley A.M.* Vol. 7 (London: Epworth, 1931), p. 203.

9 Journal of John Wesley, 14 August - 6 September 1787. W. Reginald Ward and Richard P. Heitzenrater (eds), *The Works of John Wesley* Vol. 24 'Journal and Diaries VII (1787-1791)' (Nashville: Abingdon, 2003), pp. 49-57.

10 'Memoir of Peter Le Sueur', p. 406.

11 *Minutes of the Methodist Conferences* Vol. 1 (London: Wesleyan Conference Office, 1862).

12 *Le Magasin Méthodiste des Iles de la Manche* was first published in January 1817. It ran continuously until the final edition was published in December 1901. The first issue contained sermons, theological articles, a story about the providential preservation of the King of Poland, and news of Methodist overseas missions in Africa, the Caribbean, North America and Ceylon.

13 William Toase, *Memorials of the Rev. William Toase: consisting principally of extracts from his journals and correspondence, illustrative of the rise and progress of Methodism in France and*

the Channel Islands (London: Wesleyan Conference Office, 1874), p. 181. Curiously, R.D. Moore, *Methodism in the Channel Islands* (London: Epworth, 1952) makes no mention of this useful source.

14 Toase, *Memorials*, pp. 53-4.

15 Toase, *Memorials*, p. 45.

16 Toase, *Memorials*, p. 51.

17 Matthieu Le Lièvre, *Histoire du Méthodisme dans les Iles de la Manche 1784-1884* (Paris: Librarie Evangélique, 1885), p. 188.

18 Le Lièvre, *Histoire du Méthodisme*, p. 318.

19 Adam Clarke to John Wesley, 2 June 1788. Cited in Le Lièvre, *Histoire du Méthodisme*, p. 313.

20 Le Lièvre, *Histoire du Méthodisme*, p. 574-7 contains a summary of Methodist chapels built in the Channel Islands between 1789 and 1881.

21 Le Lièvre, *Histoire du Méthodisme*, p. 430. Wesleyan Methodist membership grew steadily in the course of the 19th century: 1800 795; 1810 1,194; 1820 1,699; 1830 2,389; 1840 3,217; 1850 3,200; 1860 3,200; 1870 4,079; 1880 3,507.

22 Extracted from the figures given in R.D. Moore, *Methodism in the Channel Islands*, p. 126.

23 Moore, *Methodism in the Channel Islands*, p. 89.

24 Letter of Jean Renier, *Le Magasin Méthodiste* (1818), p. 90.

25 François Guiton, *Histoire du Méthodisme Wesleyen dans les Iles de la Manche* (London: John Mason, 1846), p. 284.

26 Guiton, *Histoire du Méthodisme Wesleyen*, p. 283.

27 Toase, *Memorials*, p. 149.

28 Toase noted the following churches and seating provision: New church (i.e. St Anne's parish church) 800; 2 Wesleyan Methodist chapels 500; Primitive Methodist chapel 300; church at Braye 100.

29 Guiton, *Histoire du Méthodisme Wesleyen*, p. 290.

Chapter 2

[1] Obituary, *Minutes of Conference* (1949), p. 133.

[2] Obituary, *Minutes of Conference* (1970), p. 183.

[3] Described in William J. Ward, *In and around the Oron Country* (London: W.J. Hammond, 1913). Obituary, *Minutes of Conference* (1947), p. 137.

[4] Obituary, *Minutes of Conference* (1967), p. 192.

[5] Obituary, *Minutes of Conference* (1970), p. 170.

[6] The nearest equivalent in the British legal system is a justice of the peace.

[7] Obituary, *Minutes of Conference* (1968), p. 184.

[8] Obituary, *Minutes of Conference* (1965), p. 176.

[9] *Conference Agenda* (1938), p. 15.

[10] Minutes of the Channel Islands District Synod; JA J/C/A/A/27; JA J/C/A/A/65.

[11] The figures in this paragraph have been calculated using *Methodist Church Buildings: Statistical Returns including seating accommodation as at July 1st 1940* (Methodist Conference,

1947). In 1940 the population of the islands was: Jersey (51,000); Guernsey (43,000); Alderney (1,450); Sark (600).

[12] Jersey (Grove Place) Circuit preaching plan, July – September 1940; JA J/C/D/E/44/4.

[13] *MR*, 4 July 1940.

[14] Citations from the Occupation Diary of Rev. R. Douglas Ord (deposited in the Priaulx Library, Guernsey) are denoted by 'Ord' together with a date. Shortly before the Occupation, Ord wisely obtained a stock of paper for his diary. By early 1942 paper was unobtainable in the shops (Ord, 17 May 1942).

[15] Paul Sanders, *The British Channel Islands under German Occupation 1940-1945* (Jersey: Jersey Heritage Trust and Société Jersiase, 2005), p. 160.

[16] Obituary, *Minutes of Conference* (1979), p. 81.

[17] Throughout his diary, Ord refers to his wife as 'G', shorthand for 'Grae'. Her maiden name was Hilda Graham, and she was affectionately known as 'Grae'.

[18] Ord, 19 June 1940.

[19] Ord, 22 June 1940. Ord was kept busy with enquiries. 'From early morning to midnight our house was besieged by people seeking advice. The 'phone, which rang incessantly, continued to do so until after midnight. It was a heavy responsibility.'

[20] Ord, 25 June 1940.

[21] As Ord noted in his diary in the final week in June. In fact, of the 363 marriages in Guernsey in 1940, 291 (80 percent) took place in the first six months of the year, and of these 122 (33.6 percent) took place in June alone. *GEP*, 8 July 1965.

[22] *MR*, 4 July 1940.

[23] This account is based on notes taken at the meeting. Minutes of the Advisory Committee of the Jersey (Wesley) Circuit 31/05/1940 – 27/05/1947; JA J/C/E/A/7.

[24] Ord, 26 June 1940.

[25] *MR*, 11 July 1940.

[26] Ord, 30 June 1940.

[27] *MR*, 4 July 1940.

[28] *The Star*, 5 July 1940.

[29] The Guernsey and Sark (French) Circuit QM, 19 December 1940, agreed to pay the Guernsey (English) Circuit £50 per quarter towards the cost of ministerial assistance from that circuit.

[30] Ord, 2 July 1940.

[31] R.D. Moore, *Methodism in the Channel Islands* (London: Epworth, 1952), p. 118.

[32] Brock Road TM, 16 February 1940; GA AQ 184/12.

[33] Cited in Alan Wood and Mary Seaton Wood, *Islands in Danger* (London: Evans, 1955), p. 128.

[34] T.X.H. Pantcheff, *Alderney: Fortress Island* (Chichester: Phillimore, 1981), p. 43. Pantcheff, a Military Intelligence officer, arrived in Alderney with the liberating troops in order to conduct a thorough investigation into reports of German war crimes. His book is based on contemporary notes.

[35] Fred Martin, 'The Churches in Guernsey during the Occupation', *Channel Islands Occupation Review* (1975), pp. 59-65 (p. 62).

[36] *The Star*, 19 May 1945.

[37] Sark LM, 23 October 1938; GA AQ 211/15.

[38] Sark LM, 7 February 1940; GA AQ 211/15.

[39] Julia Tremayne, *War on Sark: The Secret Letters of Julia Tremayne* (Exeter: Webb and Bower, 1981), p. 15.

[40] Tremayne, *War on Sark*, p. 22.

[41] Guernsey and Sark (French) Circuit QM, 16 December 1943; 28 June 1945.

[42] See Michael Marshall, *Hitler Invaded Sark* (St Peter Port: Guernsey Lithoprint, 1963), pp. 46-7.

[43] The full story of the Guernsey Underground News Service is told in Frank Falla, *The Silent War* (London: New English Library, 1967).

[44] Letter of Mabel Tardif (widow) to Herbert White, 23 January 1996 (Herbert White collection).

Chapter 3

[1] *GEP*, 2 July 1940.

[2] Ord, 1 August 1940.

[3] Ord, 1 August 1940.

[4] Jersey (Aquila Road) Circuit QM, 11 September 1940; JA J/C/B/A/2.

[5] Letter from Dr Maass to Major Ferguson, 10 July 1940; GA FK 30-11.

[6] Richard Heaume, 'Marie Ozanne', *Channel Islands Occupation Review* 23 (1995), pp. 79-81.

[7] *JEP*, 25 January 1941.

[8] Letter of Colonel Schumacher to the Salvation Army in Jersey, 27 January 1941; JA B/A/W30/13.

[9] *JEP*, 29 June 1945.

[10] Letter of Br Brosch to Bailiff, 13 November 1941; JA B/A/W41/19.

[11] Letter of Attorney General to Bailiff, 21 November 1941; JA B/A/W41/19.

[12] Letter of Dr Casper to Bailiff, 28 November 1941; JA B/A/W41/19.

[13] Letter of Attorney General to Bailiff, 16 December 1941; JA B/A/W41/19.

[14] Jersey (Grove Place) Circuit LPM, 5 September 1940; JA J/C/D/A/5.

[15] Roy Rabey Notes, Herbert White Collection. Roy Rabey and Alan Grut were the two members of the mission band that went on to become local preachers.

[16] The final gathering of the mission band was announced in *The Star*, 3 July 1945.

[17] St Martin's LM, 9 November 1944; JA J/C/AE/A/3.

[18] Jersey (Grove Place) Circuit preaching plan, October – December 1940; JA J/C/D/E/44/1.

[19] Horses were considerably weakened by the shortage of food during the Occupation. In November 1943 Douglas Ord, in 'robes and bands', was being transported by box cart to conduct a funeral at Castel church when the 'skeleton horse' collapsed. At first, Ord thought it was dead. Only with the greatest difficulty could the animal be coaxed to resume the journey. Ord, 15 November 1943.

[20] Jersey (Grove Place) Circuit preaching plan, October – December 1940; JA J/C/D/E/

44/1.

[21] Guernsey and Sark (French) Circuit LPM, 30 May 1940; GA AQ 213/1.

[22] Guernsey and Sark (French) Circuit LPM, 28 August 1940; GA AQ 213/1.

[23] Guernsey (English) Circuit LPM, 6 June 1940; GA AQ 213/7.

[24] Guernsey (English) Circuit LPM, 5 December 1940; GA AQ213/7.

[25] Guernsey (English) Circuit LPM, 4 June 1941; GA AQ 213/7.

[26] Guernsey (English) Circuit LPM, 1 September 1941; GA AQ 213/7.

[27] For example, the Guernsey and Sark (French) Circuit QM, 19 June 1941 recorded thanks to the local preachers of both circuits for their conduct of worship in the previous twelve months since the Occupation began.

[28] Guernsey (English) Circuit LPM, 31 August 1944; GA AQ 213/7.

[29] 'Preaching Appointments J. Simon 1923-1946'; GA AQ 188/24.

[30] Jersey Free Church Ministers' Fraternal, 19 August 1940; JA J/C/AW/A/2.

[31] *JEP*, 27 January 1945; 10 February 1945.

[32] Georgetown Pulpit Notices, 6 January 1944; 20 February 1944; JA J/C/T/D/2.

[33] Nan Le Ruez, *Jersey Occupation Diary: Her Story of the German Occupatin 1940-1945* (St Helier: Seaflower Books, 1994), p. 164-6.

[34] E.g. Edwin Langlois, a local preacher in the Guernsey and Sark (French) Circuit, was appointed lay pastor in 1943 (see Chapter 8). His diary for 1944 (Herbert White Collection) indicates that he preached on the following texts on several occasions: 'Jesus said to Peter, "Put your sword back into its sheath. Am I not to drink the cup that the Father has given me"' (John 18.11); 'Rejoice and be glad, for your reward is great in heaven, for in the same way they persecuted the prophets who were before you' (Matthew 5.12); 'But strive first for the kingdom of God and his righteousness, and all these things will be given to you as well' (Matthew 6.33). Other biblical texts mentioned in his diary for 1944 include: Psalm 78.34; Psalm 119.31; Matthew 16.15; Acts 8.15; Acts 8.31.

[35] *Methodist Hymn Book* (Methodist Conference, 1933) 157. Leslie Roussel, *Evacuation* (Bognor Regis: New Horizon, 1980), p. 47.

[36] *Methodist Hymn Book*, 488.

[37] *Methodist Hymn Book*, 916. This is borne out by St Martin's church in the Jersey (Grove Place) Circuit where in 1941 the Sunday service once a month included a roll call of those associated with the church presently serving in the armed forces or mercantile marine, followed by the singing of the hymn 'Holy Father, in thy mercy'. St Martin's LM, 23 May 1941; J/C/AE/A/1.

[38] Paul Sanders, *The British Channel Islands under German Occupation 1940-1945* (Jersey: Jersey Heritage Trust and Société Jersiaise, 2005), p. 117.

[39] Heaume, 'Marie Ozanne'. Since it was forbidden for the Salvation Army to hold services, Philip Romeril conducted the funeral service at the cemetery. In 1947 she was posthumously awarded the Salvation Army's highest honour, 'The Order of the Founder'.

[40] Robin was an avid listener to sermons and forthright in his opinion of preachers' efforts. He praises Ord more highly than any other preacher. See the entries in his diary for: 28 July 1940; 8 December 1940; 20 April 1941; 11 May 1941; 18 May 1941; 1 June 1941; 20 July 1941; 30 November 1941; 8 March 1942; 2 August 1942; 13 September 1942; 28 February 1943; 4 May 1943; 23 May 1943; 26 December 1943; 30 July 1944; 6 May 1945. His criticisms

of Ord are rare: 'Sermon very long and uninteresting', 13 February 1944; 'Ord's sermon thoroughly spoilt by numerous and most unnecessary asides', 4 February 1945. Other commentators confirm Robin's opinion of Ord. For example, the Diary of Ken Lewis, 20/21 July 1941; 'as always he [Ord] was extremely interesting', 2 October 1942. No other preacher made such a positive impression on the young Lewis. According to Leslie Roussel, Ord 'made many brave and daring remarks during his services', Roussel, *Evacuation*, p. 45.

[41] Ord, 23 May 1943.

[42] Ord, 14 September 1942.

[43] 'It is splendid to watch the congregation rising to the veiled references. They are alert to gather all the encouragement and guidance one can give them, and their instant response is reward for all the purgatorial efforts in my study.' Ord, 12 September 1943.

[44] Ord, 19 December 1943.

[45] Roussel, *Evacuation*, p. 46.

[46] *GEP*, 6 October 1944.

[47] *JEP*, 19 July 1943.

[48] *GEP*, 23 April 1945. The Guernsey and Sark (French) Circuit QM, 22 March 1945, sent Corbet a letter of appreciation marking his diamond anniversary as a preacher.

[49] Herbert White, *A Safe Stronghold: An Account of Methodism in the Bailiwick of Guernsey during the German Occupation 1940-1945* (unpublished manuscript, 1998), p. 33. For health reasons, Brockway was obliged to retire early from the active ministry in 1938 whereupon he returned to his native Guernsey. He lived near St Martin's Mission where he regularly attended worship. After his death, his ashes were interred under the pulpit. Rev. Frederick Paine also retired from the ministry early because of ill health and moved to Guernsey, his wife's home. He was exempted from deportation on health grounds but nevertheless managed to preach regularly during the Occupation.

[50] Sark LM, 7 February 1940; GA AQ 211/15.

[51] 'Travel permit for Rev. Théodule Maré to travel to France to import articles for religious purposes, including communion wine and candles, 24 July 1942'; JA B/A/W68/18.

[52] Les Capelles LM, 18 February 1945; GA AQ 410/12.

[53] Jersey (Grove Place) Circuit QM, 4 September 1941; JA J/C/D/A/7.

[54] Diary of Ken Lewis, 28 September 1941.

[55] Ord, 12 September 1943.

[56] St Andrew's Pulpit Notices, 10 September 1944; GA AQ 185/11.

[57] Ord, 17 September 1944.

[58] Jersey (Aquila Road) Circuit QM, 11 December 1940; JA J/C/B/A/2.

[59] Jersey (Aquila Road) Circuit QM, 7 December 1944; JA J/C/B/A/2.

[60] Georgetown LM, 27 August 1941; JA J/C/T/A/4. In 1942 St Martin's church in the Jersey (Grove Place) Circuit celebrated their church anniversary with a watch-night service on New Year's Eve; *JEP*, 6 January 1943.

[61] *Channel Islands Monthly Review* Vol. 9/1 July 1945.

[62] Frank Stroobant, *One Man's War* (Guernsey: Guernsey Press, 1967), p. 26.

[63] Diary of Ambrose Robin, 23 August 1942.

[64] Roy Rabey Notes, Herbert White Collection. On the other hand, Leslie Roussel,

Evacuation p. 47 suggests a higher percentage of the population attended worship during the Occupation. Roussel offers no evidence to substantiate this claim.

[65] Diary of Ambrose Robin, 2 November 1941.

[66] Diary of Ambrose Robin, 14 February 1943.

[67] Diary of Ambrose Robin, 27 February 1944.

[68] Diary of Ambrose Robin, 12 March 1944.

[69] Diary of Ambrose Robin, 5 September 1943.

[70] V.V. Cortvriend, *Isolated Island: A History and Personal Reminiscences of the German Occupation of the Island of Guernsey June 1940 – May 1945* (Guernsey: Guernsey Star, 1946), p. 112.

[71] J.C. Sauvary, *Diary of the German Occupation of Guernsey 1940-1945* (Guernsey: Guernsey Press, 1990), p. 27.

[72] Le Ruez, *Jersey Occupation Diary*, p. 163.

[73] 1941 0.2%; 1942 1.3%; 1943 1.3%; 1944 0.62%; 1945 0.85%.

[74] St Martin's LM, 6 March 1939; JA J/C/AE/A/3.

[75] St Ouen's TM, 15 February 1939. JA J/C/AF/A/2.

[76] St Martin's TM, 20 February 1941; JA J/C/AE/A/1.

[77] Carmel TM, 27 January 1945; JA J/C/M/A/1.

[78] There were exceptions: Tabor chapel continued to record pew rentals in French until 1950; JA J/C/AM/C/5.

[79] Jersey (Grove Place) Circuit QM, 14 June 1945; JA J/C/D/A/7.

[80] From 194 in 1940 to 161 in 1945. The statistics for French services are: 1940 46.6%; 1941 53.2%; 1942 51.4%; 1943 50.7%; 1944 48.7%; 1945 45.9%. The percentage increase in the number of French services in 1941 is explained by the fact that two English-language churches (Victoria Road and Forest) closed in September 1940, whilst another (Wesley) held only one Sunday service.

[81] Guernsey and Sark (French) Circuit LPM, February 1944; GA AQ 213/1.

[82] Guernsey and Sark (French) Circuit LPM, 30 May 1941; GA AQ 213/1.

[83] Les Capelles LM, 10 March 1943; 26 May 1943; GA AQ 410/12.

[84] Notes from Roy Rabey, Herbert White Collection.

[85] *The Star*, 28 July 1945.

Chapter 4

[1] *JEP*, 9 July 1940.

[2] *GEP*, 4 September 1940.

[3] *GEP*, 9 May 1941.

[4] Ord, 9 November 1940.

[5] Letter of Dean of Guernsey to Bailiff of Guernsey, 11 November 1940; GA CC/3-17. The Dean was not exaggerating: a concert in July was reported in the press. *GEP*, 12 July 1940.

[6] GA CC/3-17.

[7] Letter of Bailiff of Jersey to Feldkommandantur, 9 November 1940; JA B/A/W30/13.

[8] Letter of Dr Reffler to Bailiff of Guernsey, 14 January 1941; GA CC/3-17.

[9] Letter of Dr Reffler, 9 June 1941; GA CC/3-17.

[10] Letter of Feldkommandantur to Bailiff of Jersey, 7 January 1941; JA B/A/W30/13.

[11] Letter of Dr Reffler to St John's Ambulance Brigade, 24 May 1941; GA CC/3-17.

[12] Letter of Southern Social Club to John Leale, 21 June 1941; reply from the Nebenstelle, 8 August 1941; GA CC/3-17.

[13] Approval of application by Mr Lawrence to hold a meeting to form a Ladies Netball League, 22 May 1944; JA B/A/W30/13.

[14] Letter of Bailiff of Guernsey to Fuerst von Oettingen, 21 November 1941; JA B/A/W30/13.

[15] Letter of Attorney General to Bailiff of Jersey, 20 December 1941; cf. Letter of Bailiff of Guernsey to Bailiff of Jersey, 13 December 1941; JA B/A/W30/13. In fact the liquidation of assets did not achieve the desired result. After the Occupation the civilian authorities restored the assets of Freemasons and Oddfellows.

[16] For example, the Rohais Wesley Guild in Guernsey ceased recording its meetings during the Occupation; GAQ 185/32.

[17] Jersey (Wesley) Circuit QM, 7 March 1945; JA J/C/E/A/8.

[18] Jersey (Wesley) Circuit QM, 9 December 1943; JA J/C/E/A/4.

[19] Samarès Wesley Guild, 24 October 1943; JA J/C/AH/A/3.

[20] Samarès Wesley Guild, 20 January 1944; JA J/C/AH/A/3.

[21] Nan Le Ruez, *Jersey Occupation Diary: Her Story of the German Occupation 1940-1945* (St Helier: Seaflower Books, 1994), p. 153.

[22] Bethlehem Wesley Guild; JA J/C/L/A/4.

[23] St Martin's Wesley Guild, 20 September 1945; JA J/C/AE/A/2.

[24] Methodist Youth Department Channel Island (Jersey Section) District Schedules; JA J/C/AY/B/2.

[25] Vale Wesley Guild; GA 215/25.

[26] Miriam M. Mahy, *There is an Occupation* (Guernsey: Guernsey Press, 1992), p. 45.

[27] Jersey (Wesley) Circuit QM, 9 December 1943; JA J/C/E/A/4.

[28] St Martin's LM, 23 May 1941; JA J/C/AE/A/3.

[29] St Sampson's Sisterhood; GA 214/20.

[30] Ord, 8 October 1944; 2 November 1944.

[31] *The Star*, 28 March 1945.

[32] *JEP*, 7 April 1945.

[33] Brock Road TM, 7 February 1945; GA AQ 184/12.

[34] A performance of Handel's *Messiah* at Easter 1942 raised £20/19s/2d for Trust funds. A repeat performance at Christmas raised £22/10s/2d. Brock Road TM, 19 February 1943. The organist's stipend at this time was around £20 per annum; GA 184/12.

[35] Les Capelles LM, 29 May 1940; GA 410/12.

[36] Ebenezer Choir, June 1942; JA J/C/H/K/2.

[37] Les Capelles LM, 6 September 1942; GA 410/12.

[38] Les Capelles LM, 3 March 1941; GA 410/12.

[39] Les Capelles LM, 6 September 1942; GA 410/12.

[40] Philadelphie TM, 15 June 1943; JA J/C/AB/A/1.

[41] Grove Place TM, 29 January 1943; JA J/C/W/A/3.

[42] Ord, 24 April 1942.

[43] Jersey Free Church Ministers' Fraternal, 8 June 1942; JA J/C/AW/A/2.

[44] Jersey (Wesley) Circuit QM, 9 March 1944; JA J/C/E/A/4.

[45] Jersey Free Church Ministers' Fraternal, 10 November 1942; JA J/C/AW/A/2.

[46] Jersey Free Church Ministers' Fraternal, 8 May 1944; JA J/C/AW/A/1.

[47] Jersey Free Church Ministers' Fraternal, 8 September 1941; JA J/C/AW/A/2.

[48] Jersey Free Church Ministers' Fraternal, 13 November 1944; JA J/C/AW/A/1.

[49] Guernsey Free Church Ministers' Fraternal; GA 213/20.

Chapter 5

[1] Charles Cruickshank, *The German Occupation of the Channel Islands* (Channel Islands: Guernsey Press, 1975), p. 194.

[2] Letter of Rev. T. Davis to Dr Maass, 16 July 1940; GA FK 30-11.

[3] Letter of Dr Maass to Rev. T. Davis, 19 July 1940; GA FK 30-11.

[4] In the early days German parade services were announced in the newspaper. *GEP*, 12 October 1940. The Germans closed Forest parish church near the airport in August 1940 after an air raid by the RAF. The church re-opened in April 1941 but only for services led by German padres for the troops. A German padre lived in the rectory next to the church. The rector, Rev. Finey, insisted that the colours of the Royal Guernsey Militia remain in the church throughout the Occupation. He also hid the key to the church, obliging the Germans to make a new key (Source: Richard Heaume).

[5] V.V. Cortvriend, *Isolated Island: A History and Personal Reminiscences of the German Occupation of the Island of Guernsey June 1940 – May 1945* (Guernsey: Guernsey Star, 1946), p. 114.

[6] For example, St Andrew's church in the Guernsey and Sark (French) Circuit was sometimes used for German parade services because of its proximity to major military installations, including the underground hospital and the arsenal at Les Naftiaux. Castel church in the same circuit was also used for German parade services because of its proximity to a large military camp at Les Beaucamps. After the Liberation, German forces were given permission to continue holding services. They would march down to the church in full parade order. In the months leading up to the Liberation, parade services were held at Les Capelles church at 9.30am on Sunday mornings before islanders gathered for their service. Fred Martin, 'The Churches in Guernsey during the Occupation', *Channel Islands Occupation Review* (1975), pp. 59-65 (p. 62).

[7] Cited in George Forty, *Channel Islands at War: A German Perspective* (Shepperton: Allan, 1999), p. 141.

[8] *JEP*, 11 December 1940.

[9] *GEP*, 18 November 1943; *JEP*, 18 November 1943.

[10] Cortvriend, *Isolated Island*, p. 113.

[11] Jersey (Wesley) Circuit QM, 11 September 1941; JA J/C/E/A/4.

[12] Ord, 16 December 1943.

[13] Ord, 14 August 1944. Not all members of the German forces were aware that they were welcome to attend events in island churches. When Ord invited a German soldier to attend a performance of Handel's *Messiah* at Brock Road church the man was surprised

and asked if the event was open to all. Ord, 18 December 1942.

[14] Ord, 8 February 1942. He was not the only German soldier to offer firewood to the church. Years later Mary Le Lacheur recalled an impromptu choir practice in a house near the church. A German officer billeted with the family heard the singing and asked if he might join in, explaining that he sang in the choir in his village church at home. He asked for 'Sing praise to God who reigns above' (*Methodist Hymn Book* (1933) 415; translated by Frances Elizabeth Cox from a German hymn by Johann Jakob Schültz). By the last verse he was almost in tears. That winter (1943?), every Saturday he sent his batman after dark with a bag of logs for the grate in the schoolroom where Sunday services were being held. The supply of logs eventually stopped and it was assumed he had been posted elsewhere. It was a risky undertaking that could have landed the officer in trouble. Letter of Mary Le Lacheur, Herbert White Collection.

[15] Ord, 6 July 1942.

[16] Herbert White, *A Safe Stronghold: An Account of Methodism in the Bailiwick of Guernsey during the German Occupation 1940 – 1945* (unpublished manuscript, 1998), p. 58.

[17] Ord, 25 August 1940.

[18] Leslie Roussel, *Evacuation* (Bognor Regis: New Horizon, 1980), pp. 46-7. According to his own reckoning, Roussel conducted more than 200 acts of public worship during the Occupation, but this was the only occasion on which a member of the German armed forces was present.

[19] Diary of Ken Lewis, 2 January 1944.

[20] Ord, 21 May 1944.

[21] Letter of Rev. Edwin Foley to Colonel Knackfuss, 16 September 1942; GA FK 12-7.

[22] Preserving the original play on words, this can be rendered into English as: 'It is possible to militarise civilians, but it is impossible to civilise the military.'

[23] Ord, 24 August 1944.

[24] Ord, 10 October 1941. 'We hate the system but try to judge each individual on his merits.' Ord, 6 February 1942.

[25] Ord, 30 July 1944.

[26] Ord, 1 April 1942.

[27] Ord, 1 April 1942.

[28] *Methodist Recorder*, 19 June 1945.

[29] It was not only the authorities that sought Ord's assistance as a translator. Islanders often asked him to translate leaflets dropped by Allied aircraft addressed to the troops. When the *Deutsche Guernsey Zeitung* was published islanders wanted him to translate articles. Ord's wife turned away numerous requests for translation because otherwise he would find himself doing nothing else. Ord, 3 September 1944.

[30] Ord, 22 July 1943.

[31] Prince von Oettingen of the Guernsey Feldkommandantur was a wealthy Bavarian landowner and a devout Catholic who saw to it that soldiers attended services led by army chaplains. Alan Wood and Mary Seaton Wood, *Islands in Danger* (London: Evans, 1955), p. 95.

[32] As Ord recalled in a short newspaper article, 'Encounters with Germans in Guernsey', *Methodist Recorder*, 14 June 1945.

[33] Ord, 6/26 October 1941.

[34] Ord, 31 October 1941. Ord thought that Ebersbach must equally have thought him 'a stuffed shirt'.

[35] Ord, 28 February 1942.

[36] Ord, 4 March 1942.

[37] Ord, 4 March 1942.

[38] Ord, 27 July 1942.

[39] For instance, in August 1942 discussions centred on Rudolf Bultmann's *Offenbarung und Heilsgeschicte*. Ord, 21 August 1942.

[40] Letter of Furst Von Oettingen, 13 March 1942; Letter of Dr Brosch, 30 June 1942; GA CC/3-17. The proximity of the Brock Road church to the Feldkommandantur headquarters at the Grange Lodge Hotel (the properties abutted each other) meant that Germans working in the censor's office often heard the choir practising. In June 1943 Ord's wife visited the German headquarters seeking approval for a concert programme. When she confirmed that the concert was to be held at the Brock Road church the officer remarked 'Then I should like to attend it. Day after day I hear such beautiful music coming from it, and I am a lover of good music.' Ord, 22 June 1943.

[41] Ord, 25 September 1943.

[42] Letter of Norman Grut to the Feldkommandantur, 16 December 1942; GA CC/3-17.

[43] *First Tower Methodist Church 1847-1997* (Jersey, 1997).

[44] A popular stage play for repertory theatre written by Walter Hackett and first performed in Edinburgh in 1922.

[45] JA B/A/W71/5.

[46] I am indebted to Reg Jeune for confirming these last details. He played the part of *Ambrose Applejohn*.

[47] L'Islet corps of the Salvation Army in Guernsey managed to publish a weekly *Joyful News* bulletin from 20 July 1940 until it was banned by the German censor after 20 weeks. *Salvation Army L'Islet Corps History, 1940-1945*.

[48] Paul Sanders, *The British Channel Islands under German Occupation 1940-1945* (Jersey: Jersey Heritage Trust and Société Jersiase, 2005), p. 97. Cf. Peter Davies, *Dangerous Liaisons: Collaboration and World War Two* (Harlow: Longman, 2004).

[49] Sanders, *The British Channel Islands*, p. 80.

[50] Speech by John Leale, 21 June 1940. Cited in Sanders, *The British Channel Islands*, p. 81.

[51] 'Report of the President of the Controlling Committee of the States of Guernsey on the activities of the Committee during the five years of German Occupation', 23 May 1945; GA.

[52] Alan Wood and Mary Seaton Wood, *Islands in Danger*, pp. 14, 98.

[53] Alan Wood and Mary Seaton Wood, *Islands in Danger*, p. 99.

[54] Alan Wood and Mary Seaton Wood, *Islands in Danger*, p. 99.

Chapter 6

[1] Controlling Committee Minutes, 6 September 1940; GA.

[2] Superior Council Minutes, 6 September 1940; JA S/05/C/1.

[3] Royal Crescent LM, 25 September 1940; JA J/C/AC/A/5.

[4] Superior Council Minutes, 23 October 1940; JA S/05/C/1.

[5] Ord, 8 December 1940.

[6] Ord, 22 December 1940.

[7] Ord, 16 January 1942.

[8] Diary of Ambrose Robin, 6 December 1942.

[9] Diary of Ambrose Robin, 28 February 1943.

[10] Diary of Ambrose Robin, 18 June 1944. This is confirmed in the diary of Adèle Lainé, 27 June 1944.

[11] Grove Place TM; JA J/C/W/A/3.

[12] Georgetown TM, 20 May 1942; JA J/C/T/A/3.

[13] Ord, 20 November 1943.

[14] Ord, 13 February 1944.

[15] Ord, 14 January 1945. The service was still too long for some members of the congregation. Ambrose Robin regretted having attended worship that day because it was 'far too cold for long services'. He did not attend worship the following week again because it was 'too cold for church'. Diary of Ambrose Robin, 14/21 January 1945.

[16] Nan Le Ruez, *Jersey Occupation Diary: Her Story of the German Occupation 1940-1945* (St Helier: Seaflower Books, 1994), p. 265.

[17] Ord, 30 October 1943.

[18] Jersey (Grove Place) Circuit preaching plan, July – September 1944; JA J/C/D/E/48.

[19] Ord, 30 July 1944.

[20] Ord, 24 February 1945.

[21] Ord, 25 February 1945.

[22] Ord, 28 September 1941.

[23] Ord, 11 April 1942. 'The tea-table was an unbelievable sight. A farm has resources!'

[24] Ord, 18 December 1943.

[25] Rev. Clement Mylne Prison Notes; JA L/C/20/D/4.

[26] Letter of John Leale, 25 July 1940; GA CC/1-12.

[27] Letter of John Leale, 18 September 1940; GA CC/1-12.

[28] Letter of Elsie Roussel to John Leale, 28 November 1940; GA CC/1-12.

[29] Letter of John Leale, 20 March 1941; GA CC/1-12.

[30] In the days leading up to the Occupation, Romeril impressed Leale because of his calm manner in the pulpit at St Sampson's Methodist Church where Leale regularly attended worship. After the Controlling Committee was formed Leale invited Romeril to work part-time in the Labour Office under the supervision of Richard Johns (another member of the same church). Romeril worked in the Labour Office without remuneration throughout the Occupation. Besides helping organise the soup kitchens, he assisted island men in finding employment, sought alternative funding for those whose pensions could no longer be received from England, and negotiated with the German authorities over the confiscation of bicycles. His ministerial colleagues were not entirely supportive: 'shorthanded as we are it is a further complication to have this withdrawal when tasks mount up' (Ord, 11 October 1940). After the war, he transferred to the United Church of Canada.

234

[31] Letter of Rev. E.L. Frossard to John Leale, 21 March 1941. GA CC/1-12.

[32] Letter or Rev. Kilshaw to John Leale, 22 March 1941. GA CC/1-12.

[33] Letter of Rev. E.N. Greenhow to John Leale, 1 April 1941. GA CC/1-12.

[34] Letter of Rev. E.N. Greenhow to John Leale, 30 August 1941. GA CC/1-12.

[35] Letter of Sir Abraham Lainé to John Leale, 22 November 1944; GA CC/1-12.

[36] As acknowledged in a newspaper report of the soup kitchen's opening, *GEP*, 21 February 1941.

[37] Letter of John Leale, 28 July 1944. GA CC/1-12.

[38] Letter of John Leale, 21 August 1944. GA CC/1-12. The church did benefit considerably from hosting the soup kitchen because the States of Guernsey paid for the premises to be connected to the island's sewerage system.

[39] Letter from Olive Kellow to John Leale, undated but probably April 1941. GA CC/1-12.

[40] *JEP*, 1 August 1944.

[41] 'Report to the Food Delegation [of the International Red Cross] of the States of Jersey of the Dinner Baking Service', 9 April 1945; JA B/A/W5/6. Complaints were categorised as: (1) 'permanent grumblers'; (2) thefts; (3) spoiled dishes (accidents or burned); (4) undercooking, chiefly in periods of bad weather when only wet wood blocks could be used.

[42] On one occasion Douglas Ord had to pay an on-the-spot fine of 1RM to a passing German police officer who noticed an infringement of the blackout regulations at his manse. Giving Ord the receipt the police officer asked Ord whereabouts his church was. On hearing that Ord was minister at Brock Road, he remarked 'It is well known. You have plenty of music.' Ord, 14 August 1942.

[43] The following paragraphs are based on Mylne's account, 'Methodist Minister and family jailed by Germans'; JA L/C/20/D/5. Mylne's account of his experience in Jersey during the Occupation was serialised in the *Methodist Recorder* in May and June 1945.

[44] Vivienne Mylne was an intelligent young woman whose academic potential was already recognised. After the war she read French at Oxford University and then joined the staff at the University of Kent, rising to become Professor of French until she retired in 1992.

[45] News of Mylne's arrest for a radio offence reached Guernsey. Ord, 15 February 1943.

[46] Diary of Ambrose Robin, 11 November 1943.

[47] Diary of Ambrose Robin, 14 February 1943.

[48] Ord, 8 September 1943.

[49] Ord, 11 April 1942.

[50] Ord, 31 December 1943.

[51] Ord, 22 December 1943.

[52] Ord, 17 May 1944.

[53] For example, Beaugié was on sick leave from October to December 1943. Ord, 24 October & 31 December 1943. He was commended for trying to carry on his ministerial duties during this time. Guernsey and Sark (French) Circuit QM, 16 December 1943. Similarly, it was reported at the Jersey (Grove Place) Circuit QM, 4 June 1942, that William Ward and Pastor Peter Hanks were both ill; JA J/C/D/A/7.

[54] Ord, 6 February 1942.

[55] Ord, 20 March 1944.

[56] Ord, 26 March 1944.

[57] Ord, 19 November 1944.

[58] Ord, 3 January 1945. Because of fuel shortages, there were no cremations in the Channel Islands between 1940 and 1945.

Chapter 7

[1] Douglas Ord built a rock garden to conceal a deed box buried in his garden. Ord, 19 September 1940.

[2] During the Occupation, Methodist treasurers banked church money in private bank accounts, contrary to regulations but necessary in the circumstances to avoid confiscation. Meticulous sets of accounts were maintained, and no thefts were reported.

[3] Letters of Agnew Giffard and John Leale, 26 June 1940; GA CC 2-20.

[4] Letter of John Leale to Agnew Giffard, 15 July 1940; GA CC 2-20.

[5] Letter of Agnew Giffard, 1 August 1940; reply of John Leale, 3 August 1940; GA CC 2-20.

[6] GA CC 2-20. On 6 August 1940 the Dean of Guernsey set out the revised stipends as follows:

Church	1939 Stipend (£)	Occupation stipend (£)
St Andrew's	423	225
St John's	459	283
Forest	387	313
Catel	301	173
St Martin's	413	253
Cobo	242	197
Vale	414	334
St Peter Port [Agnew]	462	279
Torteval	427	310
St Peter's	431	277
St Saviour's	397	314
St Stephen's	585	220
Sark	344	291
St Sampson's	495	253
Total (£)	5780	3722

The Dean later pointed out that Trinity church in St Peter Port was without an incumbent. He would pay for clergy duties at the church and then claim these from the States of Guernsey.

[7] Jersey (Wesley) Circuit Advisory Committee, 28 June 1940; JA J/C/E/A/7.

[8] Jersey (Aquila Road) Circuit QM, 11 September 1940; JA J/C/B/A/2.

[9] Jersey (Wesley) Circuit QM, 7 December 1944; JA J/C/E/A/8.

[10] Jersey (Wesley) Circuit Advisory Committee, 15 July 1940; JA J/C/E/A/7.

[11] Jersey (Great Union Road) Circuit QM, 17 September 1940; JA J/C/C/A/2.

[12] Ord, 19 July 1940.

[13] As reported to the Guernsey and Sark (French) Circuit QM, 19 September 1940. For some reason, this news of Guernsey Methodism was reported in the *JEP*, 8 August 1940.

[14] Guernsey and Sark (French) Circuit QM, 23 April 1944. Noting that the English Circuit had already agreed to increase stipends to the full amount with effect from the current quarter, the French Circuit unanimously agreed to do the same. Beaugié felt able to accept only if organists and chapel keepers were treated in the same way.

[15] Jersey (Aquila Road) Circuit QM, 12 March 1941; JA J/C/B/A/2.

[16] Jersey (Grove Place) Circuit QM, 4 September 1941; JA J/C/D/A/7.

[17] Jersey (Wesley) Circuit QM, 7 March 1945; JA J/C/E/A/8.

[18] Les Capelles LM, 25 August 1940; GA AQ 410/12.

[19] Les Capelles LM, 14 December 1940. GA AQ 410/12.

[20] Guernsey and Sark (French) Circuit QM, 17 June 1943.

[21] 1939 £10/18s/4d; 1940 £21/8s/9d; 1941 £36/16s/2d; 1942 £76/12s/8d; 1943 £117/1s/5d; 1944 £189/2s/8d; 1945 £236/10s/0d. St Martin's Mission TM, 22 January 1940; 23 February 1941; 24 February 1942; 25 February 1943; 16 February 1944; 14 February 1945; 29 January 1946; GA AQ 185/27.

[22] St Martin's Mission TM, 16 February 1944; 29 January 1946; GA AQ 185/27.

[23] Brock Road TM, 5 March 1941; GA AQ 184/12.

[24] Brock Road TM, 19 February 1943; GA AQ 184/12.

[25] Brock Road TM, 9 February 1944; GA AQ 184/12.

[26] Brock Road TM, 7 February 1945; 24 January 1947; GA AQ 184/12.

[27] *The Star*, 18 May 1937.

[28] Salem LM, 18 October 1939; GA AQ 185/31.

[29] Jersey (Aquila Road) Circuit QM, 11 December 1941; JA J/C/B/A/2.

[30] St Martin's Pulpit Notices, 5 September 1943; JA J/C/AE/G/3.

[31] Letter of Percy Chalker (Herbert White Collection).

[32] Sark LM, 27 September 1943; GA AQ 211/15. Following the Liberation, a description of the bumper harvest festival on Sark appeared in the *Methodist Recorder*. 'The church was beautifully decorated. The choicest gifts lay around the pulpit and communion table: bread, soap, tobacco leaves, cotton wool, butter, eggs, raisins, apple rings, matches and a Bunny Rabbit. The children's gift service brought in milk, sugar, saccharine, pepper and vinegar. The sale of goods was held in the schoolroom with Mr W. Giffard as auctioneer, and never before have prices soared so high. £100 was the amazing result. A bar of Lifebuoy soap fetched £8.10.11d. 2oz. of tea £5.6.10d.½oz. pepper £1.6.8d and a reel of cotton £1.2.4½d. Of this truly amazing result £30 was allocated to the Red Cross Fund in appreciation of their help given to Sark families interned in Germany.' *MR*, 21 June 1945. Note the discrepancy in the sum donated to the Red Cross.

[33] Sark LM, 22 September 1944; GA AQ 211/15.

[34] Jersey (Aquila Road) Circuit QM, 11 December 1940; JA J/C/B/A/2.

[35] Grove Place LM, 2 June 1942; JA J/C/W/A/4.

[36] Royal Crescent LM, 13 February 1943; JA J/C/AC/A/5.

[37] *GEP*, 30 August 1943.

[38] Wesley church seat rent account book; JA J/C/AN/C/7.

[39] Jersey (Aquila Road) Circuit QM, 7 June 1944; JA J/C/B/A/2.

[40] Salem Trust and Church Accounts 1939; GA AQ 823/10.

[41] St Andrew's Pulpit Notices, 2/9 January 1944. Similar announcements are recorded for 27 December 1942, 3 January 1943, 7 January 1945, 14 January 1945; GA AQ 185/11.

[42] Brock Road TM, 25 January 1946; GA AQ 184/12.

[43] St Sampson's LM, 3 October 1940; GA AQ 214/11.

[44] Grove Place LM, 28 November 1940; 3 June 1941; 2 June 1942; 22 May 1945; JA J/C/W/A/4.

[45] Guernsey and Sark (French) Circuit Poor Fund Accounts; GA AQ 188/21.

[46] Tabor LM, 19 March 1942; 29 February 1944; JA J/C/AM/A/3.

[47] Carmel LM, 7 November 1944; JA J/C/M/A/4.

[48] Georgetown LM, 3 December 1940; 10 December 1941; JA J/C/T/A/4.

[49] St Martin's Pulpit Notices, 21 December 1941; JA J//C/AE/G/2.

[50] St Martin's LM, 25 March 1942; 26 November 1942; JA J/C/AE/A/3.

[51] Jersey (Aquila Road) Circuit QM, 10 September 1941; JA J/C/B/A/2.

[52] Jersey (Aquila Road) Circuit QM, 11 March 1943; JA J/C/B/A/2.

[53] Sark LM, 27 January 1942; GA AQ 211/15.

[54] Sark LM, 19 May 1944. GA AQ 211/15.

[55] Samarès LM, 16 December 1942; JA J/C/AH/A/1.

[56] Jersey (Grove Place) Circuit preaching plan, July – September 1940; JA J/C/D/E/44/4.

[57] Guernsey and Sark (French) Circuit LPM, 30 November 1944; GA AQ 213/1.

[58] St Andrew's Pulpit Notices, 7 January 1945; 22 April 1945; GA AQ 185/11.

[59] Diary of Ken Lewis, 7 January 1945; Les Capelles LM, 18 February 1945; GA AQ 410/12.

[60] Sark LM, 22 September 1944; GA AQ 211/15.

[61] Jersey (Grove Place) Circuit QM, 14 June 1945; JA J/C/D/A/7.

[62] Jersey (Grove Place) Circuit preaching plan, January – March 1941; JA J/C/D/E/45.

[63] 'Galaad Chapel Pulpit Notice Book, 31.08.1941 – 04.11.1945'; JA J/C/S/G/2. Entries for 8 March 1942 and two preceding Sundays.

[64] Correspondence relating to a donation given by Women's Work in Jersey to the Methodist Missionary Society; JA J/C/A/E/2.

[65] Channel Islands District Chapel Affairs Committee, 8 May 1946; JA J/C/A/A/1.

[66] Tabor LM, 15 May 1941; 10 July 1941; JA J/C/AM/A/3.

Chapter 8

[1] Sark LM, 23 April 1941; GA AQ 211/15.

[2] Sark LM, 27 January 1942; GA AQ 211/15.

[3] Fred Martin, 'The Churches in Guernsey during the Occupation', *Channel Islands Occupation Review* (1975), pp. 59-65 (p. 62) claims that Tardif was 'authorized by the Dean of Guernsey to adminster Holy Communion'. This is almost certainly incorrect. Martin's article contains several inaccuracies: he refers to 'Tardil' instead of Tardif; he states that 'the vicar Rev. W. Bunting was interned' (whereas Bunting was the Methodist minister who died in May 1940). In referring here to the Dean of Guernsey, Martin appears to be

confusing Anglican and Methodist structures.

[4] Guernsey and Sark (French) Circuit QM, 18 March 1943. The meeting unanimously approved the appointments. Simon had been a local preacher for 43 years and a Jurat in the States of Guernsey for 23; Langlois had been a local preacher for 37 years. Simon was appointed lay pastor for Les Adams and Rocquaine. Langlois was appointed for Sion, Torteval and Carmel.

[5] Edwin Langlois' diary for 1944 (Herbert White Collection) reveals that during the course of the year he led Sunday worship on at least 40 occasions; presided at the Lord's Supper on 12 occasions; conducted 4 baptisms and 18 funerals.

[6] Jersey (Great Union Road) Circuit QM, 21 June 1943; JA J/C/C/A/2.

[7] Jersey (Wesley) Circuit QM, 8 June 1944; JA J/C/E/A/8.

[8] Jersey (Wesley) Circuit Advisory Committee, 21 June 1940; JA J/C/E/A/7.

[9] Jersey Free Church Ministers' Fraternal, 22 July 1940; JA J/C/AW/A/2.

[10] Jersey (Wesley) Circuit LPM, 13 September 1940; JA J/C/E/A/3.

[11] A number of conscientious objectors sent to Jersey to assist with the potato harvest were members of the Peace Pledge Union, which was widely suspected of disloyalty to Britain. Shortly before the Occupation one of them appeared in court in Liverpool having stowed away on a ship leaving St Helier. When arrested, he was found to be carrying peace literature in English and German. *JEP*, 27 June 1940.

[12] Jersey (Wesley) Circuit QM, 13 March 1941; JA J/C/E/A/4.

[13] Jersey (Grove Place) Circuit LPM, 27 February 1941; JA J/C/D/A/5.

[14] Jersey (Aquila Road) Circuit QM, 10 September 1941; JA J/C/B/A/2.

[15] Jersey (Wesley) Circuit LPM, 8 December 1941; JA J/C/E/A/3.

[16] Jersey (Wesley) Circuit LPM, 7 December 1942; JA J/C/E/A/3.

[17] Jersey (Wesley) Circuit LPM, 8 September 1943; 6 December 1943; JA J/C/E/A/3.

[18] Jersey (Grove Place) Circuit LPM, 3 December 1942; JA J/C/D/A/5.

[19] Jersey (Grove Place) Circuit LPM, 4 March 1943; JA J/C/D/A/5.

[20] Jersey (Grove Place) LPM, 28 August 1941; 27 August 1942; 3 December 1942; JA J/C/D/A/5. The service of accreditation at Grove Place was reported in the *JEP*, 5 February 1943.

[21] Jersey (Wesley) Circuit LPM, 1 September 1944; JA J/C/E/A/3.

[22] Guernsey and Sark (French) Circuit QM, 28 June 1945.

[23] Guernsey (English) Circuit LPM, 29 November 1945; GA AQ 213/8.

[24] Guernsey and Sark (French) Circuit LPM, February 1944; GA AQ 213/1.

[25] Roy Rabey Notes (Herbert White Collection). He died in January 2008 aged 86. An obituary can be found in the *Minutes of Conference* (2008), p. 54.

[26] His story is published in Leslie Roussel, *Evacuation* (Bognor Regis: New Horizon, 1980).

[27] Circuits recognised that any recommendations concerning the annual invitation of ministers was redundant in the circumstances created by the German Occupation. In spring 1941, the Guernsey and Sark (French) Circuit QM noted that it would not be possible formally to consider the re-invitation of ministers; 'times had changed and under the existing conditions this could not be done'. The following spring it was again noted that invitations could not be considered but 'sincere thanks' were expressed to ministers. In spring 1943 Beaugié (the only minister remaining in the circuit) was 'unanimously

invited' to remain in his appointment, 'a formality in the circumstances' but probably intended to affirm his ministry. Guernsey and Sark (French) Circuit QM, 20 March 1941; 19 March 1942; 18 March 1943. The other circuits in Jersey and Guernsey similarly continued to record their thanks annually to ministers at the spring QM.

[28] Jersey (Wesley) Circuit QM, 7 March 1940; JA J/C/E/A/4.

[29] Jersey (Wesley) Circuit Advisory Committee, 13 February 1941; JA J/C/E/A/7.

[30] Jersey (Wesley) Circuit QM, 13 March 1941; JA J/C/E/A/4.

[31] Stuart's wife owned a family property in Guernsey. During the First World War, Stuart's father, Rev. George Stuart, served in Guernsey where Donald met and married Gertrude Stranger.

[32] Wesley TM, 3 June 1941; JA J/C/AN/A/7.

[33] Jersey (Wesley) Circuit QM, 12 June 1941; JA J/C/E/A/4.

[34] Jersey (Wesley) Circuit QM, 19 March 1942; JA J/C/E/A/4.

[35] Jersey (Wesley) Circuit QM, 9 March 1944; JA J/C/E/A/4.

[36] Jersey (Wesley) Circuit QM, 9 December 1943; JA J/C/E/A/4.

[37] Jersey (Grove Place) Circuit QM; JA J/C/D/A/7.

[38] The Jersey (Wesley) Circuit QM, 7 December 1944, reported the current membership of the circuit as 336 of whom 57 had evacuated in 1940. The meeting accepted that many of these would probably not resume their involvement with the church when they returned to the island; JA J/C/E/A/8.

[39] As reported at the Channel Islands District Synod and subsequently in the *GEP*, 20 May 1940.

[40] Brock Road LM, 16 January 1940; GA AQ 184/14.

[41] St Sampson's LM, 3 October 1940; 29 April 1945; GA AQ 214/11.

[42] Guernsey and Sark (French) Circuit QM, 20 December 1945.

Chapter 9

[1] *Le Magasin Méthodiste* (1901), p. 143f.

[2] For example, 'Order of Service for the Aquila Road church Sunday school anniversary, 19/20 May 1940.' JA J/C/H/K/2.

[3] Jersey (Grove Place) Circuit Sunday school council, 23 February 1940; JA J/C/D/A/6.

[4] Jersey (Grove Place) Circuit Sunday school council, 5 September 1940; JA J/C/D/A/6.

[5] Jersey (Grove Place) Circuit Sunday school council, 9 January 1941; JA J/C/D/A/6.

[6] Jersey (Grove Place) Circuit Sunday school council, 9 January 1941; JA J/C/D/A/6.

[7] Jersey (Grove Place) Circuit QM, 6 March 1941; JA J/C/D/A/7. See Chapter 8, Table 8.2.

[8] Jersey (Grove Place) Circuit Sunday school council, 8 January 1942; JA J/C/D/A/8.

[9] Jersey (Grove Place) Circuit QM, 9 March 1944; JA J/C/D/A/7.

[10] Jersey (Grove Place) Circuit QM, 8 March 1945; JA J/C/D/A/7. See Chapter 8, Table 8.2.

[11] Ebenezer Sunday School, 29 October 1944; JA J/C/N/A/6.

[12] Jersey (Grove Place) Circuit Sunday school council, 26 March 1943; JA J/C/D/A/8.

[13] Jersey (Grove Place) Circuit Sunday school council, 28 September 1945; JA J/C/D/A/8.

[14] 'Methodist Youth Department Channel Island (Jersey Section) District Schedules (1946)';

JA J/C/AY/B/2. The breakdown of the 1945 total (815) shows the relative strength of each Sunday school in the circuit: Grove Place (98); Georgetown (78); Bethel (20); Philadelpie (49); St Ouen (62); Bethlehem (42); Tabor (30); Bethesda (15); Sion (56); Les Fréres (27); Six Roads (29); Galaad (33); Les Augrés (29); St Martin (94); Ebenezer (38); La Rocque (51); Eden (50); Carmel (14).

[15] Jersey (Wesley) Circuit QM, 11 June 1942; JA J/C/E/A/4.

[16] Jersey (Wesley) Circuit QM, 7 March 1945; JA J/C/E/A/8. 'Methodist Youth Department Channel Island (Jersey Section) District Schedules (1946)'; JA J/C/AY/B/2.

[17] Jersey (Wesley) Circuit Advisory Committee, 28 May 1945; JA J/C/E/A/7. The figures in brackets have been extrapolated from Table 9.2.

[18] St Martin's LM, 6 March 1939; JA J/C/AE/A/3.

[19] Jersey (Aquila Road) Circuit QM, 9 September 1943; JA J/C/B/A/2.

[20] Jersey (Wesley) Circuit preaching plan, October – December 1940; JA J/C/D/E/44/1.

[21] Bethlehem Wesley Guild; JA J/C/L/A/4.

[22] Jersey (Wesley) Circuit QM, 9 December 1943; JA J/C/E/A/4.

[23] Royal Crescent LM, 31 July 1940; JA J/C/AC/A/5.

[24] 'Methodist Youth Department Channel Island (Jersey Section) District Schedules'; JA J/C/AY/B/2.

[25] *JEP*, 27 September 1948.

[26] Guernsey (English) Circuit Sunday school council, 29 May 1940; GA AQ 210/11.

[27] *GEP*, 8 July 1940.

[28] This and the following paragraph are based on 'Report of the Occupation period', Les Camps Sunday School; GA AQ 293/11.

[29] Cf. Diary of Ken Lewis, 20/21 July 1941. According to Lewis, 19 children and 8 teachers attended.

[30] Diary of Ken Lewis, 19 October 1941.

[31] Cf. Diary of Ken Lewis, 18 February 1945.

[32] Diary of Ken Lewis, 11 January 1942.

[33] Diary of Ken Lewis, 9 May 1943.

[34] Diary of Ken Lewis, 15 October 1944.

[35] Within a few days of Ord appealing for books, 140 had been donated. Diary of Ken Lewis, 12 November 1944.

[36] Les Capelles Sunday school, 6 August 1940; GA AQ 410/6.

[37] Les Capelles Sunday school, ? December 1943; 10 June 1944; GA AQ 410/6.

[38] *GEP*, 6 July 1940.

[39] Diary of Ambrose Robin, 18 July 1943.

[40] St Sampson's LM, 23 April 1942; GA AQ 214/11.

[41] St Martin's Mission Sunday school, 10 July 1939, 26 May 1940; GA AQ 185/24.

[42] St Martin's Mission Sunday school, 30 August 1942; GA AQ 185/24.

[43] St Martin's Mission Sunday school, 12 June 1945, 28 December 1945; GA AQ 185/24.

[44] St Martin's Mission Sunday school, 30 August 1942; GA AQ 185/24.

[45] Leslie Roussel, *Evacuation* (Bognor Regis: New Horizon, 1980), pp. 76-7.

[46] Vale church baptismal roll; GA AQ 215/28. Wesley church baptism register; JA J/C/AN/B/9.

Chapter 10

[1] *MR*, 11 July 1940.

[2] Her story is told in Lois M. Ainger, *My Case Unpacked* (Stroud: Alan Sutton, 1995).

[3] The Methodist Conference temporarily stationed Moore in the Medway Towns Circuit from 1 September 1940 but, apart from conducting Sunday services in the circuit, he was given (or assumed) considerable latitude to conduct his mission to Channel Island refugees. *Minutes of Conference* (1940).

[4] *MR*, 4 July 1940.

[5] *MR*, 11 July 1940.

[6] *MR*, 1 August 1940.

[7] *MR*, 18 July 1940.

[8] *MR*, 16 January 1941.

[9] *MR*, 8 January 1942.

[10] *MR*, 29 May 1941.

[11] *MR*, 11 July 1940.

[12] *MR*, 8 August 1940.

[13] *MR*, 29 August 1940.

[14] *MR*, 8 August 1940.

[15] *MR*, 27 February 1941.

[16] *MR*, 16 January 1941.

[17] *MR*, 12 September 1940.

[18] Among the flow of Red Cross messages were a small number of official communications between Methodism in the Channel Islands and the Methodist Conference. For example, ministers serving in the Channel Islands received an individual message of good wishes from the Conference meeting in July 1941. Cf. Jersey (Grove Place) Circuit QM, 4 September 1941; JA J/C/D/A/7. The following is typical of the exchange of greetings between the Conference and Methodism in the Channel Islands during the Occupation. From the Secretary of the Methodist Conference to the Jersey (Wesley) Circuit, 24 August 1942: 'Conference received with joy news of your well-being and lovingly greets you holding you both ministers and members in prayer. God be with you (Finch).' Reply: 'The Wesley Circuit December Quarterly Meeting now assembled receives yours gladly. We send cordial greetings to you and evacuees particularly. Our work goes on (South).' Jersey (Wesley) Circuit QM, 10 December 1942; JA J/C/E/A/4. The following year there was a further exchange of messages. 'With sincere assurances of continual remembrance Conference sends to you and your people cordial greetings and earnest hopes that our separation will soon be ended.' Reply: 'Our people reciprocate cordial greetings. Glad to report our work continues with undiminished vigour. Our folks loyalty to church and adaptability to circumstances excellent.' Jersey (Wesley) Circuit QM, 9 December 1943; JA J/C/E/A/4.

[19] *MR*, 17 September 1942.

[20] *MR*, 8 August 1940.

[21] *MR*, 29 August 1940; 12 September 1940.

[22] *MR*, 21 November 1940; 19 December 1940.

[23] *MR*, 28 August 1941.

[24] *MR*, 17 September 1942.

[25] *MR*, 27 February 1941.

[26] *MR*, 12 December 1940.

[27] *MR*, 17 February 1944.

[28] *MR*, 18 July 1940.

[29] *MR*, 8 August 1940.

[30] *MR*, 15 August 1940.

[31] *MR*, 12 September 1940.

[32] *MR*, 18 July 1940.

[33] The format of the regular meeting suggests a church setting: 'Procedure on Sunday afternoons: (1) Lord's Prayer and hymn, "Absent Friends" (2) Welcome to Visitors (3) Announcements (4) News (5) Tea.' *Channel Islands Monthly Review* Vol. 1/1 May 1941. The Stockport and District Channel Islands Society met at Tiviot Dale Methodist Church where the minister was Rev. Mark Lund. In 1945 Lund was stationed in the Guernsey (English) Circuit, presumably because of his knowledge of Channel Island refugees. The inaugural meeting in January 1941 attracted 250 people from Guernsey, 3 or 4 from Jersey, and 1 from Sark. In addition to the fortnightly meeting on Sunday afternoons, social evenings were held every Saturday. In 1944 the President of the Methodist Conference, Rev. Dr Leslie Church, made an official visit to the society. *Channel Islands Monthly Review* Vol. 7/1 July 1944.

[34] *MR*, 12 December 1940.

[35] *MR*, 8 January 1942.

[36] Cf. *Channel Islands Monthly Review* Vol. 2/1 November 1941; *Channel Islands Monthly Review* Vol. 2/2 December 1941.

[37] *Channel Islands Monthly Review* Vol. 2/3 January 1942.

[38] *Channel Islands Monthly Review* Vol. 2/4 February 1942.

[39] *Channel Islands Monthly Review* Vol. 2/4 February 1942; Vol. 2/5 March 1942; Vol. 3/2 August 1942.

[40] *Channel Islands Monthly Review* Vol. 2/6 April 1942.

[41] *Channel Islands Monthly Review* Vol. 3/2 August 1942. In the summer of 1944 the BBC broadcast an appeal for the Channel Islands Refugee Committee as 'the week's good cause'. The appeal raised £7,416/0s/9d. *Channel Islands Monthly Review* Vol. 7/1 July 1944.

[42] *Channel Islands Monthly Review* Vol. 8/5 May 1945.

[43] *Channel Islands Monthly Review* Vol. 4/1 January 1943.

[44] *Channel Islands Monthly Review* Vol. 4/2 February 1943.

[45] *GEP*, 4 July 1945.

[46] *Conference Agenda* (1941), p. 10.

[47] *Wisbeach Advertiser*, 20 January 1943.

[48] Ord, 17 September 1942.

[49] Beaugié's letter has survived in a German file that contains appeals against deportation. GA FK 12-7. The appeal was endorsed by the Guernsey and Sark (French) Circuit quarterly meeting on 17 September 1942.

[50] Obituary, *Minutes of Conference* (1967), p.188f.

[51] Ord, 15 September 1942.

[52] Stuart believed that had he remained in Jersey he would have avoided deportation, as he ruefully pointed out in his letter to HM Greffier, dated 19 September 1942, registering for deportation; GA FK 12-7. It is not clear why Stuart was confident he would not have been deported had he still been resident in Jersey.

[53] Ord, 19 September 1942. However, an Elim Pentecostal minister, Gilbert Dunk, believed that his own exemption was due to Stuart: 'In the course of the evening service at Eldad Elim Church last evening, the Rev. G.S. Dunk announced that the Rev. Donald Stuart had very kindly offered to replace him as an evacuee to leave one representative of the Elim church here.' *GEP*, 21 September 1942. (Reference here to 'evacuee' rather than 'deportee' was of course a euphemism intended to placate the German censor.) The reasons for the discrepancy can only be conjectured.

[54] Marie Ozanne's letter to the German authorities gives her home address as 'The Guernsey Prison'; GA FK 12-7.

[55] GA FK 12-7.

[56] One of Foley's church members wrote to the Commandant (on church notepaper) explaining that he had lived in Guernsey since 1919. His hairdressing business was 'patronized extensively by the German Forces, and, as I believe doing a useful service'. He was also church secretary 'and in this respect I feel I am doing a faithful and religious work to which I have been called'. He was deported. GA FK 12-7.

[57] Diary of Ken Lewis, 27 September 1942.

[58] Ord, 20 September 1942.

[59] Diary of Joan Coles, 27 September 1942; JA L/C/01/1/1.

[60] Diary of Joan Coles, 24 December 1942; JA L/C/01/1/1.

[61] Diary of Joan Coles, 23/25 April 1943; JA L/C/01/1/1.

[62] Diary of Joan Coles, 26 December 1943; 3 January 1944; JA L/C/01/1/1.

[63] *Peace News*, 19 February 1943.

[64] *Peace News*, 19 February 1943.

[65] Letter of Milly Grieve, 23 May 1943; Farmer Collection of Letters to and from Internees, Priaulx Library, Guernsey.

[66] Bailiff's Chambers, Occupation Files, Biberach Papers; JA B/A/W80/2/1-100.

[67] Letter of Ambrose Sherwill, Camp Senior at Laufen, to Bailiff of Guernsey, 10 October 1943. Rev. Hartley Jackson was transferred to Stalag Luft VI in East Prussia; Rev. Percival to Stalag VI C. Bailiff's Chambers, Occupation Files, Laufen Papers; JA B/A/W80/3/1-44.

[68] Entry for 1 July 1943 in Sherwill's Internment Diary, privately published in Ambrose Sherwill, *A Fair and Honest Book* (no publication details, copy in Priaulx Library, Guernsey).

[69] In his Preface to Frank Stroobant, *One Man's War* (Guernsey: Guernsey Press, 1967).

[70] Ken Lewis, a clerk in John Leale's office, typed out the list of names of those to be deported. Of the 81 names, 50 were listed as 'ex-officers', and 31 'undesirables'. Diary of Ken Lewis, 4 February 1943.

[71] Letter of Beaugié to German authorities, 2 February 1943; GA FK 12-7. Ord, 4 February 1943.

[72] As noted in the *Channel Islands Monthly Review* Vol. 5/5, November 1943.

[73] Letter to *GEP*, 23 June 1964 (following Foss' death). Cited in Herbert White, *A Safe Stronghold: An Account of Methodism in the Bailiwick of Guernsey during the German Occupation 1940-1945* (unpublished manuscript, 1998).

[74] Stuart and the other Channel Island internees were amongst 270 British civilians who arrived in Liverpool on 23 March 1945 on board a Swedish cruise liner. *Channel Islands Monthly Review* Vol. 8/4 April 1945.

[75] Joan Coles made eight small wreaths from greenery in the form of a cross for the funeral service, which was conducted by Rev. James of Guernsey. Six friends bore the coffin. Diary of Joan Coles, 27/28 February 1945; JA L/C/01/1/1. The death was announced in the *JEP*, 16 May 1945.

[76] Bailiff's Chambers, Occupation Files, Biberach Papers; JA B/A/W80/2/201-264.

[77] Letter of Deputy Camp Senior to Bailiff of Jersey, 29 June 1943; JA B/A/W80/3/1-44.

Chapter 11

[1] Ord, 7 June 1944.

[2] Ord, 11 June 1944. This was one of the few occasions when Ambrose Robin was critical of Ord's preaching: 'An attempt at a popular topic – not very impressive'. Diary of Ambrose Robin, 11 June 1944.

[3] Guernsey and Sark (French) Circuit QM, 16 September 1943.

[4] Guernsey and Sark (French) Circuit LPM, 3 August 1944; GA AQ 213/1. The timing of the service changed during the following months.

[5] Sark LM, 22 September 1944; GA AQ 211/15.

[6] Bordeaux Mission LM, 20 September 1944; GA AQ 220/42.

[7] Ord, 28 February 1943.

[8] Jersey Free Church Ministers' Fraternal, 8 May 1944; JA J/C/AW/A/1.

[9] Jersey (Grove Place) Circuit QM, 8 June 1944; JA J/C/D/A/7.

[10] Jersey (Great Union Road) Circuit QM, 12 June 1944; JA J/C/C/A/2.

[11] *JEP*, 8 May 1945.

[12] *JEP*, 9 May 1945.

[13] *JEP*, 15 May 1945. A collection for the International Red Cross raised £80.

[14] Order of service for the Jersey Free Church Council United Thanksgiving for the Liberation; JA J/C/AS/G/6.

[15] Ord, 9 May 1945.

[16] Ord, 20 September 1944.

[17] A copy is preserved in the Jersey Archives; JA J/C/AS/F/4. The service was reported in the *GEP*, 18 May 1945.

[18] At a press conference on 5 June 1945 (a few days after Ord's liberation address), Niemöller admitted he had volunteered to serve in the German navy following the outbreak of war in 1939. He also admitted that he had never quarrelled with Hitler on political issues but only on religious grounds. These admissions seriously damaged his reputation as a hero of the German opposition to Hitler. In the summer of 1945 the *Daily Telegraph* led a campaign against him being allowed to visit Britain. The Home Secretary

refused him permission to enter Britain.

[19] Les Camps Sunday school, 4 January 1945; GA AQ 302/1.

[20] Les Camps Sunday school, 13 May 1945; GA AQ 302/1.

[21] Jersey (Wesley) Circuit Advisory Committee, 2 June 1944; JA J/C/E/A/7.

[22] Jersey (Wesley) Circuit QM, 8 June 1944; JA J/C/E/A/8.

[23] Jersey (Wesley) Circuit QM, 7 September 1944; JA J/C/E/A/8.

[24] 'Official Report of the English Circuit for the period of the German Occupation of Jersey'; JA J/C/E/H/6.

[25] Guernsey and Sark (French) Circuit LPM, 31 May 1945; GA AQ 213/1.

[26] Jersey (Grove Place) Circuit QM, 14 June 1945; JA J/C/D/A/7.

[27] In May 1945 the indefatigable Moore appealed for bedding for Channel Island refugees in transit to the islands. *Methodist Recorder*, 31 May 1945.

[28] Lois M. Ainger, *My Case Unpacked* (Stroud: Alan Sutton, 1995), p. 223.

[29] *JEP*, 15 May 1945.

[30] *JEP*, 11 July 1945.

[31] *GEP*, 18 June 1945.

[32] *GEP*, 26 May 1945. Salvation Army leaders visited the Channel Islands in July 1945. In Guernsey a Salvation Army rally was held at Ebenezer Church. In Jersey the Salvation Army held its first meeting since 1940 on 20 June 1945. *JEP*, 29 June 1956.

[33] *GEP*, 12 July 1945; *MR*, 19 July 1945.

[34] *JEP*, 13 July 1945.

[35] The Conference had already taken note of the following suggestion from the Bradford District Synod: 'Reconstruction of Channel Islands Methodism – In view of the known as well as of the likely needs of Channel Islands Methodism – a Church notable for its loyalty – Synod urges that preparation for re-building our work in the Islands be taken in hand without delay. This would stimulate our refugee flock, and rally the sympathy of friends.' *Conference Agenda* (1944), p. 16.

[36] Letter of Douglas Moore to Sidney Beaugié, 5 July 1945. Herbert White Collection.

[37] For example, the Jersey (Wesley) Circuit QM, 13 September 1945, noted with relief that the connexional assessment (levy) on the circuit was being waived for the period 1940-1945. In addition, the Conference was to make an emergency grant to the circuit towards the cost of Rev. Ronald South's stipend for 1945/46; JA J/C/E/A/8.

[38] The Channel Islands District Chapel Commission was able to vote a sum of £300 to St Andrew's church in the Guernsey and Sark (French) Circuit 'for the purpose of rehabilitation following the German Occupation'. The church was extensively used by German forces for parade services. Channel Islands District Chapel Commission, 15 May 1946; JA J/C/A/A/1.

[39] Grove Place LM, 22 May 1945; JA J/C/W/A/4.

[40] Brock Road marriage register, 1935-55; GA AQ 193/3.

[41] An example is preserved in the Herbert White Collection addressed to Thomas Vidamour, formerly of Carmel Methodist Sunday school who evacuated in June 1940 aged 8. Thomas rejoined the Sunday school and later became a Methodist minister.

[42] Les Capelles Sunday school, 12 June 1945; 25 September 1945; GA AQ 410/6.

[43] Les Camps Sunday school, 13 September 1945; GA AQ 302/1.

44 Torteval Sunday school, no date; GA AQ 821/22.

45 St Sampson's Sisterhood; GAQ 214/20.

Chapter 12

1 A good example of wartime reflection on the future of the Channel Islands is *Nos Iles: A Symposium on the Channel Islands* published by the Channel Islands Study Group in March 1944.

2 *Minutes of Conference* (1945), p. 38.

3 The full membership of the Conference commission was: Rev. Wilbert Howard (Ex-President); Sir George Knight (Vice-President); Rev. Edwin Finch (Secretary of Conference); Rev. Oliver Hornabrook; Rev. Samuel Magor; Rev. Benson Perkins; Rev. Colin Roberts (Home Missions Department, convenor); Mr Arthur Wilks; Mr Ashton Davies CVO OBE; Rt Hon Isaac Foot. *Conference Agenda* (1945), p. 38.

4 Local newspapers carried a report of the Methodist stationing committee summarising changes in the Channel Islands. *JEP*, 7 July 1945.

5 *Minutes of Conference* (1949), p. 133.

6 'Report on the proposed union of the English Circuit and the French Circuit'. JA J/C/E/H/7.

7 Ord, 13 December 1943.

8 Guernsey (English) Circuit QM, 14 June 1945; GA AQ 823/10.

9 *GEP*, 4 September 1945. When church officials re-entered the premises in May 1945 they found the hymn board still in place showing the numbers of the hymns sung at the last service in 1940. The final hymn was Joseph Hart's 'This, this is the God we adore' (*Methodist Hymn Book* (1933) 69). The last verse is "Tis Jesus, the first and the last,/ Whose Spirit shall guide us safe home;/ We'll praise Him for all that is past,/ And trust Him for all that's to come.' The hymn was sung at the re-opening of the church. Roy Helyar, *Salem: A Peep into the Past* (pamphlet, 1987).

10 Ord, 21 June 1944.

11 Ord, 25 June 1944.

12 Ord, 2 July 1944.

13 Diary of Ambrose Robin, 9 July 1944.

14 Diary of Ambrose Robin, 13 August 1944.

15 In particular Ord, 18 September 1942.

16 Morley TM; GA AQ 213/5.

17 Jersey (Wesley) Circuit QM, 9 March 1944; JA J/C/E/A/4.

18 Jersey (Wesley) Circuit QM, ? June 1945; JA J/C/E/A/8.

19 Channel Islands District Synod, 6 May 1948; JA J/C/A/A/27.

SOURCES

Jersey Archives (JA)
Methodist Collection
Feldkommandantur Files
Superior Council of the States of Jersey, Minutes & Files (1940-1945)
Vivian Mylne Collection
Diary of Joan Coles

Guernsey Archives (GA)
Methodist Collection
Controlling Committee of the States of Guernsey, Minutes & Files (1940-1945)
Feldkommandantur Files
Diary of Ken Lewis
Diary of Adèle Lainé

Priaulx Library, Guernsey
Diary of Rev. Douglas Ord
Diary of Ambrose Robin
Farmer Collection of Letters to and from Internees
Ambrose Sherwill, *A Fair and Honest Book* (privately published)

German Occupation Museum, Guernsey
Herbert White Collection

Periodicals and Newspapers
Channel Islands Monthly Review
Channel Islands Occupation Review
Evening Post
Guernsey Evening Press
Magasin Méthodiste des Iles de la Manche
Methodist Magazine
Methodist Recorder
Star

Methodist Church Publications
Minutes of the Methodist Conferences Vol. 1 (Wesleyan Conference Office, 1862)
Minutes of Conference (1936-2008)
Conference Agenda (1938-1948)
Methodist Church Buildings: Statistical Returns including seating accommodation as at July 1ˢᵗ 1940 (Methodist Conference, 1947)
Methodist Hymn Book (Methodist Conference, 1933)

BIBLIOGRAPHY

Ainger, Lois M., *My case unpacked* (Stroud: Alan Sutton, 1995)

Arnett, H. *Handbook of Methodist History in Jersey* (Jersey: Evening Post, 1909)

Atkin, Nicholas *Church and Schools in Vichy France 1940-1944* (London: Garland, 1991)

Balleine, G. R. *A history of the Island of Jersey from the cave men to the German occupation and after* (London: Staples, 1950; revd edn 1998)

Bunting, Madeleine, *The Model Occupation: The Channel Islands under German Rule 1940-1945* (London: Harper Collins, 1995)

Burkert, Wilhelm, 'Four Years as an Occupation Soldier in Guernsey', *Channel Islands Occupation Review* 26 (2000), pp. 22-33

Channel Islands Study Group, *Nos Iles: A Symposium on the Channel Islands* (Teddington, 1944)

Cohen, Frederick, *The Jews in the Channel Islands during the German Occupation 1940-1945* 2nd edition (Jersey: Jersey Heritage Trust, 2000)

Comte, Bernard *L'honneur et la conscience: catholiques français en résistance 1940-1944* (Paris: Editions de l'atelier, 1998)

Cortvriend, V.V. *Isolated Island: A History and Personal Reminiscences of the German Occupation of the Island of Guernsey June 1940 – May 1945* (Guernsey: Guernsey Star, 1946)

Cruickshank, Charles, *The German Occupation of the Channel Islands* (Channel Islands: Guernsey Press, 1975)

Dantinne, L.G. *The Catholic Church in Belgium under the German Occupation* (London: Lincolns-Prager, 1944)

Davies, C.S.L., 'International Politics and the Establishment of Presbyterianism in the Channel Islands: The Coutances Connection', *Journal of Ecclesiastical History* 50/3 (1999), pp. 498-522

Davies, Peter *Dangerous Liaisons: Collaboration and World War Two* (Harlow: Longman, 2004)

Durand, Ralph, *Guernsey under German Rule* (London: The Guernsey Society, 1946)

Duquesne, Jacques *Les Catholiques français sous l'Occupation* (Paris: Bernard Grasset, 1996)

Eagleston, A.J., *The Channel Islands under Tudor Government, 1485-1642* (Cambridge: Cambridge University Press, 1949)

Fabre, Emile C. *God's Underground* (St Louis: Bethany, 1970)

Falla, Frank *The Silent War* (London: New English Library, 1967)

Forty, George *Channel Islands at War: A German Perspective* (Shepperton: Allan, 1999)

Ginns, Michael, 'Wolff of the Gestapo', *Channel Islands Occupation Review* 31 (2003), pp. 112-25

Guiton, François, *Histoire du Méthodisme Wesleyen dans les Iles de la Manche* (London: John Mason, 1846)

Halls, W.D. *Politics, Society and Christianity in Vichy France* (Oxford: Berg, 1995)

Harris, Roger E., *Islanders Deported* (London: Channel Islands Specialist Society, 1979)

Heaume, Richard 'Marie Ozanne', *Channel Islands Occupation Review* 23 (1995), pp. 79-81

Hempton, David *Methodism: Empire of the Spirit* (Yale: Yale University Press, 2005)

Knowles-Smith, Hazel R. *The Changing Face of the Channel Islands Occupation: Record, Memory and Myth* (Basingstoke: Palgrave MacMillan, 2007)

Le Lièvre, Matthieu, *Histoire du Méthodisme dans les Iles de la Manche 1784-1884* (Paris: Librarie Evangélique, 1885)

Le Pelley, Paul, 'The Evacuation of Guernsey Schoolchildren', *Channel Islands Occupation Review* (1988), pp. 21-29

Le Poidevin, Francis, *Les Capelles Methodist Church: the story of two hundred years 1786-1986* (Isle of Mann: Chapelles, 1986)

Le Ruez, Nan *Jersey Occupation Diary: Her Story of the German Occupation 1940-1945* (Jersey: Seaflower Books, 1994)

Le Sueur, Peter 'A Short Account of Peter Le Sueur, of Jersey. By his eldest son', *Methodist Magazine* (1820), pp. 401-8

Lemprière, Raoul *Portrait of the Channel Islands*, 2nd edn (London: Hale, 1975)

—— *A History of the Channel Islands* (London: Hale, 1980)

Mahy, Miriam M. *There is an Occupation* (Guernsey: Guernsey Press, 1992)

Malinowski-Krum, Horsta *Frankreich am Kreuz: Protestanten Frankreichs unter deutscher Okkupation, 1940-1944* (Berlin: Wichem-Verlag, 1993)

Marshall, Michael, *Hitler Invaded Sark* (St Peter Port: Guernsey Lithoprint, 1963)

Martin, Fred, 'The Churches in Guernsey during the Occupation', *Channel Islands Occupation Review* (1975), pp. 59-65

Mollet, Ralph *Jersey under the Swastika: An Account of the Occupation of the Island of Jersey by the German Forces 1st July 1940 to 12th May 1945* (London: Hyperion, 1945)

Moore, Diane *Deo Gratias: A History of the French Catholic Church in Jersey: 1790-2007* (St Helier: Les Amitiés Franco-Britannique de Jersey, 2007)

Moore, R.D., *Methodism in the Channel Islands* (London: Epworth, 1952)

Ogier, Darryl *Reformation and Society in Guernsey* (Woodbridge: Boydell, 1996)

Pantcheff, T.X.H. *Alderney: Fortress Island* (Chichester: Phillimore, 1981)

Patton, Mark *Jersey in Prehistory* (La Haule: La Haule Books, 1987)

Read, Brian Ahier, *No Cause for Panic: Channel Islands refugees 1940-45* (Jersey: Seaflower Books, 1995)

Roussel, Leslie, *Evacuation* (Bognor Regis: New Horizon, 1980)

Sanders, Paul, *The British Channel Islands under German Occupation 1940-1945* (Jersey: Jersey Heritage Trust and Société Jersiaise, 2005)

Sauvary, J.C., *Diary of the German Occupation of Guernsey 1940-1945* (Guernsey: Guernsey Press, 1990)

Stroobant, Frank *One Man's War* (Guernsey: Guernsey Press, 1967)

Telford, John (ed.) *The Letters of the Rev. John Wesley A.M.* 7 Vols (London: Epworth, 1931)

Toase, William 'The Grace of God manifested: A Memoir of the late Mrs Elizabeth Arrivé of Guernsey', *Methodist Magazine* (1820), pp. 144-151, 186-195

—— *Memorials of the Rev. William Toase: consisting principally of extracts from his journals and correspondence, illustrative of the rise and progress of Methodism in France and the Channel Islands* (London: Wesleyan Conference Office, 1874)

Tough, Ken, 'Deportation from Guernsey 1942 – Two personal accounts and a German assessment', *Channel Islands Occupation Review* 20 (1995), pp. 63-76

Tremayne, Julia, *War on Sark: The Secret Letters of Julia Tremayne* (Exeter: Webb and Bower, 1981)

Vickers, John (ed.) *A Dictionary of Methodism in Britain and Ireland* (Peterborough: Epworth, 2000)

Ward, W. Reginald and Richard P. Heitzenrater (eds), *The Works of John Wesley* Vol. 24 'Journal and Diaries VII (1787-1791)' (Nashville: Abingdon, 2003)

White, Herbert, 'Methodism Occupied', *Channel Islands Occupation Review* 22 (1997), pp. 51-60

—— *A Safe Stronghold: An Account of Methodism in the Bailiwick of Guernsey during the German Occupation 1940-1945* (Unpublished manuscript, 1998)

Wood, Alan and Mary Seaton Wood, *Islands in Danger* (London: Evans, 1955)

INDEX OF NAMES AND SUBJECTS